PENGUIN TWENTIETHCENTURY CLASSICS

SELECTED ESSAYS

David Herbert Lawrence was born at Eastwood, Nottinghamshire, in 1885, fourth of the five children of a miner and his middle-class wife. He attended Nottingham High School and Nottingham University College. His first novel, *The White Peacock*, was published in 1911, just a few weeks after the death of his mother to whom he had been abnormally close. At this time he finally ended his relationship with Jessie Chambers (the Miriam of *Sons and Lovers*) and became engaged to Louie Burrows. His career as a schoolteacher was ended in 1911 by the illness which was ultimately diagnosed as tuberculosis.

In 1912 Lawrence eloped to Germany with Frieda Weekley, the German wife of his former modern languages tutor. They were married on their return to England in 1914. Lawrence was now living, precariously, by his writing. His greatest novels, *The Rainbow* and *Women in Love*, were completed in 1915 and 1916. The former was suppressed, and he could not find a publisher for the latter.

After the war Lawrence began his 'savage pilgrimage' in search of a more fulfilling mode of life than industrial Western civilization could offer. This took him to Sicily, Ceylon, Australia and, finally, New Mexico. The Lawrences returned to Europe in 1925. Lawrence's last novel, *Lady Chatterley's Lover*, was banned in 1928, and his paintings confiscated in 1929. He died at Vence in 1930 at the age of 44.

Lawrence spent most of his short life living. Nevertheless he produced an amazing quantity of work – novels, stories, poems, plays, essays, travel books, translations and letters . . . After his death Frieda wrote: 'What he had seen and felt and known he gave in his writings to his fellow men, the splendour of living, the hope of more and more life . . . a heroic and immeasurable gift.'

D. H. LAWRENCE

Selected Essays

PENGUIN BOOKS
IN ASSOCIATION WITH
WILLIAM HEINEMANN LTD

PENGUIN BOOKS

Published by the Penguin Group
Penguin Books Ltd, 27 Wrights Lane, London W8 5TZ, England
Penguin Books USA Inc., 375 Hudson Street, New York, New York 10014, USA
Penguin Books Australia Ltd, Ringwood, Victoria, Australia
Penguin Books Canada Ltd, 10 Alcorn Avenue, Toronto, Ontario, Canada M4V 3B2
Penguin Books (NZ) Ltd, 182–190 Wairau Road, Auckland 10, New Zealand

Penguin Books Ltd, Registered Offices: Harmondsworth, Middlesex, England

This selection first published in Penguin Books 1950
15 17 19 20 18 16

Printed in England by Clays Ltd, St Ives plc
Set in Monotype Garamond

CONTENTS

MEXICO AND NEW MEXICO

III. WRITING AND PAINTING

IV. LAWRENCE AND MAGNUS

INTRODUCTION
BY RICHARD ALDINGTON

LAWRENCE'S great literary output is remarkable for its diversity in originality, its versatility. As the impulse took him he attempted different kinds of writing, and failed only as a writer of plays. His was not a long career, a quarter of a century of writing and less than twenty years of publishing at most; but he was inexhaustibly fertile. From 1911 to 1930 not a year passed without the publication of at least one and often several books, and the amount of material unpublished or lost in periodicals which has been recovered since his death exceeds the total output of more sterile authors. All this mass of writing is held together by no formal links but by the magical power of Lawrence's unique temperament.

Consider the variety of his achievements. *Sons and Lovers, Women in Love, Aaron's Rod, Kangaroo, The Plumed Serpent,* how different they are, what different worlds they explore. How unlike other novels of the time! Lawrence took up the short novel or novelette, and made it his own mouth-piece, from the curious psychology of *The Captain's Doll* to the virulent satire of *St Mawr*. In the short story he produced such masterpieces as *The Prussian Officer*, *England, my England,* and *The Woman Who Rode Away,* and such scathing satires as *Jimmy and the Desperate Woman* and *The Man Who Loved Islands.* Think of his travel books, the matchless *Sea and Sardinia, Twilight in Italy, Mornings in Mexico, Etruscan Places.* As poet, basing himself on Hardy and Whitman, he kept vividly alive and honest an art which is dying out in a series of parlour tricks. Yet it was after his death that some of his best work as a poet was revealed, and that he was discovered to be one of the most entertaining of English letter-writers.

As if all these achievements were not more than enough triumph for one man, Lawrence left an abundance of essays, many of which were never printed or at least collected in book form until after his death, and still remain unknown to the wide non-specialist reading public. How many of my readers know, for instance, the long and witty Introduction to the edition of his reproduced paintings? Or possess the 850-page *Phoenix*, which has long been out of print, and at present costs at least three or four guineas second-hand?

'Essays' is a poor word for these brilliantly-varied writings, since 'an essay' unhappily implies something formal and academic and highbrow, whereas Lawrence was always intensely personal and spontaneous, with such a horror of pedantry and the university manner that he vastly preferred to be slangy and jaunty. 'Non-fictional prose' is worse than 'essay', so until somebody coins a better word we must stick to essays, though in Lawrence's case the word is more like a reference number than a description of literary form.

The suggestion that I should make a selection from these half-buried writings and thus bring them to the wide public who will certainly delight in them was naturally an opportunity to be grasped; though the few, the very few people, who know the whole of this work of Lawrence's can alone guess how anyone must quail at the difficulties and the responsibility. I eliminated all extracts from longer books, though Mr Middleton Murry's extracts from *Fantasia of the Unconscious* published in the *Adelphi* during 1923 show what could be done here by skilful editing. And I naturally also eliminated such works as *Etruscan Places* which are in Penguin Books.

Even the limitation to pieces complete in themselves and not in Penguin Books left plenty to choose from. Since the intention is to win new readers for Lawrence or to bring to readers of his other books prose pieces of charm and vivacity as well as rarity, I made another almost complete elimination. Probably because of his intensely religious upbringing, Lawrence at times has a tendency to hold forth in a didactically moral way. He was a persistent metaphysical and reforming thinker, and produced works which he loosely called 'philosophical'. But in trying to express ideas Lawrence never bothered to acquire the language of philosophy, and almost always discussed abstruse ideas in terms of myth and symbol. Interesting and sometimes beautiful as these writings are, they are baffling and irritating to any unprepared reader. So I have eliminated his long tract on Education, his writings about War or coming out of War, such as *The Crown*, *The Reality of Peace*, *Blessed are the Powerful*, as well as the long *Study of Thomas Hardy* which as Lawrence said himself is '*about* anything but Hardy'. However, I have given a taste of this sort of prose in *Democracy* and *Reflections on the Death of a Porcupine*, and in parts of one or two others.

As well as the Hardy chapters I have left out most of Lawrence's literary criticism, of which he wrote more than one might suppose in view of his dislike for touching life at second-hand and his detestation of 'the literary world'. Indeed, all writings about books are rather tepid after Lawrence's other work, which beyond that of any other writer of his time brings to the reader the immediate sensation of actual life. But if anyone is tempted to 'cut' the longish article on Galsworthy I would ask him at least to read and to meditate upon the opening pages which put so admirably and lucidly the commonsense of literary criticism. How much Lawrence detested the pompous quasi-philosophical sort of criticism which was the vogue in his day! Lawrence used to say that such critics merely looked at a book in order to paint their own portraits from the mirror, and referred to that 'ad.' on the old South-Eastern Railway of a simial looking at himself in a burnished frying pan with the stern caption: Monkey Soap Won't Wash Clothes. It won't you know.

I have grouped these pieces roughly in three sections. The first, *Love and Life*, contains some of the newspaper articles Lawrence wrote in his last years, thereby demonstrating that on top of all his other gifts as a writer he had the power to be a successful free-lance journalist. *The Spirit of Place*, which was an important conception to Lawrence, seemed a reasonable title to hold together his essays on Nature and travel and foreign countries. The three pieces on England may give the impression that Lawrence had little but hostile criticism to make of his native island, but all his earlier novels and stories abound with passages of the tenderest love for country England, and even in Australia he longed for the primroses and bluebells of an English spring. But his hatred of the blind industrial destruction of the old rural England was vehement and implacable. In the section on *Writing and Painting*, the very amusing yet appreciative essays on American writers strike me as bringing real freshness to the stale and frowsty ways of literary criticism.

In giving bibliographical information and personal details about how and where Lawrence wrote I have been indebted, in introducing the various volumes of this Penguin series, to his letters and to internal evidence and personal knowledge of his life. But here, as in the other Penguin Book introductions, I want to acknowledge how much I have learned from the writings of three Americans on the bibliography and manuscripts of Lawrence. To Edward D. McDonald, Lawrence C. Powell, and E. W. Tedlock, Jr, my grateful thanks for many a hint and piece of exact information.

Love and Life

SEX *VERSUS* LOVELINESS

Written 1928. *Sunday Dispatch*, 25 November, 1928. *Vanity Fair*, July, 1929. *Assorted Articles*, 1930

It is a pity that *sex* is such an ugly word. An ugly little word, and really almost incomprehensible. What *is* sex, after all? The more we think about it the less we know.

Science says it is an instinct; but what is an instinct? Apparently an instinct is an old, old habit that has become ingrained. But a habit, however old, has to have a beginning. And there is really no beginning to sex. Where life is, there it is. So sex is no 'habit' that has been formed.

Again, they talk of sex as an appetite, like hunger. An appetite; but for what? An appetite for propagation? It is rather absurd. They say a peacock puts on all his fine feathers to dazzle the peahen into letting him satisfy his appetite for propagation. But why should the peahen not put on fine feathers, to dazzle the peacock, and satisfy *her* desire for propagation? She has surely quite as great a desire for eggs and chickens as he has. We cannot believe that her sex-urge is so weak that she needs all that blue splendour of feathers to rouse her. Not at all.

As for me, I never even saw a peahen so much as look at her lord's bronze and blue glory. I don't believe she ever sees it. I don't believe for a moment that she knows the difference between bronze, blue, brown, or green.

If I had ever seen a peahen gazing with rapt attention on her lord's flamboyancy, I might believe that he had put on all those feathers just to 'attract' her. But she never looks at him. Only she seems to get a little perky when he shudders all his quills at her, like a storm in the trees. Then she does seem to notice, just casually, his presence.

These theories of sex are amazing. A peacock puts on his glory for the sake of a wall-eyed peahen who never looks at him. Imagine a scientist being so naive as to credit the peahen with a profound, dynamic appreciation of a peacock's colour and pattern. Oh, highly aesthetic peahen!

And a nightingale sings to attract his female. Which is mighty curious, seeing he sings his best when courtship and honeymoon are over and the female is no longer concerned with him at all, but with the young. Well, then, if he doesn't sing to attract her, he must sing to distract her and amuse her while she's sitting.

How delightful, how naive theories are! But there is a hidden will behind them all. There is a hidden will behind all theories of sex, implacable. And that is the will to deny, to wipe out the mystery of beauty.

Because beauty is a mystery. You can neither eat it nor make flannel out of it. Well, then, says science, it is just a trick to catch the female and induce her to propagate. How naive! As if the female needed inducing. She will propagate in the dark, even – so where, then, is the beauty trick?

Science has a mysterious hatred of beauty, because it doesn't fit in the cause-and-effect chain. And society has a mysterious hatred of sex, because it perpetually interferes with the nice money-making schemes of social man. So the two hatreds made a combine, and sex and beauty are mere propagation appetite.

Now sex and beauty are one thing, like flame and fire. If you hate sex you hate beauty. If you love *living* beauty, you have a reverence for sex. Of course you can love old, dead beauty and hate sex. But to love living beauty you must have a reverence for sex.

Sex and beauty are inseparable, like life and consciousness. And the intelligence which goes with sex and beauty, and arises out of sex and beauty, is intuition. The great disaster of our civilization is the morbid hatred of sex. What, for example, could show a more poisoned hatred of sex than Freudian psycho-analysis? – which carries with it a morbid fear of beauty, 'alive' beauty, and which causes the atrophy of our intuitive faculty and our intuitive self.

The deep psychic disease of modern men and women is the diseased, atrophied condition of the intuitive faculties. There is a whole world of life that we might know and enjoy by intuition, and by intuition alone. This is denied us, because we deny sex and beauty, the source of the intuitive life and of the insouciance which is so lovely in free animals and in plants.

Sex is the root of which intuition is the foliage and beauty the flower. Why is a woman lovely, if ever, in her twenties? It is the time when sex rises softly to her face, as a rose to the top of a rose bush.

And the appeal is the appeal of beauty. We deny it wherever we can. We try to make the beauty as shallow and trashy as possible. But, first and foremost, sex appeal is the appeal of beauty.

Now beauty is a thing about which we are so uneducated we can hardly speak of it. We try to pretend it is a fixed arrangement: straight nose, large eyes, etc. We think a lovely woman must look like Lilian Gish, a handsome man must look like Rudolph Valentino. So we *think*.

In actual life we behave quite differently. We say: 'She's quite beautiful, but I don't care for her.' Which shows we are using the word *beautiful* all wrong. We should say: 'She has the stereotyped attributes of beauty, but she is not beautiful to me.'

Beauty is an *experience*, nothing else. It is not a fixed pattern or an arrangement of features. It is something *felt*, a glow or a communicated sense of fineness. What ails us is that our sense of beauty is so bruised and blunted, we miss all the best.

But to stick to the films – there is a greater essential beauty in Charlie Chaplin's odd face than ever there was in Valentino's. There is a bit of true beauty in Chaplin's brows and eyes, a gleam of something pure.

But our sense of beauty is so bruised and clumsy, we don't see it, and don't know it when we do see it. We can only see the blatantly obvious, like the so-called beauty of Rudolph Valentino, which only pleases because it satisfies some ready-made notion of handsomeness.

But the plainest person can look beautiful, can *be* beautiful. It only needs the fire of sex to rise delicately to change an ugly face to a lovely one. That is really sex appeal: the communicating of a sense of beauty.

And in the reverse way, no one can be quite so repellent as a really pretty woman. That is, since beauty is a question of experience, not of concrete form, no one can be as acutely ugly as a really pretty woman. When the sex-glow is missing, and she moves in ugly coldness, how hideous she seems, and all the worse for her externals of prettiness.

What sex is, we don't know, but it must be some sort of fire. For it always communicates a sense of warmth, of glow. And when the glow becomes a pure shine, then we feel the sense of beauty.

But the communicating of the warmth, the glow of sex, is true sex appeal. We all have the fire of sex slumbering or burning inside us. If we live to be ninety, it is still there. Or, if it dies, we become one of those ghastly living corpses which are unfortunately becoming more numerous in the world.

Nothing is more ugly than a human being in whom the fire of sex has gone out. You get a nasty clayey creature whom everybody wants to avoid.

But while we are fully alive, the fire of sex smoulders or burns in us. In youth it flickers and shines; in age it glows softer and stiller, but there it is. We have some control over it; but only partial control. That is why society hates it.

While ever it lives, the fire of sex, which is the source of beauty and anger, burns in us beyond our understanding. Like actual fire, while it lives it will burn our fingers if we touch it carelessly. And so social man, who only wants to be 'safe', hates the fire of sex.

Luckily, not many men succeed in being merely social men. The fire of the old Adam smoulders. And one of the qualities of fire is that it calls to fire. Sex-fire here kindles sex-fire there. It may only rouse the smoulder into a soft glow. It may call up a sharp flicker. Or rouse a flame and then flame leans to flame, and starts a blaze.

Whenever the sex-fire glows through, it will kindle an answer somewhere or other. It may only kindle a sense of warmth and optimism. Then you say: 'I like that girl; she's a real good sort.' It may kindle a glow that makes the world look kindlier, and life feel better. Then you say: 'She's an attractive woman. I like her.'

Or she may rouse a flame that lights up her own face first, before it lights up the universe. Then you say: 'She's a lovely woman. She looks lovely to me.'

It takes a rare woman to rouse a real sense of loveliness. It is not that a woman is born beautiful. We say that to escape our own poor, bruised, clumsy understanding of beauty. There have been thousands and thousands of women quite as good-looking as Diane de Poitiers, or Mrs Langtry, or any of the famous ones. There are to-day thousands and thousands of superbly good-looking women. But oh, how few lovely women!

And why? Because of the failure of their sex appeal. A good-looking woman becomes lovely when the fire of sex rouses pure and fine in her and flickers through her face and touches the fire in me.

Then she becomes a lovely woman to me, then she is in the living flesh a lovely woman: not a mere photograph of one. And how lovely a lovely woman! But, alas! how rare! How bitterly rare in a world full of unusually handsome girls and women!

Handsome, good-looking, but not lovely, not beautiful. Handsome and good-looking women are the women with good features and the right hair. But a lovely woman is an experience. It is a question of communicated fire. It is a question of sex appeal in our poor, dilapidated modern phraseology. Sex appeal applied to Diane de Poitiers, or even, in the lovely hours, to one's wife – why, it is a libel and a slander in itself. Nowadays, however, instead of the fire of loveliness, it is sex appeal. The two are the same thing, I suppose, but on vastly different levels.

The business man's pretty and devoted secretary is still chiefly valuable because of her sex appeal. Which does not imply 'immoral relations' in the slightest.

Even to-day a girl with a bit of generosity likes to feel she is helping a man if the man will take her help. And this desire that he shall take her help is her sex appeal. It is the genuine fire, if of a very mediocre heat.

Still, it serves to keep the world of 'business' alive. Probably, but for the introduction of the lady secretary into the business man's office, the business man would have collapsed entirely by now. She calls up the sacred fire in her and she communicates it to her boss. He feels an added flow of energy and optimism, and – business flourishes.

There is, of course, the other side of sex appeal. It can be the destruction of the one appealed to. When a woman starts using her sex appeal to her own advantage it is usually a bad moment for some poor devil. But this side of sex appeal has been overworked lately, so it is not nearly as dangerous as it was.

The sex-appealing courtesans who ruined so many men in Balzac no longer find it smooth running. Men have grown canny. They fight shy even of the emotional vamp. In fact, men are inclined to think they smell a rat the moment they feel the touch of feminine sex appeal to-day.

Which is a pity, for sex appeal is only a dirty name for a bit of life-flame. No man works so well and so successfully as when some woman has kindled a little fire in his veins. No woman does her housework with real joy unless she is in love – and a woman may go on being quietly in love for fifty years almost without knowing it.

If only our civilization had taught us how to let sex appeal flow properly and subtly, how to keep the fire of sex clear and alive, flickering or glowing or blazing in all its varying degrees of strength and communication, we might, all of us, have lived all our lives in love, which means we should be kindled and full of zest in all kinds of ways and for all kinds of things...

Whereas, what a lot of dead ash there is in life now.

GIVE HER A PATTERN

Written 1928–9. *Assorted Articles*, 1930

THE real trouble about women is that they must always go on trying to adapt themselves to men's theories of women, as they always have done. When a woman is thoroughly herself, she is being what her type of man wants her to be. When a woman is hysterical it's because she doesn't quite know what to be, which pattern to follow, which man's picture of woman to live up to.

For, of course, just as there are many men in the world, there are many masculine theories of what women should be. But men run to type, and it is the type, not the individual, that produces the theory, or 'ideal' of woman. Those very grasping gentry, the Romans, produced a theory or ideal of the matron, which fitted in very nicely with the Roman property lust. 'Caesar's wife should be above suspicion.' – So Caesar's wife kindly proceeded to be above it, no matter how far below it the Caesar fell. Later gentlemen like Nero produced the 'fast' theory of woman, and later ladies were fast enough for everybody. Dante arrived with a chaste and untouched Beatrice, and chaste and untouched Beatrices began to march self-importantly through the centuries. The Renaissance discovered the learned woman, and learned women buzzed mildly into verse and prose. Dickens invented the child-wife, so child-wives have swarmed ever since. He also fished out his version of the chaste Beatrice, a chaste but marriageable Agnes. George Eliot imitated this pattern, and it became confirmed. The noble woman, the pure spouse, the devoted mother took the field, and was simply worked to death. Our own poor mothers were this sort. So we younger men, having been a bit frightened of our noble mothers, tended to revert to the child-wife. We weren't very inventive. Only the child-wife must be a boyish little thing – that was the new touch we added. Because young men are definitely frightened of the real female. She's too risky a quantity. She is too untidy, like David's Dora. No, let her be a boyish little thing, it's safer. So a boyish little thing she is.

There are, of course, other types. Capable men produce the capable woman ideal. Doctors produce the capable nurse. Business men produce the capable secretary. And so you get all sorts. You can produce the masculine sense of honour (whatever that highly mysterious quantity may be) in women, if you want to.

There is also the eternal secret ideal of men – the prostitute. Lots of women live up to this idea, just because men want them to.

And so, poor woman, destiny makes away with her. It isn't that she hasn't got a mind – she has. She's got everything that man has. The only difference is that she asks for a pattern. Give me a pattern to follow! That will always be woman's cry. Unless of course she has already chosen her pattern quite young, then she will declare she is herself absolutely, and no man's idea of women has any influence over her.

Now the real tragedy is not that women ask and must ask for a pattern of womanhood. The tragedy is not, even, that men give them such abominable patterns, child-wives, little-boy-baby-face girls, perfect secretaries, noble spouses, self-sacrificing mothers, pure women who bring forth children in virgin coldness, prostitutes who just make themselves low, to please men; all the atrocious patterns of womanhood that men have supplied to woman; patterns all perverted from any real natural fulness of a human being. Man is willing to accept woman as an equal, as a man in skirts, as an angel, a devil, a baby-face, a machine, an instrument, a bosom, a womb, a pair of legs, a servant, an encyclopedia, an ideal, or an obscenity; the one thing he won't accept her as, is a human being, a real human being of the feminine sex.

And, of course, women love living up to strange patterns, weird patterns – the more uncanny the better. What could be more uncanny than the present pattern of the Eton-boy girl with flower-like artificial complexion? It is just weird. And for its very weirdness women like living up to it. What can be more gruesome than the little-boy-baby-face pattern? Yet the girls take it on with avidity.

But even that isn't the real root of the tragedy. The absurdity, and often, as in the Dante-Beatrice business, the inhuman nastiness of the pattern – for Beatrice had to go on being chaste and untouched all her life, according to Dante's pattern, while Dante had a cosy wife and kids at home – even that isn't the worst of it. The worst of it is, as soon as a woman has really lived up to the man's pattern the man dislikes her for it. There is intense secret dislike for the Eton-young-man girl, among the boys, now that she is actually produced. Of course, she's very nice to show in public, absolutely the thing. But the very young men who have brought about her production detest her in private and in their private hearts are appalled by her.

When it comes to marrying, the pattern goes all to pieces. The boy marries the Eton-boy girl, and instantly he hates the *type*. Instantly his mind begins to play hysterically with all the other types, noble Agneses, chaste Beatrices, clinging Doras and lurid *filles de joie*. He is in a wild welter of confusion. Whatever the pattern the poor woman tries to live up to, he'll want another. And that's the condition of modern marriage.

Modern woman isn't really a fool. But modern man is. That seems to me the only plain way of putting it. The modern man is a fool, and the modern young man a prize fool. He makes a greater mess of his women than men have ever made. Because he absolutely doesn't know *what* he wants her to be. We shall see the changes in the woman-pattern follow one another fast and furious now, because the young men hysterically don't know what they want. Two years hence women may be in crinolines – there was a pattern for you! – or a bead flap, like naked negresses in mid-Africa – or they may be wearing brass armour, or the uniform of the Horse Guards. They may be anything. Because the young men are off their heads, and don't know what they want.

The women aren't fools, but they *must* live up to some

pattern or other. They *know* the men are fools. They don't really respect the pattern. Yet a pattern they must have, or they can't exist.

Women are not fools. They have their own logic, even if it's not the masculine sort. Women have the logic of emotion, men have the logic of reason. The two are complementary and mostly in opposition. But the woman's logic of emotion is no less real and inexorable than the man's logic of reason. It only works differently.

And the woman never really loses it. She may spend years living up to a masculine pattern. But in the end, the strange and terrible logic of emotion will work out the smashing of that pattern, if it has not been emotionally satisfactory. This is the partial explanation of the astonishing changes in women. For years they go on being chaste Beatrices or child-wives. Then on a sudden – bash! The chaste Beatrice becomes a roaring lioness! The pattern didn't suffice, emotionally.

Whereas men are fools. They are based on a logic of reason, or are supposed to be. And then they go and behave, especially with regard to women, in a more-than-feminine unreasonableness. They spend years training up the little-boy-baby-face type, till they've got her perfect. Then the moment they marry her, they want something else. Oh, beware, young women, of the young men who adore you! The moment they've got you they'll want something utterly different. The moment they marry the little-boy-baby-face, instantly they begin to pine for the noble Agnes, pure and majestic, or the infinite mother with deep bosom of consolation, or the perfect business woman, or the lurid prostitute on black silk sheets; or, most idiotic of all, a combination of the lot of them at once. And that is the logic of reason! When it comes to women, modern men are idiots. They don't know what they want, and so they never want, permanently, what they get. They want a cream cake that is at the same time ham and eggs and at the same time porridge. They are fools. If only women weren't bound by fate to play up to them!

For the fact of life is that women *must* play up to man's pattern. And she only gives her best to a man when he gives her a satisfactory pattern to play up to. But to-day, with a stock of ready-made, worn-out idiotic patterns to live up to, what can women give to men but the trashy side of their emotions? What could a woman possibly give to a man who wanted her to be a boy-baby-face? What could she possibly give him but the dribblings of an idiot? – And, because women aren't fools, and aren't fooled even for very long at a time, she gives him some nasty cruel digs with her claws, and makes him cry for mother dear! – abruptly changing his pattern.

Bah! men are fools. If they want anything from women, let them give women a decent, satisfying idea of womanhood – not these trick patterns of washed-out idiots.

LOVE

Written *circa* 1917. *English Review*, January, 1918. *Phoenix*, 1936

LOVE is the happiness of the world. But happiness is not the whole of fulfilment. Love is a coming together. But there can be no coming together without an equivalent going asunder. In love, all things unite in a oneness of joy and praise. But they could not unite unless they were previously apart. And, having united in a whole circle of unity, they can go no further in love. The motion of love, like a tide, is fulfilled in this instance; there must be an ebb.

So that the coming together depends on the going apart; the systole depends on the diastole; the flow depends upon the ebb. These can never be love universal and unbroken. The sea can never rise to high tide over all the globe at once. The undisputed reign of love can never be.

Because love is strictly a travelling. 'It is better to travel than to arrive', somebody has said. This is the essence of unbelief. It is a belief in absolute love, when love is by nature relative. It is a belief in the means, but not in the end. It is strictly a belief in force, for love is a unifying force.

How shall we believe in force? Force is instrumental and functional; it is neither a beginning nor an end. We travel in order to arrive; we do not travel in order to travel. At least, such travelling is mere futility. We travel in order to arrive.

And love is a travelling, a motion, a speed of coming together. Love is the force of creation. But all force, spiritual or physical, has its polarity, its positive and its negative. All things that fall, fall by gravitation to the earth. But has not the earth, in the opposite of gravitation, cast off the moon and held her at bay in our heavens during all the aeons of time?

So with love. Love is the hastening gravitation of spirit towards spirit, and body towards body, in the joy of creation. But if all be united in one bond of love, then there is no more love. And therefore, for those who are in love with love, to travel is better than to arrive. For in arriving one passes beyond love, or, rather, one encompasses love in a new transcendence. To arrive is the supreme joy after all our travelling.

The bond of love! What worse bondage can we conceive than the bond of love? It is an attempt to wall in the high tide; it is a will to arrest the spring, never to let May dissolve into June, never to let the hawthorn petal fall for the berrying.

This has been our idea of immortality, this infinite of love, love universal and triumphant. And what is this but a prison and a bondage? What is eternity but the endless passage of time? What is infinity but an endless progressing through space? Eternity, infinity, our great ideas of rest and arrival, what are they but ideas of endless travelling? Eternity is the endless travelling through time, infinity is the endless travelling through space; no more, however we try to argue it. And immortality, what is it, in our idea, but an endless continuing in the same sort? A continuing, a living for ever, a lasting and enduring for ever – what is this but travelling? An assumption into heaven, a becoming one with God – what is the infinite on arrival? The infinite is no arrival. When we come to find exactly what we mean by God, by the infinite, by our immortality, it is a meaning of endless continuing in the same line and in the same sort, endless travelling in one direction. This is infinity, endless travelling in one direction. And the God of Love is our idea of the progression *ad infinitum* of the force of love. Infinity is no arrival. It is as much a cul-de-sac as is the bottomless pit. And what is the infinity of love but a cul-de-sac or a bottomless pit?

Love is a progression towards the goal. Therefore it is a progression away from the opposite goal. Love travels heavenwards. What then does love depart from? Hellwards, what is there? Love is at last a positive infinite. What then is the negative infinite? Positive and negative infinite are the same, since there is only one infinite. How then will it matter if we travel heavenwards, *ad infinitum*, or in the opposite direction, to infinity? Since the infinity obtained is the same in either case, the infinite of pure homogeneity, which is nothingness, or everythingness, it does not matter which.

Infinity, the infinite, is no goal. It is a cul-de-sac, or, in another sense, it is the bottomless pit. To fall down the bottomless pit is to travel for ever. And a pleasant-walled cul-de-sac may be a perfect heaven. But to arrive in a sheltered, paradisiacal cul-de-sac of peace and unblemished happiness, this will not satisfy us. And to fall for ever down the bottomless pit of progression, this will not do either.

Love is not a goal; it is only a travelling. Likewise death is not a goal; it is a travelling asunder into elemental chaos. And from the elemental chaos all is cast forth again into creation. Therefore death also is but a cul-de-sac, a melting-pot.

There is a goal, but the goal is neither love nor death. It is a goal neither infinite nor eternal. It is the realm of calm delight, it is the other-kingdom of bliss. We are like a rose, which is a miracle of pure centrality, pure absolved equilibrium. Balanced in perfection in the midst of time and space, the rose is perfect in the realm of perfection, neither temporal nor spatial, but absolved by the quality of perfection, pure immanence of absolution.

We are creatures of time and space. But we are like a rose; we accomplish perfection, we arrive in the absolute. We are creatures of time and space. And we are at once creatures of pure transcendence, absolved from time and space, perfected in the realm of the absolute, the other-world of bliss.

And love, love is encompassed and surpassed. Love always has been encompassed and surpassed by the fine lovers. We are like a rose, a perfect arrival.

Love is manifold, it is not of one sort only. There is the love between man and woman, sacred and profane. There is Christian love, 'thou shalt love thy neighbour as thyself.' And there is the love of God. But always love is a joining together.

Only in the conjunction of man and woman has love kept a duality of meaning. Sacred love and profane love, they are opposed, and yet they are both love. The love between man and woman is the greatest and most complete passion the world will ever see, because it is dual, because it is of two opposing kinds. The love between man and woman is the perfect heart-beat of life, systole, diastole.

Sacred love is selfless, seeking not its own. The lover serves his beloved and seeks perfect communion of oneness with her. But whole love between man and woman is sacred and profane together. Profane love seeks its own. I seek my own in the beloved, I wrestle with her to wrest it from her. We are not clear, we are mixed and mingled. I am in the beloved also, and she is in me. Which should not be, for this is confusion and chaos. Therefore I will gather myself complete and free from the beloved, she shall single herself out in utter contradistinction to me. There is twilight in our souls, neither light nor dark. The light must draw itself together in purity, the dark must stand on the other hand; they must be two complete in opposition, neither one partaking of the other, but each single in its own stead.

We are like a rose. In the pure passion for oneness, in the pure passion for distinctness and separateness, a dual passion of unutterable separation and lovely conjunction of the two, the new configuration takes place, the transcendence, the two in their perfect singleness, transported into one surpassing heaven of a rose-blossom.

But the love between a man and a woman, when it is whole, is dual. It is the melting into pure communion, and it is the friction of sheer sensuality, both. In pure communion I become whole in love. And in pure, fierce passion of sensuality I am burned into essentiality. I am driven from the matrix into sheer separate distinction. I become my single self, inviolable and unique, as the gems were perhaps once driven into themselves out of the confusion of earths. The woman and I, we are the confusion of earths. Then in the fire of their extreme sensual love, in the friction of intense, destructive flames, I am destroyed and reduced to her essential otherness. It is a destructive fire, the profane love. But it is the only fire that will purify us into singleness, fuse us from the chaos into our own unique gem-like separateness of being.

All whole love between man and woman is thus dual, a love which is the motion of melting, fusing together into oneness, and a love which is the intense, frictional, and sensual gratification of being burnt down, burnt apart into separate clarity of being, unthinkable otherness and separateness. But not all love between man and woman is whole. It may be all gentle, the merging into oneness, like St Francis and St Clare, or Mary of Bethany and Jesus. There may be no separateness discovered, no singleness won, no unique otherness admitted. This is a half love, what is called sacred love. And this is the love which knows the purest happiness. On the other hand, the love may be all a lovely battle of sensual gratification, the beautiful but deadly counterposing of male against female, as Tristan and Isolde. These are the lovers that top the sum of pride, they go with the grandest banners, they are the gem-like beings, he pure male singled and separated out in superb jewel-like isolation of arrogant manhood, she purely woman, a lily balanced in rocking pride of beauty and perfume of womanhood. This is the profane love, that ends in flamboyant and lacerating tragedy when the two which are so singled out are torn finally apart by death. But if profane love ends in piercing tragedy, none the less the sacred love ends in a poignant yearning and exquisite submissive grief. St Francis dies and leaves St Clare to her pure sorrow.

There must be two in one, always two in one – the sweet love of communion and the fierce, proud love of sensual fulfilment, both together in one love. And then we are like a rose. We surpass even love, love is encompassed and surpassed. We are two who have a pure connexion. We are two, isolated like gems in our unthinkable otherness. But the rose contains and transcends us, we are one rose, beyond.

The Christian love, the brotherly love, this is always sacred. I love my neighbour as myself. What then? I am enlarged, I surpass myself, I become whole in mankind. In the whole of perfect humanity I am whole. I am the microcosm, the epitome of the great microcosm. I speak of the perfectibility of man. Man can be made perfect in love, he can become a creature of love alone. Then humanity shall be one whole of love.

This is the perfect future for those who love their neighbours as themselves.

But, alas! however much I may be the microcosm, the exemplar of brotherly love, there is in me this necessity to separate and distinguish myself into gem-like singleness, distinct and apart from all the rest, proud as a lion, isolated as a star. This is a necessity within me. And this necessity is unfulfilled, it becomes stronger and stronger and it becomes dominant.

Then I shall hate the self that I am, powerfully and profoundly shall I hate this microcosm that I have become, this epitome of mankind. I shall hate myself with madness the more I persist in adhering to my achieved self of brotherly love. Still I shall persist in representing a whole loving humanity, until the unfulfilled passion for singleness drives me into action. Then I shall hate my neighbour as I hate myself. And then, woe betide my neighbour and me! Whom the gods wish to destroy they first make mad. And this is how we become mad, by being impelled into activity by the subconscious reaction against the self we maintain, without ever ceasing to maintain this detested self. We are bewildered, dazed. In the name of brotherly love we rush into stupendous blind activities of brotherly hate. We are made mad by the split, the duality in ourselves. The gods wish to destroy us because we serve them too well. Which is the end of brotherly love, *liberté*, *fraternité*, *égalité*, how can there be liberty when I am not free to be other than fraternal and equal? I must be free to be separate and unequal in the finest sense, if I am to be free. *Fraternité* and *égalité*, these are tyranny of tyrannies.

There must be brotherly love, a wholeness of humanity. But there must also be pure, separate individuality, separate and proud as a lion or a hawk. There must be both. In the duality lies fulfilment. Man must act in concert with man, creatively and happily. This is greatest happiness. But man must also act separately and distinctly, apart from every other man, single and self-responsible and proud with unquenchable pride, moving for himself without reference to his neighbour. These two movements are opposite, yet they do not negate each other. We have understanding. And if we understand, then we balance perfectly between the two motions, we are single, isolated individuals, we are a great concordant of humanity, both, and then the rose of perfection transcends us, the rose of the world which has never yet blossomed, but which will blossom from us when we begin to understand both sides and to live in both directions, freely and without fear, following the inmost desires of our body and spirit, which arrive to us out of the unknown.

Lastly, there is the love of God; we become whole with God. But God as we know Him is either infinite love or infinite pride and power, always one or the other, Christ or Jehovah, always one half excluding the other. Therefore, God is for ever jealous. If we love one God, we must hate this one sooner or later, and choose the other. This is the tragedy of religious experience. But the Holy Spirit, the unknowable, is single and perfect for us.

There is that which we cannot love, because it surpasses either love or hate. There is the unknown and the unknowable which propounds all creation. This we cannot love, we can only accept it as a term of our own limitation and ratification. We can only know that from the unknown, profound desires enter in upon us, and that the fulfilling of these desires is the fulfilling of creation. We know that the rose comes to blossom. We know that we are incipient with blossom. It is our business to go as we are impelled, with faith and pure spontaneous morality, knowing that the rose blossoms, and taking that knowledge for sufficient.

COCKSURE WOMEN AND HENSURE MEN

Written 1928. *The Forum*, January, 1929.
Assorted Articles, 1930

It seems to me there are two aspects to women. There is the demure and the dauntless. Men have loved to dwell, in fiction at least, on the demure maiden whose inevitable reply is: Oh, yes, if you please, kind sir! The demure maiden, the demure spouse, the demure mother – this is still the ideal. A few maidens, mistresses, and mothers *are* demure. A few pretend to be. But the vast majority are not. And they don't pretend to be. We don't expect a girl skilfully driving her car to be demure, we expect her to be dauntless. What good would demure and maidenly Members of Parliament be, inevitably responding: Oh, yes, if you please, kind sir! – Though of course there are masculine members of that kidney. And a demure telephone girl? Or even a demure stenographer? Demureness, to be sure, is outwardly becoming, it is an outward mark of femininity, like bobbed hair. But it goes with inward dauntlessness. The girl who has got to make her way in life has got to be dauntless, and if she has a pretty, demure manner with it, then lucky girl. She kills two birds with two stones.

With the two kinds of femininity go two kinds of confidence: there are the women who are cocksure, and the women who are hensure. A really up-to-date woman is a cocksure woman. She doesn't have a doubt nor a qualm. She is the modern type. Whereas the old-fashioned demure woman was sure as a hen is sure, that is, without knowing anything about it. She went quietly and busily clucking around, laying the eggs and mothering the chickens in a kind of anxious dream that still was full of sureness. But not mental sureness. Her sureness was a physical condition, very soothing, but a condition out of which she could easily be startled or frightened.

It is quite amusing to see the two kinds of sureness in chickens. The cockerel is, naturally, cocksure. He crows because he is *certain* it is day. Then the hen peeps out from under her wing. He marches to the door of the hen-house and pokes out his head assertively: *Ah ha! daylight! of course! just as I said!* – and he majestically steps down the chicken ladder towards *terra firma*, knowing that the hens will step cautiously after him, drawn by his confidence. So after him, cautiously, step the hens. He crows again: *Ha-ha! here we are!* – It is indisputable, and the hens accept it entirely. He marches towards the house. From the house a person ought to appear, scattering corn. Why does the person not appear? The cock will see to it. He is cocksure. He gives a loud crow in the doorway, and the person appears. The hens are suitably impressed, but immediately devote all their henny consciousness to the scattered corn, pecking absorbedly, while the cock runs and fusses, cocksure that he is responsible for it all.

So the day goes on. The cock finds a tit-bit, and loudly calls the hens. They scuffle up in henny surety, and gobble the tit-bit. But when they find a juicy morsel for themselves, they devour it in silence, hensure. Unless, of course, there are little chicks, when they most anxiously call the brood. But in her own dim surety, the hen is really much surer than the cock, in a different way. She marches off to lay her egg, she secures obstinately the nest she wants, she lays her egg at last, then steps forth again with prancing confidence, and gives that most assured of all sounds, the hensure cackle of a bird who has laid her egg. The cock, who is never so sure about anything as the hen is about the egg she has laid, immediately starts to cackle like the female of his species. He is pining to be hensure, for hensure is so much surer than cocksure.

Nevertheless, cocksure is boss. When the chicken-hawk appears in the sky, loud are the cockerel's calls of alarm. Then the hens scuffle under the verandah, the cock ruffles his feathers on guard. The hens are numb with fear, they say: Alas, there is no health in us! How wonderful to be a cock so bold!

– And they huddle, numbed. But their very numbness is hensurety.

Just as the cock can cackle, however, as if he had laid the egg, so can the hen bird crow. She can more or less assume his cocksureness. And yet she is never so easy, cocksure, as she used to be when she was hensure. Cocksure, she is cocksure, but uneasy. Hensure, she trembles, but is easy.

It seems to me just the same in the vast human farmyard. Only nowadays all the cocks are cackling and pretending to lay eggs, and all the hens are crowing and pretending to call the sun out of bed. If women to-day are cocksure, men are hensure. Men are timid, tremulous, rather soft and submissive, easy in their very henlike tremulousness. They only want to be spoken to gently. So the women step forth with a good loud *cock-a-doodle-do!*

The tragedy about cocksure women is that they are more cocky, in their assurance, than the cock himself. They never realize that when the cock gives his loud crow in the morning, he listens acutely afterwards, to hear if some other wretch of a cock dare crow defiance, challenge. To the cock, there is always defiance, challenge, danger, and death on the clear air; or the possibility thereof.

But alas, when the hen crows, she listens for no defiance or challenge. When she says *cock-a-doodle-do!* then it is unanswerable. *Cock-a-doodle-do!* and there it is, take it or leave it!

And it is this that makes the cocksureness of women so dangerous, so devastating. It is really out of scheme, it is not in relation to the rest of things. So we have the tragedy of cocksure women. They find, so often, that instead of having laid an egg, they have laid a vote, or an empty ink-bottle, or some other absolutely unhatchable object, which means nothing to them.

It is the tragedy of the modern woman. She becomes cocksure, she puts all her passion and energy and years of her life into some effort or assertion, without ever listening for the denial which she ought to take into account. She is cocksure, but she is a hen all the time. Frightened of her own henny self, she rushes to mad lengths about votes, or welfare, or sports, or business: she is marvellous, out-manning the man. But alas, it is all fundamentally disconnected. It is all an attitude, and one day the attitude will become a weird cramp, a pain, and then it will collapse. And when it has collapsed, and she looks at the eggs she has laid, votes, or miles of typewriting, years of business efficiency – suddenly, because she is a hen and not a cock, all she has done will turn into pure nothingness to her. Suddenly it all falls out of relation to her basic henny self, and she realizes she has lost her life. The lovely henny surety, the hensureness which is the real bliss of every female, has been denied her: she had never had it. Having lived her life with such utmost strenuousness and cocksureness, she has missed her life altogether. Nothingness!

NOBODY LOVES ME

Written 1929. *Phoenix*, 1936

LAST year, we had a little house up in the Swiss mountains, for the summer. A friend came to tea: a woman of fifty or so, with her daughter: old friends. 'And how are you all?' I asked, as she sat, flushed and rather exasperated after the climb up to the chalet on a hot afternoon, wiping her face with a too-small handkerchief. 'Well!' she replied, glancing almost viciously out of the window at the immutable slopes and peaks opposite, 'I don't know how *you* feel about it – but – these mountains! – well! – I've lost *all* my *cosmic consciousness* and *all* my *love for humanity*.'

She is, of course, New England of the old school – and usually transcendentalist calm. So that her exasperated frenzy of the moment – it was really a frenzy – coupled with the New England language and slight accent, seemed to me really funny. I laughed in her face, poor dear, and said: 'Never mind! Perhaps you can do with a rest from your cosmic consciousness and your love of humanity.'

I have often thought of it since: of what she really meant. And every time, I have had a little pang, realizing that I was a bit spiteful to her. I admit, her New England transcendental habit of loving the cosmos *en bloc* and humanity *en masse* did rather get on my nerves, always. But then she had been brought up that way. And the fact of loving the cosmos didn't prevent her from being fond of her own garden – though it did, a bit; and her love of humanity didn't prevent her from having a real affection for her friends, except that she felt that she *ought* to love them in a selfless and general way, which was rather annoying. Nevertheless, that, to me, rather silly language about cosmic consciousness and love of humanity did stand for something that was not merely cerebral. It stood, and I realized it afterwards, for her peace, her inward peace with the universe and with man. And this she could *not* do without. One may be at war with society, and still keep one's deep peace with mankind. It is not pleasant to be at war with society, but sometimes it is the only way of preserving one's peace of soul, which is peace with the living, struggling, *real* mankind. And this latter one cannot afford to lose. So I had no right to tell my friend she could do with a rest from her love of humanity. She couldn't, and none of us can: if we interpret *love of humanity* as that feeling of being at one with the struggling soul, or spirit, or whatever it is, of our fellow-men.

Now the wonder to me is that the young do seem to get on without any 'cosmic consciousness' or 'love of humanity'. They have, on the whole, shed the cerebral husk of generalizations from their emotional state: the cosmic and humanity touch. But it seems to me they have also shed the flower that was inside the husk. Of course, you can hear a girl exclaim: '*Really*, you know, the colliers are darlings, and it's a shame the way they're treated.' She will even rush off and register a vote for her darlings. But she doesn't really care – and one can sympathize with her. This caring about the wrongs of unseen people has been rather overdone. Nevertheless, though the colliers or cotton-workers or whatever they be are a long way off and we can't do anything about it, still, away in some depth of us, we know that we are connected vitally, if remotely, with these colliers or cotton-workers, we dimly realize that mankind is one, almost one flesh. It is an abstraction, but it is also a physical fact. In some way or other, the cotton-workers of Carolina, or the rice growers of China, are connected with me and, to a faint yet real degree, part of me. The vibration of life which they give off reaches me, touches me, and affects me all unknown to me. For we are more or less connected, all more or less in touch: all humanity. That is, until we have killed the sensitive responses in ourselves, which happens to-day only too often.

Dimly, this is what my transcendentalist meant by her 'love of humanity', though she tended to kill the real thing by labelling it so philanthropically and bossily. Dimly, she meant her sense of participating in the life of all humanity, which is a sense we all have, delicately and deeply, when we are at peace in ourselves. But let us lose our inward peace, and at once we are likely to substitute for this delicate inward sense of participating in the life of all mankind another thing, a nasty pronounced benevolence, which wants to do good to all mankind, and is only a form of self-assertion and of bullying. From this sort of love of humanity, good Lord deliver us! and deliver poor humanity. My friend was a tiny bit tainted with this form of self-importance, as all transcendentalists were. So if the mountains, in their brutality, took away the tainted love, good for them. But my dear Ruth – I shall call her Ruth – had more than this. She had, woman of fifty as she was, an almost girlish naive sense of living at peace, real peace, with her fellow-men. And this she could not afford to lose. And save for that taint of generalization and *will*, she would never have lost it, even for that half-hour in the Swiss mountains. But she meant the 'cosmos' and 'humanity' to fit her will and her feelings, and the mountains made her realize that the cosmos *wouldn't*. When you come up against the cosmos, your consciousness is likely to suffer a jolt. And humanity, when you come down to it, is likely to give your 'love' a nasty jar. But there you are.

When we come to the younger generation, however, we realize that 'cosmic consciousness' and 'love of humanity' have really been left out of their composition. They are like a lot of brightly-coloured bits of glass and they only feel just what they bump against, when they're shaken. They make an accidental pattern with other people, and for the rest they know nothing and care nothing.

So that cosmic consciousness and love of humanity, to use the absurd New England terms, are really dead. They were tainted. Both the cosmos and humanity were too much manufactured in New England. They weren't the real thing. They were, very often, just noble phrases to cover up self-assertion, self-importance, and malevolent bullying. They were just activities of the ugly, self-willed ego, determined that humanity and the cosmos should exist as New England allowed them to exist, or not at all. They were tainted with bullying egoism, and the young, having fine noses for this sort of smell, would have none of them.

The way to kill any feeling is to insist on it, harp on it, exaggerate it. Insist on loving humanity, and sure as fate you'll come to hate everybody. Because, of course, if you insist on loving humanity, then you insist that it shall be lovable: which half the time it isn't. In the same way, insist on loving your husband, and you won't be able to help hating him secretly. Because of course nobody is *always* lovable. If you insist they shall be, this imposes a tyranny over them, and they become less lovable. And if you force yourself to love them – or pretend to – when they are not lovable, you falsify everything, and fall into hate. The result of forcing any feeling is the death of that feeling, and the substitution of some sort of opposite. Whitman insisted on sympathizing with everything and everybody: so much so, that he came to believe in death only, not just his own death, but the death of all people. In the same way the slogan 'Keep Smiling!' produces at last a sort of savage rage in the breast of the smilers, and the famous 'cheery morning greeting' makes the gall accumulate in all the cheery ones.

It is no good. Every time you force your feelings, you damage yourself and produce the opposite effect to the one you want. Try to force yourself to love somebody, and you are bound to end by detesting that same somebody. The only thing to do is to have the feelings you've really got, and not make up any of them. And that is the only way to leave the other person free. If you feel like murdering your husband, then don't say, 'Oh, but I love him dearly. I'm devoted to him.' That is not only bullying yourself, but bullying him. He doesn't want to be *forced*, even by love. Just say to yourself: 'I could murder him, and that's a fact. But I suppose I'd better not.' And then your feelings will get their own balance.

The same is true of love of humanity. The last generation, and the one before that *insisted* on loving humanity. They cared terribly for the poor suffering Irish and Armenians and Congo rubber Negroes and all that. And it was a great deal of it fake, self-conceit, self-importance. The bottom of it was the egoistic thought: 'I'm so good, I'm so superior, I'm so benevolent, I care intensely about the poor suffering Irish and the martyred Armenians and the oppressed Negroes, and I'm going to save them, even if I have to upset the English and the Turks and the Belgians severely.' This love of mankind was half self-importance and half a desire to interfere and put a spoke in other people's wheels. The younger generation, smelling the rat under the lamb's-wool of Christian Charity, said to themselves: No love of humanity for me!

They have, if the truth be told, a secret detestation of all oppressed or unhappy people who need 'relief'. They rather hate 'the poor colliers', 'the poor cotton-workers', 'the poor starving Russians', and all that. If there came another war, how they would loathe 'the stricken Belgians'! And so it is: the father eats the pear, and the son's teeth are set on edge.

Having overdone the sympathy touch, especially the love of humanity, we have now got the recoil away from sympathy. The young don't sympathize, and they don't want to. They are egoists, and frankly so. They say quite honestly: 'I don't give a hoot in hell for the poor oppressed this-that-and-the-other'. And who can blame them? Their loving forbears brought on the Great War. If love of humanity brought on the Great War, let us see what frank and honest egoism will do. Nothing so horrible, we can bet.

The trouble about frank and accepted egoism is its unpleasant effect on the egoist himself. Honesty is very good, and it is good to cast off all the spurious sympathies and false emotions of the pre-war world. But casting off spurious sympathy and false emotion need not entail the death of all sympathy and all deep emotion, as it seems to do in the young. The young quite deliberately *play* at sympathy and emotion. 'Darling child, how lovely you look to-night! I *adore* to look at you!' – and in the next breath, a little arrow of spite. Or the young wife to her husband: 'My beautiful love, I feel so precious when you hold me like that, my perfect dear! But shake me a cocktail, angel, would you? I need a good kick – you *angel* of light!'

The young, at the moment, have a perfectly good time strumming on the keyboard of emotion and sympathy, tinkling away at all the exaggerated phrases of rapture and tenderness, adoration and delight, while they feel – nothing, except a certain amusement at the childish game. It is so *chic* and charming to use all the most precious phrases of love and endearment amusingly, just amusingly, like the tinkling in a music-box.

And they would be very indignant if told they had no love of humanity. The English ones profess the most amusing and histrionic love of England, for example. 'There is only one thing I care about, except my beloved Philip, and that is England, our precious England. Philip and I are both prepared to die for England, at any moment.' At the moment, England does not seem to be in any danger of asking them, so they are quite safe. And if you gently enquire: 'But what, in your imagination, is England?' they reply fervently: 'The great tradition of the English, the great idea of England' – which seems comfortably elastic and non-committal.

And they cry: 'I would give everything for the cause of freedom. Hope and I have wept tears, and saddened our precious marriage-bed, thinking of the trespass on English liberty. But we are calmer now, and determined to fight calmly to the utmost.' Which calm fight consists in taking another cocktail and sending out a wildly emotional letter to somebody perfectly irresponsible. Then all is over, and freedom is forgotten, and perhaps religion gets a turn, or a wild outburst over some phrase in the burial service.

This is the advanced young of to-day. I confess it is amusing, while the coruscation lasts. The trying part is when the fireworks have finished – and they don't last very long, even with cocktails – and the grey stretches intervene. For with the advanced young, there is no warm daytime and silent night. It is all fireworks of excitement and stretches of grey emptiness; then more fireworks. And, let the grisly truth be owned, it is rather exhausting.

Now in the grey intervals in the life of the modern young one fact emerges in all its dreariness, and makes itself plain to the young themselves, as well as the onlooker. The fact that they are empty: that they care about nothing and nobody: not even the Amusement they seek so strenuously. Of course this skeleton is not to be taken out of the cupboard. 'Darling angel man, don't start being a nasty white ant. Play the game, angel-face, play the game; don't start saying unpleasant things and rattling a lot of dead men's bones! Tell us something nice, something amusing. Or let's be *really* serious, you know, and talk about bolshevism or *la haute finance*. Do be an angel of light, and cheer us up, you YOU nicest precious pet!'

As a matter of fact, the young are becoming afraid of their own emptiness. It's awful fun throwing things out of the window. But when you've thrown everything out, and you've spent two or three days sitting on the bare floor, your bones begin to ache, and you begin to wish for some of the old furniture, even if it was the ugliest Victorian horsehair.

At least, that's how it seems to me the young women begin to feel. They are frightened at the emptiness of their house of life, now they've thrown everything out of the window. Their young Philips and Peters and so on don't seem to make the slightest move to put any new furniture in the house of the young generation. The only new piece they introduce is a cocktail-shaker and perhaps a wireless set. For the rest, it can stay blank.

And the young women begin to feel a little uneasy. Women don't like to feel empty. A woman hates to feel that she believes in nothing and stands for nothing. Let her be the silliest woman on earth, she will take something seriously: her appearance, her clothes, her house, something. And let her be not so very silly, and she wants more than that. She wants to feel, instinctively, that she amounts to something and that her life stands for something. Women, who so often are angry with men because men cannot 'just live', but must always be wanting some purpose in life, are themselves, perhaps, the very root of the male necessity for a purpose in life. It seems to me that in a woman the need to feel that her life *means* something, stands for something, and amounts to something is much more imperative than in a man. The woman herself may deny it emphatically; because, of course, it is the man's business to supply her life with this 'purpose'. But a man can be a tramp, purposeless, and be happy. Not so a woman. It is a very, very rare woman who can be happy if she feels herself 'outside' the great purpose of life. Whereas, I verily believe, vast numbers of men would gladly drift away as wasters, if there were anywhere to drift to.

A woman cannot bear to feel empty and purposeless. But a man may take a real pleasure in that feeling. A man can take real pride and satisfaction in pure negation: 'I am quite empty of feeling, I don't care the slightest bit in the world for anybody or anything except myself. But I do care for myself, and I'm going to survive in spite of them all, and I'm going to have my own success without caring the least in the world how I get it. Because I'm cleverer than they are, I'm cunninger than they are, even if I'm weak. I must build myself proper protections, and entrench myself, and then I'm safe. I can sit inside my glass tower and feel nothing and be touched by nothing, and yet exert my power, my will, through the glass walls of my ego.'

That, roughly, is the condition of a man who accepts the condition of true egoism, and emptiness, in himself. He has a certain pride in the condition, since in pure emptiness of real feeling he can still carry out his ambition, his will to egoistic success.

Now I doubt if any woman can feel like this. The most egoistic woman is always in a tangle of hate, if not of love. But the true male egoist neither hates nor loves. He is quite empty, at the middle of him. Only on the surface he has feelings: and these he is always trying to get away from. Inwardly, he feels nothing. And when he feels nothing, he exults in his ego and knows he is safe. Safe, within his fortifications, inside his glass tower.

But I doubt if women can even understand this condition in a man. They mistake the emptiness for depth. They think the false calm of the egoist who really feels nothing, is strength. And they imagine that all the defences which the confirmed egoist throws up, the glass tower of imperviousness, are screens to a real man, a positive being. And they throw themselves madly on the defences, to tear them down and come at the real man, little knowing that there *is* no real man, the defences are only there to protect a hollow emptiness, an egoism, not a human man.

But the young are beginning to suspect. The young women are beginning to respect the defences, for they are more afraid of coming upon the ultimate nothingness of the egoist, than of leaving him undiscovered. Hollowness, nothingness – it frightens the woman. They cannot be *real* nihilists. But men can. Men can have a savage satisfaction in the annihilation of all feeling and all connexion, in a resultant state of sheer negative emptiness, when there is nothing left to throw out of the window, and the window is sealed.

Women wanted freedom. The result is a hollowness, an emptiness which frightens the stoutest heart. Women then turn to women for love. But that doesn't last. It can't. Whereas the emptiness persists and persists.

The love of humanity is gone, leaving a great gap. The cosmic consciousness has collapsed upon a great void. The egoist sits grinning furtively in the triumph of his own emptiness. And now what is woman going to do? Now that the house of life is empty, now that she's thrown all the emotional furnishing out of the window, and the house of life, which is her eternal home, is empty as a tomb, now what is dear forlorn woman going to do?

BOOKS

Written 1924. *Phoenix*, 1936

ARE books just toys? the toys of consciousness?

Then what is man? The everlasting brainy child?

Is man nothing but a brainy child, amusing himself for ever with the printed toys called books?

That also. Even the greatest men spend most of their time making marvellous fine toys. Like *Pickwick* or *Two on a Tower*.

But there is more to it.

Man is a thought-adventurer.

Man is a great venture in consciousness.

Where the venture started, and where it will end, nobody knows. Yet here we are – a long way gone already, and no glimpse of any end in sight. Here we are, miserable Israel of the human consciousness, having lost our way in the wilderness of the world's chaos, giggling and babbling and pitching camp. We needn't go any further.

All right, let us pitch camp, and see what happens. When the worst comes to the worst, there is sure to be a Moses to set up a serpent of brass. And then we can start off again.

Man is a thought-adventurer. He has thought his way down the far ages. He used to think in little images of wood or stone. Then in hieroglyphs on obelisks and clay rolls and papyrus. Now he thinks in books, between two covers.

The worst of a book is the way it shuts up between covers. When man had to write on rocks and obelisks, it was rather difficult to lie. The daylight was too strong. But soon he took his venture into caves and secret holes and temples, where he could create his own environment and tell lies to himself. And a book is an underground hole with two lids to it. A perfect place to tell lies in.

Which brings us to the real dilemma of man in his long adventure with consciousness. He is a liar. Man is a liar unto himself. And once he has told himself a lie, round and round he goes after that lie, as if it was a bit of phosphorus on his nose-end. The pillar of cloud and the pillar of fire wait for him to have done. They stand silently aside, waiting for him to rub the *ignis fatuus* off the end of his nose. But man, the longer he follows a lie, becomes all the surer he sees a light.

The life of man is an endless venture into consciousness. Ahead goes the pillar of cloud by day, the pillar of fire by night, through the wilderness of time. Till man tells himself a lie, another lie. Then the lie goes ahead of him, like the carrot before the ass.

There are, in the consciousness of man, two bodies of knowledge: the things he tells himself, and the things he finds out. The things he tells himself are nearly always pleasant, and they are lies. The things he finds out are usually rather bitter to begin with.

Man is a thought-adventurer. But by thought we mean, of course, discovery. We don't mean this telling himself stale facts and drawing false deductions, which usually passes as thought. Thought is an adventure, not a trick.

And of course it is an adventure of the whole man, not merely of his wits. That is why one cannot quite believe in Kant, or Spinoza. Kant thought with his head and his spirit, but he never thought with his blood. The blood also thinks, inside a man, darkly and ponderously. It thinks in desires and revulsions, and it makes strange conclusions. The conclusion of my head and my spirit is that it would be perfect, this world of men, if men all loved one another. The conclusion of my blood says nonsense, and finds the stunt a bit disgusting. My blood tells me there is no such thing as perfection. There is the long endless venture into consciousness down an ever-dangerous valley of days.

Man finds that his head and his spirit have led him wrong. We are at present terribly off the track, following our spirit, which says how nice it would be if everything was perfect, and listening to our head, which says we might have everything perfect if we would only eliminate the tiresome reality of our obstinate blood-being.

We are sadly off the track, and we're in a bad temper, like a man who has lost his way. And we say: I'm not going to bother. Fate must work it out.

Fate doesn't work things out. Man is a thought-adventurer, and only his adventuring in thought rediscovers a way.

Take our civilization. We are in a tantrum because we don't really like it now we've got it. There we've been building it for a thousand years, and built so big we can't shift it. And we hate it, after all.

Too bad! What's to be done?

Why, there's nothing to be done! Here we are, like sulky children, sulking because we don't like the game we're playing, feeling that we've been *made* to play it against our will. So play it we do: badly: in the sulks.

We play the game badly, so of course it goes from bad to worse. Things go from bad to worse.

All right, let 'em! Let 'em go from bad to worse. *Après moi le déluge.*

By all means! But a deluge presupposes a Noah and an Ark. The old adventurer on the old adventure.

When you come to think of it, Noah matters more than the deluge, and the ark is more than all the world washed out.

Now we've got the sulks, and are waiting for the flood to come and wash out our world and our civilization. All right, let it come. But somebody's got to be ready with Noah's Ark.

We imagine, for example, that if there came a terrible crash and terrible bloodshed over Europe, then out of the crash and bloodshed a remnant of regenerated souls would inevitably arise.

We are mistaken; if you look at the people who escaped the terrible times of Russia, you don't see many regenerated souls. They are more scared and senseless than ever. Instead of the great catastrophe having restored them to manhood, they are finally unmanned.

What's to be done? If a huge catastrophe is going only to unman us more than we are already unmanned, then there's no good in a huge catastrophe. Then there's no good in anything, for us poor souls who are trapped in the huge trap of our civilization.

Catastrophe alone never helped man. The only thing that ever avails is the living adventurous spark in the souls of men. If there is no living adventurous spark, then death and disaster are as meaningless as tomorrow's newspaper.

Take the fall of Rome. During the Dark Ages of the fifth, sixth, seventh centuries A.D., the catastrophes that befell the Roman Empire didn't alter the Romans a bit. They went on just the same, rather as we go on to-day, having a good time when they could get it, and not caring. Meanwhile Huns, Goths, Vandals, Visigoths, and all the rest wiped them out.

With what result? The flood of barbarism rose and covered Europe from end to end.

But, bless your life, there was Noah in his Ark with the animals. There was young Christianity. There were the lonely fortified monasteries, like little arks floating and keeping the adventure afloat. There is no break in the great adventure in consciousness. Throughout the howlingest deluge, some few brave souls are steering the ark under the rainbow.

The monks and bishops of the Early Church carried the soul and spirit of man unbroken, unabated, undiminished over the howling flood of the Dark Ages. Then this spirit of undying courage was fused into the barbarians, in Gaul, in Italy, and the new Europe began. But the germ had never been allowed to die.

Once all men in the world lost their courage and their newness, the world would come to an end. The old Jews said the same: unless in the world there was at least one Jew passionately praying, the race was lost.

So we begin to see where we are. It's no good leaving everything to fate. Man is an adventurer, and he must never give up the adventure. The venture is the venture: fate is the circumstance around the adventurer. The adventurer at the quick of the venture is the living germ inside the chaos of circumstance. But for the living germ of Noah in his Ark, chaos would have redescended on the world in the waters of the flood. But chaos *couldn't* redescend, because Noah was afloat with all the animals.

The same with the Christians when Rome fell. In their little fortified monasteries they defended themselves against howling invasions, being too poor to excite much covetousness. When wolves and bears prowled through the streets of Lyons, and a wild boar was grunting and turning up the pavement of Augustus's temple, the Christian bishops also roved intently and determinedly, like poor forerunners, along the ruined streets, seeking a congregation. It was the great adventure, and they did not give it up.

But Noah, of course, is always in an unpopular minority. So, of course, were the Christians, when Rome began to fall. The Christians now are in a hopelessly popular majority, so it is their turn to fall.

I know the greatness of Christianity: it is a past greatness. I know that, but for those early Christians, we should never have emerged from the chaos and hopeless disaster of the Dark Ages. If I had lived in the year 400, pray God, I should have been a true and passionate Christian. The adventurer.

But now I live in 1924, and the Christian venture is done. The adventure is gone out of Christianity. We must start on a new venture towards God.

CLIMBING DOWN PISGAH

Written 1924. *Phoenix*, 1936

SOMETIMES one pulls oneself up short, and asks: 'What am I doing this for?' One writes novels, stories, essays: and then suddenly: 'What on earth am I doing it for?'

What indeed?

For the sake of humanity?

Pfui! The very words *human*, *humanity*, *humanism* make one sick. For the sake of humanity as such, I wouldn't lift a little finger, much less write a story.

For the sake of the Spirit?

Tampoco! – But what do we mean by the Spirit? Let us be careful. Do we mean that One Universal Intelligence of which every man has his modicum? Or further, that one Cosmic Soul, or Spirit, of which every individual is a broken fragment, and towards which every individual strives back, to escape the raw edges of his own fragmentariness, and to experience once more the sense of wholeness?

The sense of wholeness! Does one write books in order to give one's fellow-men a sense of wholeness: first, a oneness with all men, then a oneness with all things, then a oneness with our cosmos, and finally a oneness with the vast invisible universe? Is that it? Is that our achievement and our peace?

Anyhow, it would be a great achievement. And this has been the aim of the great ones. It was the aim of Whitman, for example.

Now it is the aim of the little ones, since the big ones are all gone. Thomas Hardy, a last big one, rings the knell of our Oneness. Virtually, he says: Once you achieve the great identification with the One, whether it be the One Spirit, or the Oversoul, or God, or whatever name you like to give it, you find that this God, this One, this Cosmic Spirit isn't human at all, hasn't any human feelings, doesn't concern itself for a second with the individual, and is, all told, a gigantic cold monster. It is a machine. The moment you attain that sense of Oneness and Wholeness, you become cold, dehumanized, mechanical, and monstrous. The greatest of all illusions is the Infinite of the Spirit.

Whitman really rang the same knell. (I don't expect anyone to agree with me.)

The sense of wholeness is a most terrible let-down. The big ones have already decided it. But the little ones, sneakingly too selfish to care, go on sentimentally tinkling away at it.

This we may be sure of: all talk of brotherhood, universal love, sacrifice, and so on, is a sentimental pose for us. We reached the top of Pisgah, and looking down, saw the graveyard of humanity. Those meagre spirits who could never get to the top, and are careful never to try, because it costs too much sweat and a bleeding at the nose, they sit below and still snivellingly invent Pisgah-sights. But strictly, it is all over. The game is up.

The little ones, of course, are writing at so many cents a word – or a line – according to their success. They may say I do the same. Yes, I demand my cents, a Shylock. Nevertheless, if I wrote for cents I should write differently, and with far more 'success'.

What, then, does one write for? There must be some imperative.

Probably it is the sense of adventure, to start with. Life is no fun for a man, without an adventure.

The Pisgah-top of spiritual oneness looks down upon a hopeless squalor of industrialism, the huge cemetery of human hopes. This is our Promised Land. 'There's a good time coming, boys, a good time coming.' Well, we've rung the bell, and here it is.

Shall we climb hurriedly down from Pisgah, and keep the secret? Mum's the word!

This is what our pioneers are boldly doing. We used, as boys, to sing parodies of most of the Sunday-school hymns.

They climbed the steep ascent of heaven
Through peril, toil, and pain:
O God, to us may grace be given
To scramble down again.

This is the grand hymn of the little ones. But it's harder getting down a height, very often, than getting up. It's a predicament. Here we are, cowering on the brinks of precipices half-way up, or down, Pisgah. The Pisgah of Oneness, the Oneness of Mankind, the Oneness of Spirit.

Hie, boys, over we go! Pisgah's a fraud, and the Promised Land is Pittsburgh, the Chosen Few, there are billions of 'em, and Canaan smells of kerosene. Let's break our necks if we must, but let's get down, and look over the brink of some other horizon. We're like the girl who took the wrong turning: thought it was the right one.

It's an adventure. And there's only one left, the venture of consciousness. Curse these ancients, they have said everything for us. Curse these moderns, they have done everything for us. The aeroplane descends and lays her egg-shells of empty tin cans on the top of Everest, in the Ultimate Thule, and all over the North Pole; not to speak of tractors waddling across the inviolate Sahara and over the jags of Arabia Petraea, laying the same addled eggs of our civilization, tin cans, in every camp-nest.

Well, then, they can have the round earth. They've got it anyhow. And they can have the firmament: they've got that too. The moon is a cold egg in the astronomical nest. *Heigho! for the world well lost!*

That's the known World, the world of the One Intelligence. That is the Human World! I'm getting out of it. *Homo sum. Omnis a me humanum alienum puto.*

Of the thing we call human, I've had enough. And enough is as good as a feast.

Inside of me, there's a little demon – maybe he's a big demon – that says *Basta! Basta!* to all my oneness. 'Farewell, a long farewell to all my greatness.' In short, come off the perch, Polly, and look what a mountain of droppings you've crouched upon.

Are you human, and do you want me to sympathize with you for that? Let me hand you a roll of toilet-paper.

After looking down from the Pisgah-top on to the oneness of all mankind safely settled these several years in Canaan, I admit myself dehumanized.

Fair waved the golden corn
In Canaan's pleasant land.

The factory smoke waves much higher. And in the sweet smoke of industry I don't care a button who loves whom, nor what babies are born. The sight of all of it *en masse* was a little too much for my human spirit, it dehumanized me. Here I am, without a human sympathy left. Looking down on Human Oneness was too much for my human stomach, so I vomited it away.

Remains a demon which says *Ha! ha! So you've conquered the earth, have you, oh man? Now swallow the pill.*

For if the proof of the pudding is in the eating, the proof of a conquest is in digesting it. Humanity is an ostrich. But even the ostrich thinks twice before it bolts a rolled hedgehog. The earth is conquered as the hedgehog is conquered when he rolls himself up into a ball, and the dog spins him with his paw.

But that is not the point, at least for anyone except the Great Dog of Humanity. The point for us is, *What then?*

'Whither, O splendid ship, thy white sails bending?' To have her white sails dismantled and a gasolene engine fitted into her guts. That is whither, oh Poet!

When you've got to the bottom of Pisgah once more, where are you? Sitting on a sore posterior, murmuring: *Oneness is all bunk. There is no Oneness, till you invented it and killed your goose to get it out of her belly. It takes millions of little people to lay the egg of the Universal Spirit, and then it's an addled omelet, and stinks in our nostrils. And all the millions of little people have over-reached themselves, trying to lay the mundane egg of oneness. They're all damaged inside, and they can't face the addled omelet they've laid. What a mess!*

What then?

Heigho! Whither, oh patched canoe, your kinked keel thrusting?

We've been over the rapids, and the creature that crawls out of the whirlpool feels that most things human are foreign to him. *Homo sum!* means a vastly different thing to him, from what it meant to his father.

Homo sum! a demon who knows nothing of oneness or of perfection. *Homo sum!* a demon who knows nothing of any First Creator who created the universe from his own perfection. *Homo sum!* a man who knows that all creation lives like some great demon inhabiting space, and pulsing with a dual desire, a desire to give himself forth into creation, and a desire to take himself back, in death.

Child of the great inscrutable demon, *Homo sum!* Adventurer from the first Adventurer, *Homo sum!* Son of the blazing-hearted father who wishes beauty and harmony and perfection, *Homo sum!* Child of the raging-hearted demon-father who fights that nothing shall surpass this crude and demonish rage, *Homo sum!*

Whirling in the midst of Chaos, the demon of the beginning who is for ever willing and unwilling to surpass the *Status Quo*. Like a bird he spreads wings to surpass himself. Then like a serpent he coils to strike at that which would surpass him. And the bird of the first desire must either soar quickly, or strike back with his talons at the snake, if there is to be any surpassing of the thing that was, the *Status Quo*.

It is the joy for ever, the agony for ever, and above all, the fight for ever. For all the universe is alive, and whirling in the same fight, the same joy and anguish. The vast demon of life has made himself habits which, except in the whitest heat of desire and rage, he will never break. And these habits are the laws of our scientific universe. But all the laws of physics, dynamics, kinetics, statics, all are but the settled habits of a vast living incomprehensibility, and they can all be broken, superseded, in a moment of great extremity.

Homo sum! child of the demon. *Homo sum!* willing and unwilling. *Homo sum!* giving and taking. *Homo sum!* hot and cold. *Homo sum!* loving and loveless. *Homo sum!* the Adventurer.

This we see, this we know as we crawl down the dark side

of Pisgah, or slip down on a sore posterior. *Homo sum!* has changed its meaning for us.

That is, if we are young men. Old men and elderly will sit tight on heavy posteriors in some crevice upon Pisgah, babbling about 'all for love, and the world well saved'. Young men with hearts still for the life adventure will rise up with their trouser-seats scraped away, after the long slither from the heights down the well-nigh bottomless pit, having changed their minds. They will change their minds and change their pants. Wisdom is sometimes in a sore bottom, and the new pants will no longer be neutral.

Young men will change their minds and their pants, having done with Oneness and neutrality. Even the stork meditates on an orange leg, and the bold drake pushes the water behind him with a red foot. Young men are the adventurers.

Let us scramble out of this ash-hole at the foot of Pisgah. The universe isn't a machine after all. It's alive and kicking. And in spite of the fact that man with his cleverness has discovered some of the habits of our old earth, and so lured him into a trap; in spite of the fact that man has trapped the great forces, and they go round and round at his bidding like a donkey in a gin, the old demon isn't quite nabbed. We didn't quite catch him napping. He'll turn round on us with bare fangs, before long. He'll turn into a python, coiling, coiling, coiling anguish till we're nicely mashed. Then he'll bolt us.

Let's get out of this vicious circle. Put on new bright pants to show that we're meditative fowl who have thought the thing out and decided to migrate. To assert that our legs are not grey machine-sections, but live and limber members who know what it is to have their rear well scraped and punished, in the slither down Pisgah, and are not going to be diddled any more into mechanical service of mountain-climbing up to the great summit of Wholeness and Bunk.

REFLECTIONS ON THE DEATH OF A PORCUPINE

Written 1925. *Reflections on the Death of a Porcupine*, Philadelphia, December, 1925. London, 1934

THERE are many bare places on the little pine trees, towards the top, where the porcupines have gnawed the bark away and left the white flesh showing. And some trees are dying from the top.

Everyone says, porcupines should be killed, the Indians, Mexicans, Americans all say the same.

At full moon a month ago, when I went down the long clearing in the brilliant moonlight, through the poor dry herbage a big porcupine began to waddle away from me, towards the trees and the darkness. The animal had raised all its hairs and bristles, so that by the light of the moon it seemed to have a tall, swaying, moonlit aureole arching its back as it went. That seemed curiously fearsome, as if the animal were emitting itself demon-like on the air.

It waddled very slowly, with its white spiky spoon-tail steering flat, behind the round bear-like mound of its back. It had a lumbering, beetle's, squalid motion, unpleasant. I followed it into the darkness of the timber, and there, squat like a great tick, it began scrapily to creep up a pine-trunk. It was very like a great aureoled tick, a bug, struggling up.

I stood near and watched, disliking the presence of the creature. It is a duty to kill the things. But the dislike of killing him was greater than the dislike of him. So I watched him climb.

And he watched me. When he had got nearly the height of a man, all his long hairs swaying with a bristling gleam like an aureole, he hesitated, and slithered down. Evidently he had decided, either that I was harmless, or else that it was risky to go up any further, when I could knock him off so easily with a pole. So he slithered podgily down again, and waddled away with the same bestial, stupid motion of that white-spiky repulsive spoon-tail. He was as big as a middle-sized pig: or more like a bear.

I let him go. He was repugnant. He made a certain squalor in the moonlight of the Rocky Mountains. As all savagery has a touch of squalor, that makes one a little sick at the stomach. And anyhow, it seemed almost more squalid to pick up a pine-bough and push him over, hit him and kill him.

A few days later, on a hot, motionless morning when the pine-trees put out their bristles in stealthy, hard assertion; and I was not in a good temper, because Black-eyed Susan, the cow, had disappeared into the timber, and I had had to ride hunting her, so it was nearly nine o'clock before she was milked: Madame came in suddenly out of the sunlight, saying: 'I got such a shock! There are two strange dogs, and one of them has got the most awful beard, all round his nose.'

She was frightened, like a child, at something unnatural.

'Beard! Porcupine quills, probably! He's been after a porcupine.'

'Ah!' she cried in relief. 'Very likely. Very likely!' – then with a change of tone; 'Poor thing, will they hurt him?'

'They will. I wonder when he came.'

'I heard dogs bark in the night.'

'Did you? Why didn't you say so? I should have known Susan was hiding –'

The ranch is lonely, there is no sound in the night, save the innumerable noises of the night, that you can't put your finger on; cosmic noises in the far deeps of the sky, and of the earth.

I went out. And in the full blaze of sunlight in the field, stood two dogs, a black-and-white, and a big, bushy, rather handsome sandy-red dog, of the collie type. And sure enough, this latter did look queer and a bit horrifying, his whole muzzle set round with white spines, like some ghastly growth; like an unnatural beard.

The black-and-white dog made off as I went through the fence. But the red dog whimpered and hesitated, and moved on hot bricks. He was fat and in good condition. I thought he might belong to some shepherds herding sheep in the forest ranges, among the mountains.

He waited while I went up to him, wagging his tail and whimpering, and ducking his head, and dancing. He daren't rub his nose with his paws any more: it hurt too much. I patted his head and looked at his nose, and he whimpered loudly.

He must have had thirty quills, or more, sticking out of his nose, all the way round: the white, ugly ends of the quills protruding an inch, sometimes more, sometimes less, from his already swollen, blood-puffed muzzle.

The porcupines here have quills only two or three inches long. But they are devilish; and a dog will die if he does not get them pulled out. Because they work further and further in, and will sometimes emerge through the skin away in some unexpected place.

Then the fun began. I got him in the yard: and he drank up the whole half-gallon of the chickens' sour milk. Then I started pulling out the quills. He was a big, bushy, handsome dog, but his nerve was gone, and every time I got a quill out, he gave a yelp. Some long quills were fairly easy. But the short ones, near his lips, were deep in, and hard to get hold of, and hard to pull out when you did get hold of them. And with every one that came out, came a little spurt of blood and another yelp and writhe.

The dog wanted the quills out: but his nerve was gone. Every time he saw my hand coming to his nose, he jerked his head away. I quieted him, and stealthily managed to jerk out another quill, with the blood all over my fingers. But with every one that came out, he grew more tiresome. I tried and tried and tried to get hold of another quill, and he jerked and jerked, and writhed and whimpered, and ran under the porch floor.

It was a curiously unpleasant, nerve-trying job. The day was blazing hot. The dog came out and I struggled with him again for an hour or more. Then we blindfolded him. But either he smelled my hand approaching his nose, or some weird instinct told him. He jerked his head, this way, that way, up, down, sideways, roundwise, as one's fingers came slowly, slowly, to seize a quill.

The quills on his lips and chin were deep in, only about a quarter of an inch of white stub protruding from the swollen, blood-oozed, festering black skin. It was very difficult to jerk them out.

We let him lie for an interval, hidden in the quiet cool place under the porch floor. After half an hour, he crept out again. We got a rope round his nose, behind the bristles, and one held while the other got the stubs with the pliers. But it was too trying. If a quill came out, the dog's yelp startled every nerve. And he was frightened of the pain, it was impossible to hold his head still any longer.

After struggling for two hours, and extracting some twenty quills, I gave up. It was impossible to quiet the creature, and I had had enough. His nose on the top was clear; a punctured, puffy, blood-darkened mess; and his lips were clear. But just on his round little chin, where the few white hairs are, was still a bunch of white quills, eight or nine, deep in.

We let him go, and he dived under the porch, and there he lay invisible: save for the end of his bushy, foxy tail, which moved when we came near. Towards noon he emerged, ate up the chicken-food, and stood with that doggish look of dejection, and fear, and friendliness, and greediness, wagging his tail.

But I had had enough.

'Go home!' I said. 'Go home! Go home to your master, and let him finish for you.'

He would not go. So I led him across the blazing hot clearing, in the way I thought he should go. He followed a hundred yards, then stood motionless in the blazing sun. He was not going to leave the place.

And I! I simply did not want him.

So I picked up a stone. He dropped his tail, and swerved towards the house. I knew what he was going to do. He was going to dive under the porch, and there stick, haunting the place.

I dropped my stone, and found a good stick under the cedar tree. Already in the heat was that sting-like biting of electricity, the thunder gathering in the sheer sunshine, without a cloud, and making one's whole body feel dislocated.

I could not bear to have that dog around any more. Going quietly to him, I suddenly gave him one hard hit with the stick, crying: 'Go home!' He turned quickly, and the end of the stick caught him on his sore nose. With a fierce yelp, he went off like a wolf, downhill, like a flash, gone. And I stood in the field full of pangs of regret, at having hit him, unintentionally, on his sore nose.

But he was gone.

And then the present moon came, and again the night was clear. But in the interval there had been heavy thunder-rains, the ditch was running with bright water across the field, and the night, so fair, had not the terrific, mirror-like brilliancy, touched with terror, so startling bright, of the moon in the last days of June.

We were alone on the ranch. Madame went out into the clear night, just before retiring. The stream ran in a cord of silver across the field, in the straight line where I had taken the irrigation ditch. The pine tree in front of the house threw a black shadow. The mountain slope came down to the fence, wild and alert.

'Come!' said she excitedly. 'There is a big porcupine drinking at the ditch. I thought at first it was a bear.'

When I got out he had gone. But among the grasses and the coming wild sunflowers, under the moon, I saw his greyish halo, like a pallid living bush, moving over the field, in the distance, in the moonlit *clair-obscur*.

We got through the fence, and following, soon caught him up. There he lumbered, with his white spoon-tail spiked with bristles, steering behind almost as if he were moving backwards, and this was his head. His long, long hairs above the quills quivering with a dim grey gleam, like a bush.

And again I disliked him.

'Should one kill him?'

She hesitated. Then with a sort of disgust:

'Yes!'

I went back to the house, and got the little twenty-two rifle. Now never in my life had I shot at any live thing: I never wanted to. I always felt guns very repugnant: sinister, mean. With difficulty I had fired once or twice at a target: but resented doing even so much. Other people could shoot if they wanted to. Myself, individually, it was repugnant to me even to try.

But something slowly hardens in a man's soul. And I knew now, it had hardened in mine. I found the gun, and with rather trembling hands, got it loaded. Then I pulled back the trigger and followed the porcupine. It was still lumbering through the grass. Coming near, I aimed.

The trigger stuck. I pressed the little catch with a safety-pin I found in my pocket, and released the trigger. Then we followed the porcupine. He was still lumbering towards the trees. I went sideways on, stood quite near to him, and fired, in the clear-dark of the moonlight.

And as usual I aimed too high. He turned, went scuttling back whence he had come.

I got another shell in place, and followed. This time I fired full into the mound of his round back, below the glistening grey halo. He seemed to stumble on to his hidden nose, and struggled a few strides, ducking his head under like a hedgehog.

'He's not dead yet! Oh, fire again!' cried Madame.

I fired, but the gun was empty.

So I ran quickly, for a cedar pole. The porcupine was lying still, with subsiding halo. He stirred faintly. So I turned him and hit him hard over the nose; or where, in the dark, his nose should have been. And it was done. He was dead.

And in the moonlight, I looked down on the first creature I had ever shot.

'Does it seem mean?' I asked aloud, doubtful.

Again Madame hesitated. Then: 'No!' she said resentfully.

And I felt she was right. Things like the porcupine, one must be able to shoot them, if they get in one's way.

One must be able to shoot. I, myself, must be able to shoot, and to kill.

For me, this is a *volte-face*. I have always preferred to walk round my porcupine, rather than kill it.

Now, I know it's no good walking round. One must kill.

I buried him in the adobe hole. But some animal dug down and ate him; for two days later there lay the spines and bones spread out, with the long skeletons of the porcupine-hands.

The only nice thing about him – or her, for I believe it was a female, by the dugs on her belly – were the feet. They were like longish, alert black hands, paw-hands. That is why a porcupine's tracks in the snow look almost as if a child had gone by, leaving naked little human foot-prints, like a little boy.

So, he is gone: or she is gone. But there is another one, bigger and blacker-looking, among the west timber. That too is to be shot. It is part of the business of ranching: even when it's only a little half-abandoned ranch like this one.

Wherever man establishes himself, upon the earth, he has to fight for his place, against the lower orders of life. Food, the basis of existence, has to be fought for even by the most idyllic of farmers. You plant, and you protect your growing crop with a gun. Food, food, how strangely it relates man with the animal and vegetable world! How important it is! And how fierce is the fight that goes on around it.

The same when one skins a rabbit, and takes out the inside; one realizes what an enormous part of the animal, comparatively, is intestinal, what a big part of him is just for food-apparatus; for *living on* other organisms.

And when one watches the horses in the big field, their noses to the ground, bite-bite-biting at the grass, and stepping absorbedly on, and bite-bite-biting without ever lifting their noses, cropping off the grass, the young shoots of alfalfa, the dandelions, with a blind, relentless, unwearied persistence, one's whole life pauses. One suddenly realizes again how all creatures devour, and *must* devour the lower forms of life.

So Susan, swinging across the field, snatches off the tops of the little wild sunflowers as if she were mowing. And down they go, down her black throat. And when she stands in her cowy oblivion chewing her cud, with her lower jaw swinging peacefully, and I am milking her, suddenly the camomiley smell of her breath, as she glances round with glaring, smoke-blue eyes, makes me realize it is the sunflowers that are her ball of cud. Sunflowers! And they will go to making her glistening black hide, and the thick cream on her milk.

And the chickens, when they see a great black beetle, that the Mexicans call a *toro*, floating past, they are after it in a rush. And if it settles, instantly the brown hen stabs it with her beak. It is a great beetle two or three inches long: but in a second it is in the crop of the chicken. Gone!

And Timsy, the cat, as she spies on the chipmunks, crouches in another sort of oblivion, soft, and still. The chipmunks come to drink the milk from the chickens' bowl. Two of them met at the bowl. They were little squirrely things with stripes down their backs. They sat up in front of one another, lifting their inquisitive little noses and humping their backs. Then each put its two little hands on the other's shoulders, they reared up, gazing into each other's faces, and finally they put their two little noses together, in a sort of a kiss.

But Miss Timsy can't stand this. In a soft, white-and-yellow leap she is after them. They skip with the darting jerk of chipmunks, to the wood-heap, and with one soft, high-leaping sideways bound Timsy goes through the air. Her snowflake of a paw comes down on one of the chipmunks. She looks at it for a second. It squirms. Swiftly and triumphantly she puts her two flowery little white paws on it, legs straight out in front of her, back arched, gazing concentratedly yet whimsically. Chipmunk does not stir. She takes it softly in her mouth, where it dangles softly, like a lady's tippet. And with a proud, prancing motion the Timsy sets off towards the house, her white little feet hardly touching the ground.

But she gets shooed away. We refuse to loan her the sitting-room any more, for her gladiatorial displays. If the chippy must be 'butchered to make a Timsy holiday', it shall be outside. Disappointed, but still high-stepping, the Timsy sets off towards the clay oven by the shed.

There she lays the chippy gently down, and soft as a little white cloud lays one small paw on its striped back. Chippy does not move. Soft as thistledown she raises her paw a tiny, tiny bit, to release him.

And all of a sudden, with an elastic jerk, he darts from under the white release of her paw. And instantly, she is up in the air and down she comes on him, with the forward-thrusting bolts of her white paws. Both creatures are motionless.

Then she takes him softly in her mouth again, and looks round, to see if she can slip into the house. She cannot. So she trots towards the wood-pile.

It is a game, and it is pretty. Chippy escapes into the wood-pile, and she softly, softly reconnoitres among the faggots.

Of all the animals, there is no denying it, the Timsy is the most pretty, the most fine. It is not her mere *corpus* that is beautiful; it is her bloom of aliveness. Her 'infinite variety'; the soft, snowflakey lightness of her, and at the same time her lean, heavy ferocity. I had never realized the latter, till I was lying in bed one day moving my toe, unconsciously, under the bedclothes. Suddenly a terrific blow struck my foot. The Timsy had sprung out of nowhere, with a hurling steely force, thud upon the bedclothes where the toe was moving. It was as if someone had aimed a sudden blow, vindictive and unerring.

'Timsy!'

She looked at me with the vacant, feline glare of her hunting eyes. It is not even ferocity. It is the dilation of the strange, vacant arrogance of power. The power is in her.

And so it is. Life moves in circles of power and of vividness, and each circle of life only maintains its orbit upon the subjection of some lower circle. If the lower cycles of life are not *mastered*, there can be no higher cycle.

In nature, one creature devours another, and this is an essential part of all existence and of all being. It is not something to lament over, nor something to try to reform. The Buddhist who refuses to take life is really ridiculous, since if he eats only two grains of rice per day, it is two grains of life.

We did not make creation, *we* are not the authors of the universe. And if we see that the whole of creation is established upon the fact that one life devours another life, one cycle of existence can only come into existence through the subjugating of another cycle of existence, then what is the good of trying to pretend that it is not so? The only thing to do is to realize what is higher, and what is lower, in the cycles of existence.

It is nonsense to declare that there *is* no higher and lower. We know full well that the dandelion belongs to a higher cycle of existence than the hartstongue fern, that the ant's is a higher form of existence than the dandelion's, that the thrush is higher than the ant, that Timsy the cat is higher than the thrush, and that I, a man, am higher than Timsy.

What do we mean by higher? Strictly, we mean more alive. More vividly alive. The ant is more vividly alive than the pine-tree. We know it, there is no trying to refute it. It is all very well saying that they are both alive in two different ways, and therefore they are incomparable, incommensurable. This is also true.

But one truth does not displace another. Even apparently contradictory truths do not displace one another. Logic is far too coarse to make the subtle distinctions life demands.

Truly, it is futile to compare an ant with a great pine-tree, in the absolute. Yet as far as *existence* is concerned, they are not only placed in comparison to one another, they are occasionally pitted against one another. And if it comes to a contest, the little ant will devour the life of the huge tree. If it comes to a contest.

And, in the cycles of *existence*, this is the test. From the lowest form of existence, to the highest, the test question is: *Can thy neighbour finally overcome thee?*

If he can, then he belongs to a higher cycle of existence.

This is the truth behind the survival of the fittest. Every cycle of existence is established upon the overcoming of the lower cycles of existence. The real question is, wherein does *fitness* lie? Fitness for what? Fit merely to survive? That which is only fit to survive will survive only to supply food or contribute in some way to the existence of a higher form of life, which is able to do more than survive, which can really *vive*, live.

Life is more vivid in the dandelion than in the green fern, or than in a palm tree.

Life is more vivid in a snake than in a butterfly.

Life is more vivid in a wren than in an alligator.

Life is more vivid in a cat than in an ostrich.

Life is more vivid in the Mexican who drives the wagon, than in the two horses in the wagon.

Life is more vivid in me, than in the Mexican who drives the wagon for me.

We are speaking in terms of *existence*: that is, in terms of species, race, or type.

The dandelion can take hold of the land, the palm tree is driven into a corner, with the fern.

The snake can devour the fiercest insect.

The fierce bird can destroy the greatest reptile.

The great cat can destroy the greatest bird.

The man can destroy the horse, or any animal.

One race of man can subjugate and rule another race.

All this in terms of *existence*. As far as existence goes, that life-species is the highest which can devour, or destroy, or subjugate every other life-species against which it is pitted in contest.

This is a law. There is no escaping this law. Anyone, or any race, trying to escape it, will fall a victim: will fall into subjugation.

But let us insist and insist again, we are talking now of existence, of species, of types, of races, of nations, not of single individuals, nor of *beings*. The dandelion in full flower, a little sun bristling with sun-rays on the green earth, is a nonpareil, a nonsuch. Foolish, foolish, foolish to compare it to anything else on earth. It is itself incomparable and unique.

But that is the fourth dimension, of *being*. It is in the fourth dimension, nowhere else.

Because, in the time-space dimension, any man may tread on the yellow sun-mirror, and it is gone. Any cow may swallow it. Any bunch of ants may annihilate it.

This brings us to the inexorable law of life.

1. Any creature that attains to its own fullness of being, its own *living* self, becomes unique, a nonpareil. It has its place in the fourth dimension, the heaven of existence, and there it is perfect, it is beyond comparison.

2. At the same time, every creature exists in time and space. And in time and space it exists relatively to all other existence, and can never be absolved. Its existence impinges on other existences, and is itself impinged upon. And in the struggle for existence, if an effort on the part of any one type or species or order of life can finally destroy the other species, then the destroyer is of a more vital cycle of existence than the one destroyed. (When speaking of existence we always speak in types, species, not individuals. Species exist. But even an individual dandelion has *being*.)

3. The force which we call *vitality*, and which is the determining factor in the struggle for existence, is, however, derived also from the fourth dimension. That is to say, the ultimate source of all vitality is in that other dimension, or region, where the dandelion blooms, and which men have called heaven, and which now they call the fourth dimension: which is only a way of saying that it is not to be reckoned in terms of space and time.

4. The primary way, in our existence, to get vitality, is to absorb it from living creatures lower than ourselves. It is thus transformed into a new and higher creation. (There are many ways of absorbing: devouring food is one way, love is often another. The best way is a pure relationship, which includes the *being* on each side, and which allows the transfer to take place in a living flow, enhancing the life in both beings.)

5. No creature is fully itself till it is, like the dandelion, opened in the bloom of pure relationship to the sun, the entire living cosmos.

So we still find ourselves in the tangle of existence and

being, a tangle which man has never been able to get out of, except by sacrificing the one to the other.

Sacrifice is useless.

The clue to all existence is being. But you can't have being without existence, any more than you can have the dandelion flower without the leaves and the long tap root.

Being is *not* ideal, as Plato would have it: nor spiritual. It is a transcendent form of existence, and as much material as existence is. Only the matter suddenly enters the fourth dimension.

All existence is dual, and surging towards a consummation into being. In the seed of the dandelion, as it floats with its little umbrella of hairs, sits the Holy Ghost in tiny compass. The Holy Ghost is that which holds the light and the dark, the day and the night, the wet and the sunny, united in one little clue. There it sits, in the seed of the dandelion.

The seed falls to earth. The Holy Ghost rouses, saying: '*Come!*' And out of the sky come the rays of the sun, and out of the earth comes dampness and dark and the death-stuff. They are called in, like those bidden to a feast. The sun sits down at the hearth, inside the seed; and the dark, damp death-returner sits on the opposite side, with the host between. And the host says to them: '*Come! Be merry together!*' So the sun looks with desirous curiosity on the dark face of the earth, and the dark damp one looks with wonder on the bright face of the other, who comes from the sun. And the host says: '*Here you are at home! Lift me up, between you, that I may cease to be a Ghost. For it longs me to look out, it longs me to dance with the dancers.*'

So the sun in the seed, and the earthly one in the seed take hands, and laugh, and begin to dance. And their dancing is like a fire kindled, a bonfire with leaping flame. And the treading of their feet is like the running of little streams, down into the earth. So from the dance of the sun-in-the-seed with the earthy death-returner, green little flames of leaves shoot up, and hard little trickles of roots strike down. And the host laughs, and says: '*I am being lifted up! Dance harder! Oh wrestle, you two, like wonderful wrestlers, neither of which can win.*' So sun-in-the-seed and the death-returner, who is earthy, dance faster and faster and the leaves rising greener begin to dance in a ring above-ground, fiercely overwhelming any outsider, in a whirl of swords and lions' teeth. And the earthy one wrestles, wrestles with the sun-in-the seed, so the long roots reach down like arms of a fighter gripping the power of earth, and strangles all intruders, strangling any intruder mercilessly. Till the two fall in one strange embrace, and from the centre the long flower-stem lifts like a phallus, budded with a bud. And out of the bud the voice of the Holy Ghost is heard crying: '*I am lifted up! Lo! I am lifted up! I am here!*' So the bud opens, and there is the flower poised in the very middle of the universe, with a ring of green swords below, to guard it, and the octopus, arms deep in earth, drinking and threatening. So the Holy Ghost, being a dandelion flower, looks round, and says: '*Lo! I am yellow! I believe the sun has lent me his body! Lo! I am sappy with golden, bitter blood! I believe death out of the damp black earth has lent me his blood! I am incarnate! I like my incarnation! But this is not all. I will keep this incarnation. It is good! But oh! if I can win to another incarnation, who knows how wonderful it will be! This one will have to give place. This one can help to create the next.*'

So the Holy Ghost leaves the clue of himself behind, in the seed, and wanders forth in the comparative chaos of our universe, seeking another incarnation.

And this will go on for ever. Man, as yet, is less than half grown. Even his flower-stem has not appeared yet. He is all leaves and roots, without any clue put forth. No sign of bud anywhere.

Either he will have to start budding, or he will be forsaken of the Holy Ghost: abandoned as a failure in creation, as the ichthyosaurus was abandoned. Being abandoned means losing his vitality. The sun and the earth-dark will cease rushing together in him. Already it is ceasing. To men, the sun is becoming stale, and the earth sterile. But the sun itself will never become stale, nor the earth barren. It is only that the *clue* is missing inside men. They are like flowerless, seedless fat cabbages, nothing inside.

Vitality depends upon the clue of the Holy Ghost inside a creature, a man, a nation, a race. When the clue goes, the vitality goes. And the Holy Ghost seeks for ever a new incarnation, and subordinates the old to the new. You will know that any creature or race is still alive with the Holy Ghost, when it can subordinate the lower creatures or races, and assimilate them into a new incarnation.

No man, or creature, or race can have vivid vitality unless it be moving towards a blossoming: and the most powerful is that which moves towards the as-yet-unknown blossom.

Blossoming means the establishing of a pure, *new* relationship with all the cosmos. This is the state of heaven. And it is the state of a flower, a cobra, a jenny-wren in spring, a man when he knows himself royal and crowned with the sun, with his feet gripping the core of the earth.

This too is the fourth dimension: this state, this mysterious other reality of things in a perfected relationship. It is into this perfected relationship that every straight line curves, as if to some core, passing out of the time-space dimension.

But any man, creature, or race moving towards blossoming will have to draw immense supplies of vitality from men, or creatures below, passionate strength. And he will have to accomplish a perfected relation with all things.

There will be conquest, always. But the aim of conquest is a perfect relation of conquerors with conquered, for a new blossoming. Freedom is illusory. Sacrifice is illusory. Almightyness is illusory. Freedom, sacrifice, almightyness, these are all human side-tracks, cul-de-sacs, bunk. All that is real is the overwhelmingness of a new inspirational command, a new relationship with all things.

Heaven is always there. No achieved consummation is lost. Procreation goes on for ever, to support the achieved revelation. But the torch of revelation itself is handed on. And this is all important.

Everything living wants to procreate more living things.

But more important than this is the fact that every revelation is a torch held out, to kindle new revelations. As the dandelion holds out the sun to me, saying: '*Can you take it!*'

Every gleam of heaven that is shown – like a dandelion flower, or a green beetle – quivers with strange passion to kindle a new gleam, never yet beheld. This is not self-sacrifice: it is self-contribution: in which the highest happiness lies.

The torch of existence is handed on, in the womb of procreation.

And the torch of revelation is handed on, by every living thing, from the protococcus to a brave man or a beautiful woman, handed to whomsoever can take it. He who can take it, has power beyond all the rest.

The cycle of procreation exists purely for the keeping alight of the torch of perfection, in any species: the torch being the dandelion in blossom, the tree in full leaf, the peacock in all his plumage, the cobra in all his colour, the frog at full leap, woman in all the mystery of her fathomless desirableness, man in the fulness of his power: every creature become its pure self.

One cycle of perfection urges to kindle another cycle, as yet unknown.

And with the kindling from the torch of revelation comes the inrush of vitality, and the need to consume and *consummate* the lower cycles of existence, into a new thing. This consuming and this consummating means conquest, and fearless mastery. Freedom lies in the honourable yielding towards the new flame, and the honourable mastery of that which shall be new, over that which must yield. As I must master my horses, which are in a lower cycle of existence. And they, they are relieved and *happy* to serve. If I turn them loose into the mountain ranges, to run wild till they die, the thrill of real happiness is gone out of their lives.

Every lower order seeks in some measure to serve a higher order: and rebels against being conquered.

It is always conquest, and it always will be conquest. If the conquered be an old, declining race, they will have handed on their torch to the conqueror: who will burn his fingers badly, if he is too flippant. And if the conquered be a barbaric race, they will consume the fire of the conqueror, and leave him flameless, unless he watch it. But it is always conquest, conquered and conqueror, for ever. The Kingdom of heaven is the Kingdom of conquerors, who can serve the conquest for ever, after their own conquest is made.

In heaven, in the perfected relation, is peace: in the fourth dimension. But there is getting there. And that, for ever, is the process of conquest.

When the rose blossomed, then the great Conquest was made by the Vegetable Kingdom. But even this conqueror of conquerors, the rose, had to lend himself towards the caterpillar and the butterfly of a later conquest. A conqueror, but tributary to the later conquest.

There is no such thing as equality. In the kingdom of heaven, in the fourth dimension, each soul that achieves a perfect relationship with the cosmos, from its own centre, is perfect, and incomparable. It has no superior. It is a conqueror, and incomparable.

But every man, in the struggle of conquest towards his own consummation, must master the inferior cycles of life, and never relinquish his mastery. Also, if there be men beyond him, moving on to a newer consummation than his own, he must yield to their greater demand, and serve their greater mystery, and so be faithful to the kingdom of heaven which is within him, which is gained by conquest and by loyal service.

Any man who achieves his own being will, like the dandelion or the butterfly, pass into that other dimension which we call the fourth, and the old people called heaven. It is the state of perfected relationship. And here a man will have his peace for ever: whether he serve or command, in the process of living.

But even this entails his faithful allegiance to the kingdom of heaven, which must be for ever and for ever extended, as creation conquers chaos. So that my perfection will but serve a perfection which still lies ahead, unrevealed and unconceived, and beyond my own.

We have tried to build walls round the kingdom of heaven: but it's no good. It's only the cabbage rotting inside.

Our last wall is the golden wall of money. This is a fatal wall. It cuts off from life, from vitality, from the alive sun and the alive earth, as *nothing* can. Nothing, not even the most fanatical dogmas of an iron-bound religion, can insulate us from the inrush of life and inspiration, as money can.

We are losing vitality: losing it rapidly. Unless we seize the torch of inspiration, and drop our moneybags, the moneyless will be kindled by the flame of flames, and they will consume us like old rags.

We are losing vitality, owing to money and money-standards. The torch in the hands of the moneyless will set our house on fire, and burn us to death, like sheep in a flaming corral.

DEMOCRACY

I – THE AVERAGE

Date of writing uncertain. *Phoenix*, 1936

WHITMAN gives two laws or principles for the establishment of Democracy. We may epitomize them as:

(1) The law of the Average; (2) The Principle of Individualism, or Personalism, or Identity.

The law of the Average is well known to us. Upon this law rests all the vague dissertation concerning equality and social perfection. Rights of Man, Equality of Man, Social Perfectibility of Man: all these sweet abstractions, once so inspiring, rest upon the fatal little hypothesis of the Average.

What is the Average? As we are well aware, there is no such animal. It is a pure abstraction. It is the reduction of the human being to a mathematical unit. Every human being numbers one, one single unit. That is the grand proposition of the Average.

Let us further examine this mysterious One, this Unit, this Average; let us examine it corporeally. The average human being: put him on the table, the little monster, and let us see what his works are like. He is just a little monster. He has two legs, two eyes, one nose – all exact. He has a stomach and a penis. He is a little organism. He is one very complicated organ, a unit, an identity.

What is he for? If he's an organ, he must have a purpose. If he's an organism, he must have a purpose. The question is premature, yet it shall be answered. Since he has a mouth, he is made for eating. Since he has feet, he is made for walking. Since he has a penis, he is made for reproducing his species. And so on, and so on.

What a loathsome little beast he is, this Average, this Unit, this Homunculus. Yet he has his purposes. He is useful to measure by. That's the purpose of all averages. An average is not invented to be an Archetype. What a really comical mistake we have made about him. He is invented to serve as a standard in the business of comparison. He is invented to serve as a standard, just like any other standard, like the metre, or the gramme, or the English pound sterling. That's what he is for – nothing else. He was never intended to be worshipped. What comical, fetish-smitten savages we are.

We use a foot-rule to tell us how big our house is. We don't proceed to say that the foot-rule is the sceptre which sways the earth and all the stars. Yet we have said as much of this little standardized invention of ours, the Average Man, the man-in-the-street. We have made prime fools of ourselves.

Now let us pull the gilt off the image, and see exactly what it is, and what we want it for. It is a mathematical quantity, like the metre or the foot-rule: a purely arbitrary institution of the human mind. Let us be quite clear about that.

But the human mind has invented the institution for its own purposes. Granted. What are the purposes? Merely for the comparing of one *living* man with another *living* man, in case of necessity: just as money is merely a contrivance for comparing a leg of mutton with a volume of Keats' poems. The money in itself is nothing. It is simply the arbitrary static measure for human desires. We mistake the measure for the thing it measures, and proceed to base our desires on money. It is nonsensical materialism.

Now for the Average Man himself. He is five-feet-six-inches high: and therefore you, John, will take an over-size pair of trousers, reach-me-downs; and you, François, mon cher, will take an under-size. The Average Man also has a mouth and a stomach, which consume two pounds of bread and six ounces of meat per day: and therefore you, Fritz, exceed the normal consumption of food, while you, dear Emily, consume less than your share. The Average Man has also a penis; and therefore all of you, François, Fritz, John, and Giacomo, you may begin begetting children at the average age, let us say, of twenty-five.

The Average Man is somehow very unsatisfactory. He is not sufficiently worked out. It is astonishing that we have not perfected him before. But this is because we have mixed the issues. How could we scientifically establish the Average, whilst he had to stand draped upon a pedestal, as an Ideal? Haul him down at once. He is no Ideal. He is just a Standard, the creature on whom Standard suits and Standard boots are fitted, to whose stomach Standard bread is adjusted, and for whose eyes the Standard Lamps are lighted, the Standard Oil Company is busy refining its gallons. He comes under the Government Weights and Measures Act.

Perfect him quickly: the Average, the Normal, the Man-in-the-street. He is so many inches high, broad, deep; he weighs so many pounds. He must eat so much, and sleep so much, and work so much, and play so much, and love so much, and think so much, and argue so much, and read so many newspapers, and have so many children. Somebody, quick – some Professor of Social Economy – draw us up a perfect Average, and let us have him before the middle of next week. He is urgently required at the moment.

This is all your Man-in-the-street amounts to: this tailor's dummy of an average. He is the image and effigy of all your equality. Men are not equal, and never were, and never will be, save by the arbitrary determination of some ridiculous human Ideal. But still, in the normal course of things, all men *do* have two eyes and one nose and a stomach and a penis. In the teeth of all opposition we assert it. In the normal course of things, all men *do* hunger and thirst and sleep and laugh and feel miserable and fall in love and ache for coition and ache to escape from the woman again. And the Average Man just represents what all men need and desire, physically, functionally, materially, and socially. *Materially* need: that's the point. The Average Man is the standard of material need in the human being.

Please keep out all Spiritual and Mystical needs. They have nothing to do with the Average. You cannot Average such things. As far as the stomach goes, it is not really true that one man's meat is another man's poison. No. The Law of

Average holds good for the stomach. All young mammals suck milk, without exception. But in the free, spontaneous self, one man's meat is truly another man's poison. And therefore you *can't* draw any average. You can't *have* an average: unless you are going to poison everybody.

Now we will settle for ever the Equality of Man, and the Rights of Man. Society means people living together. People *must* live together. And to live together, they must have some Standard, some *Material* Standard. This is where the Average comes in. And this is where Socialism and Modern Democracy come in. For Democracy and Socialism rest upon the Equality of Man, which is the Average. And this is sound enough, so long as the Average represents the real basic material needs of mankind: basic material needs: we insist and insist again. For Society, or Democracy, or any Political State or Community exists not for the sake of the individual, nor should ever exist for the sake of the individual, but simply to establish the Average, in order to make living together possible: that is, to make proper facilities for every man's clothing, feeding, housing himself, working, sleeping, mating, playing, according to his necessity as a common unit, an average. Everything beyond that common necessity depends on himself alone.

The proper adjustment of material means of existence: for this the State exists, but for nothing further. The State is a dead ideal. *Nation* is a dead ideal. Democracy and Socialism are dead ideals. They are one and all just *contrivances* for the supplying of the lowest material needs of a people. They are just vast hotels, or hostels, where every guest does some scrap of the business of the day's routine – if it's only lounging gracefully to give the appearance of ease – and for this contribution gets his suitable accommodation. England, France, Germany – these great nations, they have no vital meaning any more, except as great Food Committees and Housing Committees for a throng of people whose material tastes are somewhat in accord. No doubt they *had* other meanings. No doubt the French individuals of the seventeenth century still felt themselves gloriously expressed in stone, in Versailles. But man loses more and more his faculty for collective self-expression. Nay, the great development in collective expression in mankind has been a progress towards the possibility of purely individual expression. The highest Collectivity has for its true goal the purest individualism, pure individual spontaneity. But once more we have mistaken the means for the end: so that Presidents, those representatives of the collected masses, instead of being accounted the chief machine-section of society, which they are, are revered as ideal beings. The thing to do is not to raise the idea of Nation, or even of Internationalism, higher. The need is to take away every scrap of ideal drapery from nationalism and from internationalism, to show it all as a material contrivance for housing and feeding and conveying innumerable people. The housing and feeding, the method of conveyance and the rules of the road may be as different as you please – just as the methods of one great business house, and even of one hotel, are different from those of another. But that is all it is. Man no longer expresses himself in his form of government, and his President is strictly only his superlative butler. This is the true course of evolution: the great collective activities are at last merely auxiliary to the purely individual activities. Business houses may be magnificent, but there is nothing divine in it. This is why the Kaiser sounded so foolish. He was really only the head of a very great business concern. His God was the most intolerable part of his stock-in-trade. Genuine business houses may quarrel and compete, but they don't go to war. Why? Because they are not ideal concerns. They are just practical material concerns. It is only Ideal concerns which go to war, and slaughter indiscriminately with a feeling of exalted righteousness. But when a business concern masquerades as an ideal concern, and behaves in this fashion, it is really unbearable.

There are two things to do. Strip off at once all the ideal drapery from nationality, from nations, peoples, states, empires, and even from Internationalism and Leagues of Nations. Leagues of Nations should be just flatly and simply committees where representatives of the various business houses, so-called Nations, meet and consult. Consultations, board-meetings of the State business men: no more. *Representatives of Peoples* – who can represent me? – I am myself. I don't intend anybody to represent me.

You, you Cabinet Minister – what are you? You are the arch-grocer, the super-hotel-manager, the foreman over the ships and railways. What else are you? You are the super-tradesman, same paunch, same ingratiating manner, same everything. Governments, what are they? Just board-meetings of big business men. Very useful, too – very thankful we are that sombeody *will* look after this business. But Ideal! An Ideal Government? What nonsense. We might as well talk of an Ideal Cook's Tourist Agency, or an Ideal Achille Serre Cleaners and Dyers. Even the ideal Ford of America is only an ideal *average* motor-car. His employees are not spontaneous, nonchalant human beings, à la Whitman. They are just well-tested, well-oiled sections of the Ford automobile.

Politics – what are they? Just another, extra-large, commercial wrangle over buying and selling – nothing else. Very good to have the wrangle. Let us have the buying and selling well done. But *ideal!* Politics *ideal! Political idealists!* What rank gewgaw and nonsense! We have just enough sense not to talk Ideal Selfridges or Ideal Krupps or Ideal Heidsiecks. Then let us have enough sense to drop the ideal of England or Europe or anywhere else. Let us be men and women, and keep our house in order. But let us pose no longer as houses, or as England, or as housemaids, or democrats.

Pull the ideal drapery off Governments, States, Nations, and Inter-nations. Show them for what they are: big business concerns for manufacturing and retailing Standard goods. Put up a statue of the Average Man, something like those abominable statues of men in woollen underwear which surmount a shop at the corner of Oxford Street and Tottenham Court Road. Let your statue be grotesque: in fact, borrow those ignominious statues of men in pants and vests: the fat one for Germany, the thin one for England, the middling one for France, the gaunt one for America. Point to these statues, which guard the entrance to the House of Commons, to the Chamber, to the Senate, to the Reichstag – and let every Prime Minister and President know the quick of his own ignominy. Let every bursting politician see himself in his commercial pants. Let every senatorial idealist and saviour of mankind be reminded that his office depends on the quality of the underwear he supplies to the State. Let every fiery and rhetorical Deputy remember that he is only held together by his patent suspenders.

And then, when the people of the world have finally got over the state of giddy idealizing of governments, nations, inter-nations, politics, democracies, empires, and so forth; when they really understand that their collective activities are only cook–housemaid to their sheer individual activities; when they at last calmly accept a business concern for what it is; then, at last, we may actually see free men in the streets.

II – IDENTITY

Let us repeat that Whitman establishes the true Democracy on two bases:

(1) The Average; (2) Individualism, Personalism, or Identity.

The Average is much easier to settle and define than is Individualism or Identity. The Average is the same as the Man-in-the-street, the unit of Humanity. This unit is in the first place just an abstraction, an invention of the human mind. In the first place, the Man-in-the-street is no more than an abstract idea. But in the second place, by application to Tom, Dick, and Harry, he becomes a substantial, material, functioning unit. This is how the ideal world is created. It is invented exactly as man invents machinery. First there is an idea; then the idea is substantiated, the inventor fabricates his machine; and then he proceeds to worship his fabrication, and himself as mouthpiece of the Logos. This is how the world, the universe, was invented from the Logos: exactly as man has invented machinery and the whole ideal of humanity. The vital universe was never created from any Logos; but the ideal universe of man was certainly so invented. Man's overweening mind uttered the Word, and the Word was God. So that the world exists to-day as a flesh-and-blood-and-iron substantiation of this uttered word. This is all the trouble: that the invented *ideal* world of man is superimposed upon living men and women, and men and women are thus turned into abstracted, functioning, mechanical units. This is all the great ideal of Humanity amounts to: an aggregation of ideally functioning units: never a man or woman possible.

Ideals, all ideals and every ideal, are a trick of the devil. They are a superimposition of the abstracted, automatic, invented universe of man upon the spontaneous creative universe. So much for the Average, the Man-in-the-street, and the great ideal of Humanity: all a little trick men have played on us. But quite a useful little trick – so long as we merely use it as one uses the trick of making cakes or pies or bread, just for feeding purposes, and suchlike.

Let us leave the Average, and look at the second basis of democracy. With the Average we settle the cooking, eating, sleeping, housing, mating, and clothing problem. But Whitman insisted on exalting his Democracy; he would not quite leave it on the cooking-eating-mating level. We cook to eat, we eat to sleep, we sleep to build houses, we build houses in order to beget and bear children in safety, we bear children in order to clothe them, we clothe them in order that they may start the old cycle over again, cook and eat and sleep and house and mate and clothe, and so on *ad infinitum*. That is the Average. It is the business of a government to superintend it.

But Whitman insisted on raising Democracy above government, or even above public service or humanity or love of one's neighbour. Heaven knows what his Democracy is – but something as yet unattained. It is something beyond governments and even beyond Ideals. It must be beyond Ideals, because it has never yet been stated. As an idea it doesn't yet exist. Even Whitman, with all his reiteration, got no further than *hinting*: and frightfully bad hints, many of them.

We've heard the Average hint – enough of that. Now for Individualism, Personalism, and Identity. We catch hold of the tail of the hint, and proceed with Identity.

What has Identity got to do with Democracy? It can't have

anything to do with politics and governments. It can't much affect one's love for one's neighbour, or for humanity. Yet, stay – it can. Whitman says there is One Identity in all things. It is only the old dogma. All things emanate from the Supreme Being. All things, being all emanations from the Supreme Being, have One Identity.

Very nice. But we don't like the look of this Supreme Being. It is too much like the Man-in-the-street. This Supreme Being, this Anima Mundi, this Logos was surely just invented to suit the human needs. It is surely the magnified Average, abstracted from men, and then clapped on to them again, like identity-medals on wretched khaki soldiers. But instead of a magnified average-function-unit, we have a magnified unit of Consciousness, or Spirit.

Like the Average, this One Identity is useful enough, if we use it aright. It is not a matter of provisioning the body, this time, but of provisioning the spirit, the consciousness. We are all one, and therefore every bit partakes of all the rest. That is, the Whole is inherent in every fragment. That is, every human consciousness has the same intrinsic value as every other human consciousness, because each is an essential part of the Great Consciousness. This is the One Identity which identifies us all.

It is very nice, theoretically. And it is a very great stimulus to universal comprehension; it leads us all to want to know everything; it even tempts us all to imagine we know everything beforehand, and need make no effort. It is the subtlest means of extending the consciousness. But when you have extended your consciousness, even to infinity, what then? Do you really become God? When in your understanding you embrace everything, then surely you are divine? But no! With a nasty bump you have to come down and realize that, in spite of your infinite comprehension, you are not really any other than you were before: not a bit more divine or superhuman or enlarged. Your *consciousness* is not *you*: that is the sad lesson you learn in your superhuman flight of infinite understanding.

This big bump of falling out of the infinite back into your

own old self leads you to suspect that the One Identity is not *the* identity. There is another, little sort of identity, which you can't get away from, except by breaking your neck. The One Identity is very like the Average. It is what you are when you aren't yourself. It is what you are when you imagine you're something hugely big – the Infinite, for example. And the consciousness is really capable of attaining infinity. But there you are! Your consciousness has to fly back to the old tree, to peck the old apples, and sleep under the leaves. It was all only an excursion. It was wearing a magic cap. You yourself invented the cap, and then puffed up your head to fit it. But a swelled head at last begins to ache, and you realize it's only your own old chump after all. All the extended consciousness that ranged the infinite heavens must sleep under the thatch of your hair at night: and you are only you; and your *spirit* is only a bird in your tree, that flies, and then settles, whistles, and then is silent.

Man is a queer beast. He spends dozens of centuries puffing himself up and drawing himself in, and at last he has to be content to be just his own size, neither infinitely big nor infinitely little. Man is tragi-comical. His insatiable desire to be *everything* has made him clean forget that he might be himself. To be everything – to be everything: the history of mankind is only a history of this insane craving in man. You can magnify yourself into a Jehovah and a huge Egyptian king-god: or you can reverse the spy-glass, and dwindle yourself away into a speck, lost in the Infinite of Love, as the later great races have done. But still you'll only be chasing the one mad reward, the reward of infinity: which, when you've got it, bursts like a bubble in your hand, and leaves you looking at your own fingers. Well, and what's wrong with your own fingers?

It is a bubble, the One Identity. But, chasing it, man gets his education. It is his education process, the chance of the All, the extension of the consciousness. He *learns* everything: except the last lesson of all, which he can't learn till the bubble has burst in his fingers.

The last lesson? – Ah, the lesson of his own fingers: himself:

the little identity; little, but real. Better, far better, to be oneself than to be any bursting Infinite, or swollen One Identity.

It is a radical passion in man, however, the passion to include *everything* in himself, grasp it all. There are two ways of gratifying this passion. The first is Alexander's way, the way of power, power over the material universe. This is what the alchemists and magicians sought. This is what Satan offered Jesus, in the Temptations: power, mystic and actual, over the material world. And power, we know, is a bubble: a platitudinous bubble.

But Jesus chose the other way: not to *have* all, but to *be* all. Not to *grasp* everything into supreme possession: but to *be* everything, through supreme acceptance. It is the same thing, at the very last. The king-god and the crucified God hold the same bubble in their hands: the bubble of the All, the Infinite. The king-god extends the dominion of his will and consciousness over all things: the crucified identifies his will and consciousness with all things. But the submission of love is at last a process of pure materialism, like the supreme extension of power. Up to a certain point, both in mastering, which is power, and in submitting, which is love, the soul *learns* and fulfils itself. Beyond a certain point, it merely collapses from its centrality, and lapses out into the material chain of cause and effect. The tyranny of Power is no worse than the tyranny of No-power. Government by the highest is no more fatal than government by the lowest. Let the Average govern, let him be called super-butler, let us have a faint but tolerant contempt for him. But let us keep our very self integral, greater than any having or knowing, centrally alive and quick.

The last lesson: the myriad, mysterious identities, no one of which can *comprehend* another. They can only exist side by side, as stars do. The lesson of lessons: not in any oneness with the rest of things do we have our pure being: but in clean, fine singleness. Oneness, and collectiveness, these are our lesser states, inferior: our impurity. They are mere states of consciousness and of having.

It is all very well to talk about a Supreme Being, an Anima

Mundi, an Oversoul, an Infinite: but it is all just human invention. Come down to actuality. Where do you see Being? – In individual men and women. Where do you find an Anima? – In living individual creatures. Where would you look for a soul? – In a man, in an animal, in a tree or flower. And all the rest, about Supreme Beings and Anima Mundis and Oversouls, is just abstractions. Show me the very animal! – you can't. It is merely a trick of the human will, trying to get power over everything, and therefore making the wish father of the thought. The cart foals the horse, and there you are: a Logos, a Supreme Being, a What-not.

But there are two sorts of individual identity. Every factory-made pitcher has its own little identity, resulting from a certain mechanical combination of Matter with Forces. These are the material identities. They sum up to the material Infinite.

The true identity, however, is the identity of the living self. If we look for God, let us look in the bush where he sings. That is, in living creatures. Every living creature is single in itself, a *ne plus ultra* of creative reality, *fons et origo* of creative manifestation. Why go further? Why begin to abstract and generalize and include? There you have it. Every single living creature is a single creative unit, a unique, incommutable self. Primarily, in its own spontaneous reality, it knows no law. It is a law unto itself. Secondarily, in its material reality, it submits to all the laws of the material universe. But the primal, spontaneous self in any creature has ascendance, truly, over the material laws of the universe; it uses these laws and converts them in the mystery of creation.

This then is the true identity: the inscrutable, single self, the little unfathomable well-head that bubbles forth into being and doing. We cannot analyse it. We can only know it is there. It is not by any means a Logos. It precedes any knowing. It is the fountain-head of everything: the quick of the self.

Not people melted into a oneness: that is not the new Democracy. But people released into their single, starry identity, each one distinct and incommutable. This will never be an ideal; for of the living self you cannot make an idea, just as you have not been able to turn the individual 'soul' into an idea. Both are impossible to idealize. An idea is an abstraction from reality, a generalization. And you can't generalize the incommutable.

So the Whitman One Identity, the *En Masse*, is a horrible nullification of true identity and being. At the best, our *en masse* activities can be but servile, serving the free soul. At the worst, they are sheer self-destruction. Let us put them in their place. Let us get over our rage of social activity, public being, universal self-estimation, republicanism, bolshevism, socialism, empire – all these mad manifestations of *En Masse* and One Identity. They are all self-betrayed. Let our Democracy be in the singleness of the clear, clean self, and let our *En Masse* be no more than an arrangement for the liberty of this self. Let us drop looking after our neighbour. It only robs him of his chance of looking after himself. Which is robbing him of his freedom, with a vengeance.

III – PERSONALITY

> One's-self I sing, a simple separate person,
> Yet utter the word Democratic, the word En-Masse.

Such are the opening words of *Leaves of Grass*. It is Whitman's whole *motif*, the key to all his Democracy. First and last he sings of 'the great pride of man in himself'. First and last he is Chanter of Personality. If it is not Personality, it is Identity; and if not Identity, it is the Individual: and along with these, Democracy and *En Masse*.

In Whitman, at all times, the true and the false are so near, so interchangeable, that we are almost inevitably left with divided feelings. The Average, one of his greatest idols, we flatly refuse to worship. Again, when we come to do real reverence to identity, we never know whether we shall be taking off our hats to that great mystery, the unique individual self, distinct and primal in every separate man, or whether we shall be saluting that old great idol of the past, the Supreme One which swallows up all true identity.

And now for Personality. What meaning does 'person' really carry? A *person* is given in the dictionary as an *individual human being*. But surely the words *person* and *individual* suggest very different things. It is not at all the same to have personality as to have individuality, though you may not be able to define the difference. And the distinction between a person and a human being is perhaps even greater. Some 'persons' hardly seem like human beings at all.

The derivation this time helps. *Persona*, in Latin, is a player's mask, or a character in a play: and perhaps the word is cognate with *sonare*, to sound. An *individual* is that which is not divided or not dividable. A *being* we shall not attempt to define, because it is indefinable.

So now, there must be a radical difference between something which was originally a player's mask, or a transmitted sound, and something which means 'the undivided'. The old meaning lingers in *person*, and is almost obvious in *personality*. A person is a human being *as he appears to others*; and personality is that which is transmitted from the person to his audience: the transmissible effect of a man.

A good actor can assume a personality; he can never assume an individuality. Either he has his own, or none. So that personality is something much more superficial, or at least more volatile than individuality. This volatile quality is the one we must examine.

Let us take a sentence from an American novel: 'My *ego* had played a trick on me, and made me think I wanted babies, when I only wanted the man.' This is a perfectly straight and lucid statement. But what is the difference between the authoress's *ego* and her *me*? The *ego* is obviously a sort of second self, which she carries about with her. It is her body of accepted consciousness, which she has inherited more or less ready-made from her father and grandfathers. This secondary self is very pernicious, dictating to her issues which are quite false to her true, deeper, spontaneous self, her creative identity.

Nothing in the world is more pernicious than the *ego* or spurious self, the conscious entity with which every individual is saddled. He receives it almost *en bloc* from the preceding generation, and spends the rest of his life trying to drag his spontaneous self from beneath the horrible incubus. And the most fatal part of the incubus, by far, is the dead, leaden weight of handed-on ideals. So that every individual is born with a mill-stone of ideals round his neck, and, whether he knows it or not, either spends his time trying to get his neck free, like a wild animal wrestling with a collar to which a log is fastened; or else he spends his days decorating his mill-stone, his log, with fantastic colours.

And a finely or fantastically decorated mill-stone is called a personality. Never trust for one moment any individual who has unmistakable *personality*. He is sure to be a life-traitor. His personality is only a sort of actor's mask. It is his self-conscious *ego*, his *ideal* self masquerading and prancing round, showing off. He may not be aware of it. But that makes no matter. He is a painted bug.

The *ideal* self: this is personality. The self that is begotten and born from the *idea*, this is the *ideal* self: a spurious, detestable product. This is man created from his own Logos. This is man born out of his own head. This is the self-conscious ego, the entity of fixed ideas and ideals, prancing and displaying itself like an actor. And this is personality. This is what makes the American authoress gush about babies. And this gush is her peculiar form of personality which renders her attractive to the American men, who prefer so much to deal with personalities and *egos*, rather than with real beings: because personalities and *egos*, after all, are quite *reasonable*, which means, they are subject to the laws of cause-and-effect; they are safe and calculable: materialists, units of the material world of Force and Matter.

Your idealist alone is a perfect materialist. This is no paradox. What is the idea, or the ideal, after all? It is only a fixed, static entity, an abstraction, an extraction from the living body of life. Creative life is characterized by spontaneous mutability: it brings forth unknown issues, impossible to preconceive. But an ideal is just a machine which is in process of being built. A man gets the idea for some engine, and proceeds to work it out in steel and copper. In exactly the same way, man gets some ideal of man, and proceeds to work it out in flesh-and-blood, as a fixed, static entity: just as a machine is a static entity, so is the ideal Humanity.

If we want to find the real enemy to-day, here it is: idealism. If we want to find this enemy incarnate, here he is: a personality. If we want to know the steam which drives this mechanical little incarnation, here it is: love of humanity, the public good.

There have been other ideals than ours, other forms of personality, other sorts of steam. We quite fail to see what sort of personality Rameses II had, or what sort of steam built the pyramids: chiefly, I suppose, because they are a very great load on the face of the earth.

Is love of humanity the same as real, warm, individual love? Nonsense. It is the moonshine of our warm day, a hateful reflection. Is personality the same as individual being? We know it is a mere mask. Is idealism the same as creation? Rubbish! Idealism is no more than a plan of a marvellous Human Machine, drawn up by the great Draughtsmen-Minds of the past. Give God a pair of compasses, and let the designs be measured and formed. What insufferable nonsense! As if creation proceeded from a pair of compasses. Better say that man is a forked radish, as Carlyle did: it's nearer the mark than this Pair of Compasses business.

You can have life two ways. Either everything is created from the mind, downwards; or else everything proceeds from the creative quick, outwards into exfoliation and blossom. Either a great Mind floats in space: God, the Anima Mundi, the Oversoul, drawing with a pair of compasses and making everything to scale, even emotions and self-conscious effusions; or else creation proceeds from the forever inscrutable quicks of living beings, men, women, animals, plants. The actual living quick itself is alone the creative reality. Once you abstract from this, once you generalize and postulate Universals, you have departed from the creative reality, and entered the realm of static fixity, mechanism, materialism.

Now let us put salt on the tail of that sly old bird of 'attractive personality'. It isn't a bird at all. It is a self-conscious, self-important, befeathered snail: and salt is good for snails. It is the snail which has eaten off our flowers till none are left. Now let us no longer be taken in by the feathers. Anyhow, put salt on his tail.

No personalities in our Democracy. No ideals either. When still more Personalities come round hawking their pretty ideals, we must be ready to upset their apple-cart. I say, a man's self is a law unto itself: not unto *himself*, mind you. When a man talks about *himself*, he is talking about his idea of himself; his own ideal self, that fancy little homunculus he has fathered in his brain. When a man is conscious of himself he is trading his own personality.

You can't make an *idea* of the living self: hence it can never become an ideal. Thank heaven for that. There it is, an inscrutable, unfindable, vivid quick, giving us off as a life-issue. It is not *spirit*. Spirit is merely our mental consciousness, a finished essence extracted from our life-being, just as alcohol, spirits of wine, is the material, finished essence extracted from the living grape. The living self is not spirit. You cannot postulate it. How can you postulate that which is *there*? The moon might as well try to hold forth in heaven, postulating the sun. Or a child hanging on to his mother's skirt might as well commence in a long diatribe to postulate his mother's existence, in order to prove his own existence. Which is exactly what man has been busily doing for two thousand years. What amazing nonsense!

The quick of self is *there*. You needn't try to get behind it. As leave try to get behind the sun. You needn't try to idealize it, for by doing so you will only slime about with feathers in your tail, a gorgeous befeathered snail of an *ego* and a personality. You needn't try to show it off to your neighbour: he'll put salt on your tail it you do. And you needn't go on trying to save the living soul of your neighbour. It's hands off. Do you think you are such a God-Almighty bird of paradise that you can grow your neighbour's goose-quills for him on your own loving house-sparrow wings? Every bird must grow his own feathers; you are not the almighty dodo; you've got nobody's wings to feather but your own.

IV – INDIVIDUALISM

It is obvious that Whitman's Democracy is not merely a political system, or a system of government – or even a social system. It is an attempt to conceive a new way of life, to establish new values. It is a struggle to liberate human beings from the fixed, arbitrary control of ideals into free spontaneity.

No, the ideal of Oneness, the unification of all mankind into the homogeneous whole, is done away with. The great *desire* is that each single individual shall be incommutably himself, spontaneous and single, that he shall not in any way be reduced to a term, a unit of any Whole.

We must discriminate between an ideal and a desire. A desire proceeds from within, from the unknown, spontaneous soul or self. But an ideal is superimposed from above, from the mind; it is a fixed, arbitrary thing, like a machine control. The great lesson is to learn to break all the fixed ideals, to allow the soul's own deep desires to come direct, spontaneous into consciousness. But it is a lesson which will take many aeons to learn.

Our life, our being depends upon the incalculable issue from the central Mystery into indefinable *presence*. This sounds in itself an abstraction. But not so. It is rather the perfect absence of abstraction. The central Mystery is no generalized abstraction. It is each man's primal original soul or self, within him. And *presence* is nothing mystic or ghostly. On the contrary. It is the actual man present before us. The fact that an actual man present before us is an inscrutable and incarnate Mystery, untranslatable, this is the fact upon which any great scheme of social life must be based. It is the fact of *otherness*.

Each human self is single, incommutable, and unique. This is its *first* reality. Each self is unique, and therefore incomparable. It is a single well-head of creation, unquestionable: it cannot be compared with another self, another well-head, because, in its prime or creative reality, it can never be comprehended by any other self.

The living self has one purpose only: to come into its own fullness of being, as a tree comes into full blossom, or a bird into spring beauty, or a tiger into lustre.

But this coming into full, spontaneous being is the most difficult thing of all. Man's nature is balanced between spontaneous creativity and mechanical-material activity. Spontaneous being is subject to no law. But mechanical-material existence is subject to all the laws of the mechanical-physical world. Man has almost half his nature in the material world. His spontaneous nature *just* takes precedence.

The only thing man has to trust to in coming to himself is his desire and his impulse. But both desire and impulse tend to fall into mechanical automatism: to fall from spontaneous reality into dead or material reality. All our education should be a guarding against this fall.

The fall is possible in a twofold manner. Desires tend to automatize into functional appetites, and impulses tend to automatize into fixed aspirations or ideals. These are the two great temptations of man. Falling into the first temptation, the whole human will pivots on some function, some material activity, which then works the whole being: like an *idée fixe* in the mental consciousness. This automatized, dominant appetite we call a lust: a lust for power, a lust for consuming, a lust for self-abnegation and merging. The second great temptation is the inclination to set up some fixed centre in the mind, and make the whole soul turn upon this centre. This we call idealism. Instead of the will fixing upon some sensational activity, it fixes upon some aspirational activity, and pivots this activity upon an idea or an ideal. The whole soul streams in the energy of aspiration and turns automatically, like a machine, upon the ideal.

These are the two great temptations of the fall of man, the fall from spontaneous, single, pure being, into what we call materialism or automatism or mechanism of the self. All education must tend against this fall; and all our efforts in all our life must be to preserve the soul free and spontaneous.

The whole soul of man must *never* be subjected to one motion or emotion, the life-activity must never be degraded into a fixed activity, there must be *no fixed direction.*

There can be no ideal goal for human life. Any ideal goal means mechanization, materialism, and nullity. There is no pulling open the buds to see what the blossom will be. Leaves must unroll, buds swell and open, and *then* the blossom. And even after that, when the flower dies and the leaves fall, *still* we shall not know. There will be more leaves, more buds, more blossoms: and again, a blossom is an unfolding of the creative unknown. Impossible, utterly impossible to preconceive the unrevealed blossom. You cannot forestall it from the last blossom. We know the flower of to-day, but the flower of to-morrow is all beyond us. Only in the material-mechanical world can man foresee, foreknow, calculate, and establish laws.

So, we more or less grasp the first term of the new Democracy. We see something of what a man will be unto himself.

Next, what will a man be unto his neighbour? – Since every individual is, in his first reality, a single incommutable soul, not to be calculated or defined in terms of any other soul, there can be no establishing of a mathematical ratio. We cannot say that all men are equal. We cannot say A=B. Nor can we say that men are unequal. We may not declare that A=B+C.

Where each thing is unique in itself, there can be no comparison made. One man is neither equal nor unequal to another man. When I stand in the presence of another man, and I am my own pure self, am I aware of the presence of an equal, or of an inferior, or of a superior? I am not. When I stand with another man, who is himself, and when I am truly myself, then I am only aware of a Presence, and of the strange reality of Otherness. There is me, and there is *another being*. That is the first part of the reality. There is no comparing or estimating. There is only this strange recognition of *present otherness*. I may be glad, angry, or sad, because of the presence of the other. But still no comparison enters in. Comparison enters only when one of us departs from his own integral being, and enters the material-mechanical world. Then equality and inequality start at once.

So, we know the first great purpose of Democracy: that each man shall be spontaneously himself – each man himself, each woman herself, without any question of equality or inequality entering in at all; and that no man shall try to determine the being of any other man, or of any other woman.

But, because of the temptation which awaits every individual – the temptation to fall out of being, into automatism and mechanization, every individual must be ready at all times to defend his own being against the mechanization and materialism forced upon him by those people who have fallen or departed from being. It is the long unending fight, the fight for the soul's own freedom of spontaneous being, against the mechanism and materialism of the fallen.

All the foregoing deals really with the integral, whole nature of man. If man would but *keep* whole, integral, everything could be left at that. There would be no need for laws and governments: agreement would be spontaneous. Even the great concerted social activities would be essentially spontaneous.

But in his present state of unspeakable barbarism, man is unable to distinguish his own spontaneous integrity from his mechanical lusts and aspirations. Hence there must still be laws and governments. But laws and governments henceforth, we see it clearly and we must never forget it, relate only to the material world: to property, the possession of property and the means of life, and to the material-mechanical nature of man.

In the past, no doubt, there were great ideals to fulfil: ideals of brotherhood, oneness, and equality. Great sections of humanity tended to cohere into particular brotherhoods, expressing their oneness and their equality and their united purpose in a manner peculiar to themselves. For no matter how single an ideal may be, even such a mathematical ideal as equality and oneness, it will find the most diverse and even opposite expressions. So that brotherhood and oneness in Germany never meant the same as brotherhood and oneness in France. Yet each was brotherhood, and each was oneness. Souls, as they work out the same ideal, work it out differently: always differently, until they reach the point where the spontaneous integrity of being finally breaks. And then, when pure mechanization or materialism sets in, the soul is automatically pivoted, and the most diverse of creatures fall into a common mechanical unison. This we see in America. It is not a homogeneous, spontaneous coherence so much as a disintegrated amorphousness which lends itself to perfect mechanical unison.

Men have reached the point where, in further fulfilling their ideals, they break down the living integrity of their being and fall into sheer mechanical materialism. They become automatic units, determined entirely by mechanical law.

This is horribly true of modern democracy – socialism, conservatism, bolshevism, liberalism, republicanism, communism: all alike. The one principle that governs all the *isms* is the same: the principle of the idealized unit, the possessor of property. Man has his highest fulfilment as a possessor of property: so they all say, really. One half says that the uneducated, being the majority, should possess the property; the other half says that the educated, being the enlightened, should possess the property. There is no more to it. No need to write books about it.

This is the last of the ideals. This is the last phase of the ideal of equality, brotherhood, and oneness. All ideals work down to the sheer materialism which is their intrinsic reality, at last.

It doesn't matter, now, who has the property. They have all lost all their being over it. Even property, that most substantial of realities, evaporates once man loses his integral nature. It is curious that it is so, but it is undeniable. So that property is now fast evaporating.

Wherein lies the hope. For with it evaporates the last ideal. Sometime, somewhere, man will wake up and realize that property is only there to be used, not to be possessed. He will realize that possession is a kind of illness of the spirit, and a hopeless burden upon the spontaneous self. The little pronouns 'my' and 'our' will lose all their mystic spell.

The question of property will never be settled till people

cease to care for property. Then it will settle itself. A man only needs so much as will help him to his own fulfilments. Surely the individual who wants a motor-car merely for the sake of having it and riding in it is as hopeless an automaton as the motor-car itself.

When men are no longer obsessed with the desire to possess property, or with the parallel desire to prevent another man's possessing it, then, and only then shall we be glad to turn it over to the State. Our way of State-ownership is merely a farcical exchange of words, not of ways. We only intend our States to be Unlimited Liability Companies instead of Limited Liability Companies.

The Prime Minister of the future will be no more than a sort of steward, the Minister for Commerce will be the great housekeeper, the Minister for Transport the head-coachman: all just chief servants, no more: servants.

When men become their own decent selves again, then we can so easily arrange the material world. The arrangement will come, as it must come, spontaneously, not by previous ordering. Until such time, what is the good of talking about it? All discussion and idealizing of the possession of property, whether individual or group or State possession, amounts now to no more than a fatal betrayal of the spontaneous self. All settlement of the property question must arise spontaneously out of the new impulse in man, to free himself from the extraneous load of possession, and walk naked and light. Every attempt at preordaining a new material world only adds another last straw to the load that already has broken so many backs. If we are to keep our backs unbroken, we must deposit all property on the ground, and learn to walk without it. We must stand aside. And when many men stand aside, they stand in a new world; a new world of man has come to pass. This is the Democracy: the new order.

THE STATE OF FUNK

Written 1928–9. *Assorted Articles*, 1930

WHAT is the matter with the English, that they are so scared of everything? They are in a state of blue funk, and they behave like a lot of mice when somebody stamps on the floor. They are terrified about money, finance, about ships, about war, about work, about Labour, about Bolshevism, and funniest of all, they are scared stiff of the printed word. Now this is a very strange and humiliating state of mind, in a people which has always been so dauntless. And for the nation, it is a very dangerous state of mind. When a people falls into a state of funk, then God help it. Because mass funk leads some time or other to mass panic, and then – one can only repeat, God help us.

There is, of course, a certain excuse for fear. The time of change is upon us. The need for change has taken hold of us. We are changing, we have got to change, and we can no more help it than leaves can help going yellow and coming loose in autumn, or than bulbs can help shoving their little green spikes out of the ground in spring. We are changing, we are in the throes of change, and the change will be a great one. Instinctively, we feel it. Intuitively, we know it. And we are frightened. Because change hurts. And also, in the periods of serious transition, everything is uncertain, and living things are most vulnerable.

But what of it? Granted all the pains and dangers and uncertainties, there is no excuse for falling into a state of funk. If we come to think of it, every child that is begotten and born is a seed of change, a danger to its mother, at childbirth a great pain, and after birth, a new responsibility, a new change. If we feel in a state of funk about it, we should cease having children altogether. *If* we fall into a state of funk, indeed, the best thing is to have no children. But why fall into a state of funk?

Why not look things in the face like men, and like women? A woman who is going to have a child says to herself: Yes, I feel uncomfortable, sometimes I feel wretched, and I have a time of pain and danger ahead of me. But I have a good chance of coming through all right, especially if I am intelligent, and I bring a new life into the world. Somewhere I feel hopeful, even happy. So I must take the sour with the sweet. There is no birth without birth-pangs.

It is the business of men, of course, to take the same attitude towards the birth of new conditions, new ideas, new emotions. And sorry to say, most modern men don't. They fall into a state of funk. We all of us know that ahead of us lies a great social change, a great social readjustment. A few men look it in the face and try to realize what will be best. We none of us *know* what will be best. There is no ready-made solution. Ready-made solutions are almost the greatest danger of all. A change is a slow flux, which must happen bit by bit. And it must *happen*. You can't drive it like a steam engine. But all the time you can be alert and intelligent about it, and watch for the next step, and watch for the direction of the main trend. Patience, alertness, intelligence, and a human goodwill and fearlessness, that is what you want in a time of change. Not funk.

Now England is on the brink of great changes, radical changes. Within the next fifty years the whole framework of our social life will be altered, will be greatly modified. The old world of our grandfathers is disappearing like thawing snow, and is as likely to cause a flood. What the world of our grandchildren will be, fifty years hence, we don't know. But in its social form it will be very different from our world of to-day. We've got to change. And in our power to change, in our capacity to make new intelligent adaptation to new conditions, in our readiness to admit and fulfil new needs, to give expression to new desires and new feelings, lies our hope and our health. Courage is the great word. Funk spells sheer disaster.

There is a great change coming, bound to come. The whole money arrangement will undergo a change: what, I don't know. The whole industrial system will undergo a change.

Work will be different and pay will be different. The owning of property will be different. Class will be different, and human relations will be modified and perhaps simplified. If we are intelligent, alert and undaunted, then life will be much better, more generous, more spontaneous, more vital, less basely materialistic. If we fall into a state of funk, impotence and persecution, then things may be very much worse than they are now. It is up to us. It is up to men to be men. While men are courageous and willing to change, nothing terribly bad can happen. But once men fall into a state of funk, with the inevitable accompaniment of bullying and repression, then only bad things can happen. To be firm is one thing. But bullying is another. And bullying of any sort whatsoever can have nothing but disastrous results. And when the mass falls into a state of funk, and you have mass bullying, then catastrophe is near.

Change in the whole social system is inevitable not merely because conditions change – though partly for that reason – but because people themselves change. We change, you and I, we change and change vitally, as the years go on. New feelings arise in us, old values depreciate, new values arise. Things we thought we wanted most intensely we realize we don't care about. The things we built our lives on crumble and disappear, and the process is painful. But it is not tragic. A tadpole that has so gaily waved its tail in the water must feel very sick when the tail begins to drop off and little legs begin to sprout. The tail was its dearest, gayest, most active member, all its little life was in its tail. And now the tail must go. It seems rough on the tadpole; but the little green frog in the grass is a new gem, after all.

As a novelist, I feel it is the change inside the individual which is my real concern. The great social change interests me and troubles me, but it is not my field. I know a change is coming – and I know we must have a more generous, more human system based on the life values and not on the money values. That I know. But what steps to take I don't know. Other men know better.

My field is to know the feelings inside a man, and to make

new feelings conscious. What really torments civilized people is that they are full of feelings they know nothing about; they can't realize them, they can't fulfil them, they can't *live* them. And so they are tortured. It is like having energy you can't use – it destroys you. And feelings are a form of vital energy.

I am convinced that the majority of people to-day have good, generous feelings which they can never know, never experience, because of some fear, some repression. I do not believe that people would be villains, thieves, murderers and sexual criminals if they were freed from legal restraint. On the contrary, I think the vast majority would be much more generous, good-hearted and decent if they felt they dared be. I am convinced that people want to be more decent, more good-hearted than our social system of money and grab allows them to be. The awful fight for money, into which we are all forced, hurts our good nature more than we can bear. I am sure this is true of a vast number of people.

And the same is true of our sexual feelings; only worse. There, we start all wrong. Consciously, there is supposed to be no such thing as sex in the human being. As far as possible, we never speak of it, never mention it, never, if we can help it, even think of it. It is disturbing. It is – somehow – wrong.

The whole trouble with sex is that we daren't speak of it and think of it naturally. We are not secretly sexual villains. We are not secretly sexually depraved. We are just human beings with living sex. We are all right, if we had not this unaccountable and disastrous *fear* of sex. I know, when I was a lad of eighteen, I used to remember with shame and rage in the morning the sexual thoughts and desires I had had the night before. Shame, and rage, and terror lest anybody else should have to know. And I *hated* the self that I had been, the night before.

Most boys are like that, and it is, of course, utterly wrong. The boy that had excited sexual thoughts and feelings was the living, warm-hearted, passionate me. The boy that in the morning remembered these feelings with such fear, shame and rage was the social mental me: perhaps a little priggish, and certainly in a state of funk. But the two were divided against one another. A boy divided against himself; a girl divided against herself; a people divided against itself; it is a disastrous condition.

And it was a long time before I was able to say to myself: I am *not* going to be ashamed of my sexual thoughts and desires, they are me myself, they are part of my life. I am going to accept myself sexually as I accept myself mentally and spiritually, and know that I am one time one thing, one time another, but I am always myself. My sex is me as my mind is me, and nobody will make me feel shame about it.

It is long since I came to that decision. But I remember how much freer I felt, how much warmer and more sympathetic towards people. I had no longer anything to hide from them, no longer anything to be in a funk about, lest they should find it out. My sex was me, like my mind and my spirit. And the other man's sex was him, as his mind was him, and his spirit was him. And the woman's sex was her, as her mind and spirit were herself too. And once this quiet admission is made, it is wonderful how much deeper and more real the human sympathy flows. And it is wonderful how difficult the admission is to make, for man or woman: the tacit, natural admission, that allows the natural warm flow of the blood-sympathy without repression and holding back.

I remember when I was a very young man I was enraged when with a woman, if I was reminded of her sexual actuality. I only wanted to be aware of her personality, her mind and spirit. The other had to be fiercely shut out. Some part of the natural sympathy for a woman had to be shut away, cut off. There was a mutilation in the relationship all the time.

Now, in spite of the hostility of society, I have learned a little better. Now I know that a woman is her sexual self too, and I can feel the normal sex sympathy with her. And this silent sympathy is utterly different from desire or anything rampant or lurid. If I can really sympathize with a woman in her sexual self, it is just a form of warm-heartedness and compassionateness, the most natural life-flow in the world. And it may be a woman of seventy-five, or a child of two, it is the same. But our civilization, with its horrible fear and funk and repression and bullying, has almost destroyed the natural flow of common sympathy between men and men, and men and women.

And it is this that I want to restore into life: just the natural warm flow of common sympathy between man and man, man and woman. Many people hate it, of course. Many men hate it that one should tacitly take them for sexual, physical men instead of mere social and mental personalities. Many women hate it the same. Some, the worst, are in a state of rabid funk. The papers call me 'lurid'; and a 'dirty-minded fellow'. One woman, evidently a woman of education and means, wrote to me out of the blue: 'You, who are a mixture of the missing-link and the chimpanzee, etc.' – and told me my name stank in men's nostrils: though, since she was Mrs Something or other, she might have said women's nostrils – And these people think they are being perfectly well-bred and perfectly 'right'. They are safe inside the convention, which also agrees that we are sexless creatures and social beings merely, cold and bossy and assertive, cowards safe inside a convention.

Now I am one of the least lurid mortals, and I don't at all mind being likened to a chimpanzee. If there is one thing I don't like it is cheap and promiscuous sex. If there is one thing I insist on it is that sex is a delicate, vulnerable, vital thing that you mustn't fool with. If there is one thing I deplore it is heartless sex. Sex must be a real flow, a real flow of sympathy, generous and warm, and not a trick thing, or a moment's excitation, or a mere bit of bullying.

And if I write a book about the sex relations of a man and a woman, it is not because I want all men and women to begin having indiscriminate lovers and love affairs, off the reel. All this horrid scramble of love affairs and prostitution is only part of the funk, bravado and *doing it on purpose*. And bravado and *doing it on purpose* is just as unpleasant and hurtful as repression, just as much a sign of secret fear.

What you have to do is to get out of the state of funk, sex funk. And to do so, you've got to be perfectly decent, and you have to accept sex fully in the consciousness. Accept sex in the consciousness, and let the normal physical awareness come back, between you and other people. Be tacitly and simply aware of the sexual being in every man and woman, child and animal; and unless the man or woman is a bully, be sympathetically aware. It is the most important thing just now, this gentle physical awareness. It keeps us tender and alive at a moment when the great danger is to go brittle, hard, and in some way dead.

Accept the sexual, physical being of yourself, and of every other creature. Don't be afraid of it. Don't be afraid of the physical functions. Don't be afraid of the so-called obscene words. There is nothing wrong with the words. It is your fear that makes them bad, your needless fear. It is your fear which cuts you off physically even from your nearest and dearest. And when men and women are physically cut off, they become at last dangerous, bullying, cruel. Conquer the fear of sex, and restore the natural flow. Restore even the so-called obscene words, which are part of the natural flow. If you don't, if you don't put back a bit of the old warmth into life, there is savage disaster ahead.

INSOUCIANCE

Written 1928. As 'Over-earnest Ladies' in *Evening News*, 12 July, 1928. *Assorted Articles*, 1930

MY balcony is on the east side of the hotel, and my neighbours on the right are a Frenchman, white-haired, and his white-haired wife; my neighbours on the left are two little white-haired English ladies. And we are all mortally shy of one another.

When I peep out of my room in the morning and see the matronly French lady in a purple silk wrapper, standing like the captain on the bridge surveying the morning, I pop in again before she can see me. And whenever I emerge during the day, I am aware of the two little white-haired ladies popping back like two white rabbits, so that literally I only see the whisk of their skirt-hems.

This afternoon being hot and thundery, I woke up suddenly and went out on the balcony barefoot. There I sat serenely contemplating the world, and ignoring the two bundles of feet of the two little ladies which protruded from their open doorways, upon the end of the two *chaises longues*. A hot, still afternoon! the lake shining rather glassy away below, the mountains rather sulky, the greenness very green, all a little silent and lurid, and two mowers mowing with scythes, downhill just near: *slush! slush!* sound the scythe-strokes.

The two little ladies become aware of my presence. I become aware of a certain agitation in the two bundles of feet wrapped in two discreet steamer rugs and protruding on the end of two *chaises longues* from the pair of doorways upon the balcony next me. One bundle of feet suddenly disappears; so does the other. Silence!

Then lo! with odd sliding suddenness a little white-haired lady in grey silk, with round blue eyes, emerges and looks straight at me, and remarks that it is pleasant now. A little cooler, say I, with false amiability. She quite agrees, and we speak of the men mowing; how plainly one hears the long breaths of the scythes!

By now we are *tête-à-tête*. We speak of cherries, strawberries, and the promise of the vine crop. This somehow leads to Italy, and to Signor Mussolini. Before I know where I am, the little white-haired lady has swept me off my balcony, away from the glassy lake, the veiled mountains, the two men mowing, and the cherry trees, away into the troubled ether of international politics.

I am not allowed to sit like a dandelion on my own stem. The little lady in a breath blows me abroad. And I was so pleasantly musing over the two men mowing: the young one, with long legs in bright blue cotton trousers, and with bare black head, swinging so lightly downhill, and the other, in black trousers, rather stout in front, and wearing a new straw hat of the boater variety, coming rather stiffly after, crunching the end of his stroke with a certain violent effort.

I was watching the curiously different motions of the two men, the young thin one in bright blue trousers, the elderly fat one in shabby black trousers that stick out in front, the different amount of effort in their mowing, the lack of grace in the elderly one, his jerky advance, the unpleasant effect of the new 'boater' on his head – and I tried to interest the little lady.

But it meant nothing to her. The mowers, the mountains, the cherry trees, the lake, all the things that were *actually* there, she didn't care about. They even seemed to scare her off the balcony. But she held her ground, and instead of herself being scared away, she snatched me up like some ogress, and swept me off into the empty desert spaces of right and wrong, politics, Fascism and the rest.

The worst ogress couldn't have treated me more villainously. I don't care about right and wrong, politics, Fascism, abstract liberty or anything else of the sort. I want to look at the mowers, and wonder why fatness, elderliness and black trousers should inevitably wear a new straw hat of the boater variety, move in stiff jerks, shove the end of the scythe-stroke with a certain violence, and win my hearty disapproval, as contrasted with young long thinness, bright blue cotton trousers, a bare black head, and a pretty lifting movement at the end of the scythe-stroke.

Why do modern people almost invariably ignore the things that are actually present to them? Why, having come out from England to find mountains, lakes, scythe-mowers and cherry trees, does the little blue-eyed lady resolutely close her blue eyes to them all, now she's got them, and gaze away to Signor Mussolini, whom she hasn't got, and to Fascism, which is invisible anyhow? Why isn't she content to be where she is? Why can't she be happy with what she's got? Why must she *care*?

I see now why her round blue eyes are so round, so noticeably round. It is because she 'cares'. She is haunted by that mysterious bugbear of 'caring'. For everything on earth that doesn't concern her she 'cares'. She cares terribly because far-off, invisible, hypothetical Italians wear black shirts, but she doesn't care a rap that one elderly mower whose stroke she can hear wears black trousers instead of bright blue cotton ones. Now if she would descend from the balcony and climb the grassy slope and say to the fat mower: '*Cher monsieur, pourquoi portez-vous les pantalons noirs?* Why, oh, why do you wear black trousers?' – then I should say: What an on-the-spot little lady! – But since she only torments me with international politics, I can only remark: What a tiresome off-the-spot old woman!

They care! They simply are eaten up with caring. They are so busy caring about Fascism or Leagues of Nations or whether France is right or whether Marriage is threatened, that they never know where they are. They certainly never live on the spot where they are. They inhabit abstract space, the desert void of politics, principles, right and wrong, and so forth. They are doomed to be abstract. Talking to them is like trying to have a human relationship with the letter *x* in algebra.

There simply is a deadly breach between actual living and this abstract caring. What is actual living? It is a question mostly of direct contact. There was a direct sensuous contact between me, the lake, mountains, cherry trees, mowers, and a certain invisible but noisy chaffinch in a clipped lime tree. All this was cut off by the fatal shears of that abstract word Fascism, and the little old lady next door was the Atropos who cut the thread of my actual life this afternoon. She beheaded me, and flung my head into abstract space. Then we are supposed to love our neighbours!

When it comes to living, we live through our instincts and our intuitions. Instinct makes me run from little over-earnest ladies; instinct makes me sniff the lime blossom and reach for the darkest cherry. But it is intuition which makes me feel the uncanny glassiness of the lake this afternoon, the sulkiness of the mountains, the vividness of near green in thunder-sun, the young man in bright blue trousers lightly tossing the grass from the scythe, the elderly man in a boater stiffly shoving his scythe-strokes, both of them sweating in the silence of the intense light.

The Spirit of Place

ENGLAND

—

WHISTLING OF BIRDS

Written 1919. *The Athenaeum*, 11 April, 1919.
Phoenix, 1936

THE frost held for many weeks, until the birds were dying rapidly. Everywhere in the fields and under the hedges lay the ragged remains of lapwings, starlings, thrushes, redwings, innumerable ragged bloody cloaks of birds, when the flesh was eaten by invisible beasts of prey.

Then, quite suddenly, one morning, the change came. The wind went to the south, came off the sea warm and soothing. In the afternoon there were little gleams of sunshine, and the doves began, without interval, slowly and awkwardly to coo. The doves were cooing, though with a laboured sound, as if they were still winter-stunned. Nevertheless, all the afternoon they continued their noise, in the mild air, before the frost had thawed off the road. At evening the wind blew gently, still gathering a bruising quality of frost from the hard earth. Then, in the yellow-gleamy sunset, wild birds began to whistle faintly in the blackthorn thickets of the stream-bottom.

It was startling and almost frightening after the heavy silence of frost. How could they sing at once, when the ground was thickly strewn with the torn carcasses of birds? Yet out of the evening came the uncertain, silvery sounds that made one's soul start alert, almost with fear. How could the little silver bugles sound the rally so swiftly, in the soft air, when the earth was yet bound? Yet the birds continued their whistling, rather dimly and brokenly, but throwing the threads of silver, germinating noise into the air.

It was almost a pain to realize, so swiftly, the new world. *Le monde est mort. Vive le monde!* But the birds omitted even the first part of the announcement, their cry was only a faint, blind, fecund *vive!*

There is another world. The winter is gone. There is a new world of spring. The voice of the turtle is heard in the land. But the flesh shrinks from so sudden a transition. Surely the call is premature while the clods are still frozen, and the ground is littered with the remains of wings! Yet we have no choice. In the bottoms of impenetrable blackthorn, each evening and morning now, out flickers a whistling of birds.

Where does it come from, the song? After so long a cruelty, how can they make it up so quickly? But it bubbles through them, they are like little well-heads, little fountain-heads whence the spring trickles and bubbles forth. It is not of their own doing. In their throats the new life distils itself into sound. It is the rising of silvery sap of a new summer, gurgling itself forth.

All the time, whilst the earth lay choked and killed and winter-mortified, the deep undersprings were quiet. They only wait for the ponderous encumbrance of the old order to give way, yield in the thaw, and there they are, a silver realm at once. Under the surge of ruin, unmitigated winter, lies the silver potentiality of all blossom. One day the black tide must spend itself and fade back. Then all-suddenly appears the crocus, hovering triumphant in the rear, and we know the order has changed, there is a new regime, sound of a new *vive! vive!*

It is no use any more to look at the torn remnants of birds that lie exposed. It is no longer any use remembering the sullen thunder of frost and the intolerable pressure of cold upon us. For whether we will or not, they are gone. The choice is not ours. We may remain wintry and destructive for a little longer, if we wish it, but the winter is gone out of us, and willy-nilly our hearts sing a little at sunset.

Even whilst we stare at the ragged horror of the birds scattered broadcast, part-eaten, the soft, uneven cooing of the pigeon ripples from the outhouses, and there is a faint silver whistling in the bushes come twilight. No matter, we stand and stare at the torn and unsightly ruins of life, we watch the weary, mutilated columns of winter retreating under our eyes. Yet in our ears are the silver bugles of a new creation advancing on us from behind, we hear the rolling of the soft and happy drums of the doves.

We may not choose the world. We have hardly any choice for ourselves. We follow with our eyes the bloody and horrid line of march of extreme winter, as it passes away. But we cannot hold back the spring. We cannot make the birds silent, prevent the bubbling of the wood-pigeons. We cannot stay the fine world of silver-fecund creation from gathering itself and taking place upon us. Whether we will or no, the daphne tree will soon be giving off perfume, the lambs dancing on two feet, the celandines will twinkle all over the ground, there will be a new heaven and new earth.

For it is in us, as well as without us. Those who can may follow the columns of winter in their retreat from the earth. Some of us, we have no choice, the spring is within us, the silver fountain begins to bubble under our breast, there is gladness in spite of ourselves. And on the instant we accept the gladness! The first day of change, out whistles an unusual interrupted paean, a fragment that will augment itself imperceptibly. And this in spite of the extreme bitterness of the suffering, in spite of the myriads of torn dead.

Such a long, long winter, and the frost only broke yesterday. Yet it seems, already, we cannot remember it. It is strangely remote, like a far-off darkness. It is as unreal as a dream in the night. This is the morning of reality, when we are ourselves. This is natural and real, the glimmering of a new creation that stirs in us and about us. We know there was winter, long, fearful. We know the earth was strangled and mortified, we know the body of life was torn and scattered broadcast. But what is this retrospective knowledge? It is something extraneous to us, extraneous to this that we are now. And what we are, and what, it seems, we always have been, is this quickening lovely silver plasm of pure creativity. All the mortification and tearing, ah yes, it was upon us, encompassing us. It was like a storm or a mist or a falling from a height. It was entangled with us, like bats in our hair driving us mad. But it was never really our innermost self. Within, we were always apart, we were this, this limpid fountain of silver, then quiescent, rising and breaking now into the flowering.

It is strange, the utter incompatibility of death with life. Whilst there is death, life is not to be found. It is all death, one overwhelming flood. And then a new tide rises, and it is all life, a fountain of silvery blissfulness. It is one or the other. We are for life, or we are for death, one or the other, but never in our essence both at once.

Death takes us, and all is torn redness, passing into darkness. Life rises, and we are faint fine jets of silver running out to blossom. All is incompatible with all. There is the silver-speckled, incandescent-lovely thrush, whistling pipingly his first song in the blackthorn thicket. How is he to be connected with the bloody, feathered unsightliness of the thrush-remnants just outside the bushes? There is no connexion. They are not to be referred the one to the other. Where one is, the other is not. In the kingdom of death the silvery song is not. But where there is life, there is no death. No death whatever, only silvery gladness, perfect, the other-world.

The blackbird cannot stop his song, neither can the pigeon. It takes place in him, even though all his race was yesterday destroyed. He cannot mourn, or be silent, or adhere to the dead. Of the dead he is not, since life has kept him. The dead must bury their dead. Life has now taken hold on him and tossed him into the new ether of a new firmament, where he bursts into song as if he were combustible. What is the past, those others, now he is tossed clean into the new, across the untranslatable difference?

In his song is heard the first brokenness and uncertainty of the transition. The transit from the grip of death into new being is a death from death, in its sheer metempsychosis, a dizzy agony. But only for a second, the moment of trajectory, the passage from one state to the other, from the grip of death to the liberty of newness. In a moment he is a kingdom of wonder, singing at the centre of a new creation.

The bird did not hang back. He did not cling to his death and his dead. There is no death, and the dead have buried their dead. Tossed into the chasm between two worlds, he lifted his wings in dread, and found himself carried on the impulse.

We are lifted to be cast away into the new beginning. Under our hearts the fountain surges, to toss us forth. Who can thwart the impulse that comes upon us? It comes from the unknown upon us, and it behoves us to pass delicately and exquisitely upon the subtle new wind from heaven, conveyed like birds in unreasoning migrations from death to life.

NOTTINGHAM AND THE MINING COUNTRY

Written 1929. *The New Adelphi*, June-August, 1930. *Phoenix*, 1936

I WAS born nearly forty-four years ago, in Eastwood, a mining village of some three thousand souls, about eight miles from Nottingham, and one mile from the small stream, the Erewash, which divides Nottinghamshire from Derbyshire. It is hilly country, looking west to Crich and towards Matlock, sixteen miles away, and east and north-east towards Mansfield and the Sherwood Forest district. To me it seemed, and still seems, an extremely beautiful countryside, just between the red sandstone and the oak-trees of Nottingham, and the cold limestone, the ash-trees, the stone fences of Derbyshire. To me, as a child and a young man, it was still the old England of the forest and agricultural past; there were no motor-cars, the mines were, in a sense, an accident in the landscape, and Robin Hood and his merry men were not very far away.

The string of coal-mines of B.W. & Co. had been opened some sixty years before I was born, and Eastwood had come into being as a consequence. It must have been a tiny village at the beginning of the nineteenth century, a small place of cottages and fragmentary rows of little four-roomed miners' dwellings, the homes of the old colliers of the eighteenth century, who worked in the bits of mines, foot-hill mines with an opening in the hillside into which the miners walked, or windlass mines, where the men were wound up one at a time, in a bucket, by a donkey. The windlass mines were still working when my father was a boy – and the shafts of some were still there, when I was a boy.

But somewhere about 1820 the company must have sunk the first big shaft – not very deep – and installed the first machinery of the real industrial colliery. Then came my grandfather, a young man trained to be a tailor, drifting from the south of England, and got the job of company tailor for the Brinsley mine. In those days the company supplied the men with the thick flannel vests, or singlets, and the moleskin trousers lined at the top with flannel, in which the colliers worked. I remember the great rolls of coarse flannel and pit-cloth which stood in the corner of my grandfather's shop when I was a small boy, and the big, strange old sewing-machine, like nothing else on earth, which sewed the massive pit-trousers. But when I was only a child the company discontinued supplying the men with pit-clothes.

My grandfather settled in an old cottage down in a quarry-bed, by the brook at Old Brinsley, near the pit. A mile away, up at Eastwood, the company built the first miners' dwellings – it must be nearly a hundred years ago. Now Eastwood occupies a lovely position on a hilltop, with the steep slope towards Derbyshire and the long slope towards Nottingham. They put up a new church, which stands fine and commanding, even if it has no real form, looking across the awful Erewash Valley at the church of Heanor, similarly commanding, away on a hill beyond. What opportunities, what opportunities! These mining villages *might* have been like the lovely hill-towns of Italy, shapely and fascinating. And what happened?

Most of the little rows of dwellings of the old-style miners were pulled down, and dull little shops began to rise along the Nottingham Road, while on the down-slope of the north side the company erected what is still known as the New Buildings, or the Square. These New Buildings consist of two great hollow squares of dwellings planked down on the rough slope of the hill, little four-room houses with the 'front' looking outward into the grim, blank street, and the 'back', with a tiny square brick yard, a low wall, and a w.c. and ash-pit, looking into the desert of the square, hard, uneven, jolting black earth tilting rather steeply down, with these little back yards all round, and openings at the corners. The squares were quite big, and absolutely desert, save for the posts for clothes lines, and people passing, children playing on the hard earth. And they were shut in like a barracks enclosure, very strange.

Even fifty years ago the squares were unpopular. It was 'common' to live in the Square. It was a little less common to live in the Breach, which consisted of six blocks of rather more pretentious dwellings erected by the company in the valley below, two rows of three blocks, with an alley between. And it was most 'common', most degraded of all to live in Dakins Row, two rows of the old dwellings, very old, black, four-roomed little places, that stood on the hill again, not far from the Square.

So the place started. Down the steep street between the squares, Scargill Street, the Wesleyans' chapel was put up, and I was born in the little corner shop just above. Across the other side of the Square the miners themselves built the big, barn-like Primitive Methodist chapel. Along the hill-top ran the Nottingham Road, with the scrappy, ugly mid-Victorian shops. The little market-place, with a superb outlook, ended the village on the Derbyshire side, and was just here left bare, with the Sun Inn on one side, the chemist across, with the gilt pestle-and-mortar, and a shop at the other corner, the corner of Alfreton Road and Nottingham Road.

In this queer jumble of the old England and the new, I came into consciousness. As I remember, little local speculators already began to straggle dwellings in rows, always in rows, across the fields: nasty red-brick, flat-faced dwellings with dark slate roofs. The bay-window period only began when I was a child. But most of the country was untouched.

There must be three or four hundred company houses in the squares and the streets that surround the squares, like a great barracks wall. There must be sixty or eighty company houses in the Breach. The old Dakins Row will have thirty to forty little holes. Then counting the old cottages and rows left with their old gardens down the lanes and along the twitchells, and even in the midst of Nottingham Road itself, there were houses enough for the population, there was no need for much building. And not much building went on when I was small.

We lived in the Breach, in a corner house. A field-path came down under a great hawthorn hedge. On the other side was the brook, with the old sheep-bridge going over into the meadows. The hawthorn hedge by the brook had grown tall as tall trees, and we used to bathe from there in the dipping-hole, where the sheep were dipped, just near the fall from the old mill-dam, where the water rushed. The mill only ceased grinding the local corn when I was a child. And my father, who always worked in Brinsley pit, and who always got up at five o'clock, if not at four, would set off in the dawn across the fields at Coney Grey, and hunt for mushrooms in the long grass, or perhaps pick up a skulking rabbit, which he would bring home at evening inside the lining of his pit-coat.

So that the life was a curious cross between industrialism and the old agricultural England of Shakespeare and Milton and Fielding and George Eliot. The dialect was broad Derbyshire, and always 'thee' and 'thou'. The people lived almost entirely by instinct, men of my father's age could not really read. And the pit did not mechanize men. On the contrary. Under the butty system, the miners worked underground as a sort of intimate community, they knew each other practically naked, and with curious close intimacy, and the darkness and the underground remoteness of the pit 'stall', and the continual presence of danger, made the physical, instinctive, and intuitional contact between men very highly developed, a contact almost as close as touch, very real and very powerful. This physical awareness and intimate *togetherness* was at its strongest down pit. When the men came up into the light, they blinked. They had, in a measure, to change their flow. Nevertheless, they brought with them above ground the curious dark intimacy of the mine, the naked sort of contact, and if I think of my childhood, it is always as if there was a lustrous sort of inner darkness, like the gloss of coal, in which we moved and had our real being. My father loved the pit. He was hurt badly, more than once, but he would never stay away. He loved the contact, the intimacy, as men in the war loved the intense male comradeship of the dark days. They did not know what they had lost till they lost it. And I think it is the same with the young colliers of to-day.

Now the colliers had also an instinct of beauty. The colliers' wives had not. The colliers were deeply alive, instinctively. But they had no daytime ambition, and no daytime intellect. They avoided, really, the rational aspect of life. They preferred to take life instinctively and intuitively. They didn't even care very profoundly about wages. It was the women, naturally, who nagged on this score. There was a big discrepancy, when I was a boy, between the collier who saw, at the best, only a brief few hours of daylight – often no daylight at all during the winter weeks – and the collier's wife, who had all the day to herself when the man was down pit.

The great fallacy is, to pity the man. He didn't dream of pitying himself, till agitators and sentimentalists taught him to. He was happy: or more than happy, he was fulfilled. Or he was fulfilled on the receptive side, not on the expressive. The collier went to the pub and drank in order to continue his intimacy with his mates. They talked endlessly, but it was rather of wonders and marvels, even in politics, than of facts. It was hard facts, in the shape of wife, money, and nagging home necessities, which they fled away from, out of the house to the pub, and out of the house to the pit.

The collier fled out of the house as soon as he could, away from the nagging materialism of the woman. With the women it was always: This is broken, now you've got to mend it! or else: We want this, that, and the other, and where is the money coming from? The collier didn't know and didn't care very deeply – his life was otherwise. So he escaped. He roved the countryside with his dog, prowling for a rabbit, for nests, for mushrooms, anything. He loved the countryside, just the indiscriminating feel of it. Or he loved just to sit on his heels and watch – anything or nothing. He was not intellectually interested. Life for him did not consist in facts, but in a flow. Very often, he loved his garden. And very often he had a genuine love of the beauty of flowers. I have known it often and often, in colliers.

Now the love of flowers is a very misleading thing. Most women love flowers as possessions, and as trimmings. They can't look at a flower, and wonder a moment, and pass on. If they see a flower that arrests their attention, they must at once pick it, pluck it. Possession! A possession! Something added on to *me!* And most of the so-called love of flowers to-day is merely this reaching out of possession and egoism: something I've *got*: something that embellishes *me*. Yet I've seen many a collier stand in his back garden looking down at a flower with that odd, remote sort of contemplation which shows a *real* awareness of the presence of beauty. It would not even be admiration, or joy, or delight, or any of those things which so often have a root in the possessive instinct. It would be a sort of contemplation: which shows the incipient artist.

The real tragedy of England, as I see it, is the tragedy of ugliness. The country is so lovely: the man-made England is so vile. I know that the ordinary collier, when I was a boy, had a peculiar sense of beauty, coming from his intuitive and instinctive consciousness, which was awakened down pit. And the fact that he met with just cold ugliness and raw materialism when he came up into daylight, and particularly when he came to the Square or the Breach, and to his own table, killed something in him, and in a sense spoiled him as a man. The woman almost invariably nagged about material things. She was taught to do it; she was encouraged to do it. It was a mother's business to see that her sons 'got on', and it was the man's business to provide the money. In my father's generation, with the old wild England behind them, and the lack of education, the man was not beaten down. But in my generation, the boys I went to school with, colliers now, have all been beaten down, what with the din-din-dinning of Board Schools, books, cinemas, clergymen, the whole national and human consciousness hammering on the fact of material prosperity above all things.

The men are beaten down, there is prosperity for a time, in their defeat – and then disaster looms ahead. The root of all disaster is disheartenment. And men are disheartened. The men of England, the colliers in particular, are disheartened. They have been betrayed and beaten.

Now though perhaps nobody knew it, it was ugliness which betrayed the spirit of man, in the nineteenth century. The great crime which the moneyed classes and promoters of industry committed in the palmy Victorian days was the condemning of the workers to ugliness, ugliness, ugliness: meanness and formless and ugly surroundings, ugly ideals, ugly religion, ugly hope, ugly love, ugly clothes, ugly furniture, ugly houses, ugly relationship between workers and employers. The human soul needs actual beauty even more than bread. The middle classes jeer at the colliers for buying pianos – but what is the piano, often as not, but a blind reaching out for beauty? To the woman it is a possession and a piece of furniture and something to feel superior about. But see the elderly colliers trying to learn to play, see them listening with queer alert faces to their daughter's execution of *The Maiden's Prayer*, and you will see a blind, unsatisfied craving for beauty. It is far more deep in the men than in the women. The women want show. The men want beauty, and still want it.

If the company, instead of building those sordid and hideous Squares, then, when they had that lovely site to play with, there on the hill top: if they had put a tall column in the middle of the small market-place, and run three parts of a circle of arcade round the pleasant space, where people could stroll or sit, and with the handsome houses behind! If they had made big, substantial houses, in apartments of five and six rooms, and with handsome entrances. If, above all, they had encouraged song and dancing – for the miners still sang and danced – and provided handsome space for these. If only they had encouraged some form of beauty in dress, some form of beauty in interior life – furniture, decoration. If they had given prizes for the handsomest chair or table, the loveliest scarf, the most charming room that the men or women could make! If only they had done this, there would never have been an industrial problem. The industrial problem arises from the base forcing of all human energy into a competition of mere acquisition.

You may say the working man would not have accepted such a form of life: the Englishman's home is his castle, etc., etc. – 'my own little home'. But if you can hear every word the next-door-people say, there's not much castle. And if you can see everybody in the square if they go to the w.c.! And if your one desire is to get out of the 'castle' and your 'own little home'! – well, there's not much to be said for it. Anyhow it's only the woman who idolizes 'her own little home' – and it's always the woman at her worst, her most greedy, most possessive, most mean. There's nothing to be said for the 'little home' any more: a great scrabble of ugly pettiness over the face of the land.

As a matter of fact, till 1800 the English people were strictly a rural people – very rural. England has had towns for centuries, but they have never been real towns, only clusters of village streets. Never the real *urbs*. The English character has failed to develop the real *urban* side of a man, the civic side. Siena is a bit of a place, but it is a real city, with citizens intimately connected with the city. Nottingham is a vast place sprawling towards a million, and it is nothing more than an amorphous agglomeration. There *is* no Nottingham, in the sense that there is Siena. The Englishman is stupidly undeveloped, as a citizen. And it is partly due to his 'little home' stunt, and partly to his acceptance of hopeless paltriness in his surroundings. The new cities of America are much more genuine cities, in the Roman sense, than is London or Manchester. Even Edinburgh used to be more of a true city than any town England ever produced.

That silly little individualism of 'the Englishman's home is his castle' and 'my own little home' is out of date. It would work almost up to 1800, when every Englishman was still a villager, and a cottager. But the industrial system has brought a great change. The Englishman still likes to think of himself as a 'cottager' – 'my home, my garden'. But it is puerile. Even the farm labourer to-day is psychologically a town-bird. The English are town-birds through and through, to-day, as the inevitable result of their complete industrialization. Yet they don't know how to build a city, how to think of one, or how to live in one. They are all suburban, pseudo-cottagy, and not one of them knows how to be truly urban – the citizens as the Romans were citizens – or the Athenians – or even the Parisians, till the war came.

And this is because we have frustrated that instinct of

community which would make us unite in pride and dignity in the bigger gesture of the citizen, not the cottager. The great city means beauty, dignity, and a certain splendour. This is the side of the Englishman that has been thwarted and shockingly betrayed. England is a mean and petty scrabble of paltry dwellings called 'homes'. I believe in their heart of hearts all Englishmen loathe their little homes – but not the women. What we want is a bigger gesture, a greater scope, a certain splendour, a certain grandeur, and beauty, big beauty. The American does far better than we, in this.

And the promoter of industry, a hundred years ago, dared to perpetrate the ugliness of my native village. And still more monstrous, promoters of industry to-day are scrabbling over the face of England with miles and square miles of red-brick 'homes', like horrible scabs. And the men inside these little red rat-traps get more and more helpless, being more and more humiliated, more and more dissatisfied, like trapped rats. Only the meaner sort of women go on loving the little home which is no more than a rat-trap to her man.

Do away with it all, then. At no matter what cost, start in to alter it. Never mind about wages and industrial squabbling. Turn the attention elsewhere. Pull down my native village to the last brick. Plan a nucleus. Fix the focus. Make a handsome gesture of radiation from the focus. And then put up big buildings, handsome, that sweep to a civic centre. And furnish them with beauty. And make an absolute clean start. Do it place by place. Make a new England. Away with little homes! Away with scrabbling pettiness and paltriness. Look at the contours of the land, and build up from these, with a sufficient nobility. The English may be mentally or spiritually developed. But as citizens of splendid cities they are more ignominious than rabbits. And they nag, nag, nag all the time about politics and wages and all that, like mean narrow housewives.

DULL LONDON

Written 1928. *Evening News*, 3 September, 1928. *Assorted Articles*, 1930

IT begins the moment you set foot ashore, the moment you step off the boat's gangway. The heart suddenly, yet vaguely, sinks. It is no lurch of fear. Quite the contrary. It is as if the life-urge failed, and the heart dimly sank. You trail past the benevolent policeman and the inoffensive passport officials, through the fussy and somehow foolish customs – we don't *really* think it matters if somebody smuggles in two pairs of false-silk stockings – and we get into the poky but inoffensive train, with poky but utterly inoffensive people, and we have a cup of inoffensive tea from a nice inoffensive boy, and we run through small, poky but nice and inoffensive country, till we are landed in the big but unexciting station of Victoria, when an inoffensive porter puts us into an inoffensive taxi and we are driven through the crowded yet strangely dull streets of London to the cosy yet strangely poky and dull place where we are going to stay. And the first half-hour in London, after some years abroad, is really a plunge of misery. The strange, the grey and uncanny, almost deathly sense of *dulness* is overwhelming. Of course, you get over it after a while, and admit that you exaggerated. You get into the rhythm of London again, and you tell yourself that it is *not* dull. And yet you are haunted, all the time, sleeping or waking, with the uncanny feeling: It is dull! It is all dull! This life here is one vast complex of dulness! I am dull! I am being dulled! My spirit is being dulled! My life is dulling down to London dulness.

This is the nightmare that haunts you the first few weeks of London. No doubt if you stay longer you get over it, and find London as thrilling as Paris or Rome or New York. But the climate is against me. I cannot stay long enough. With pinched and wondering gaze, the morning of departure, I look out of the taxi upon the strange dulness of London's arousing; a sort of death; and hope and life only return when I get my seat in the boat-train, and hear all the Good-byes! Good-bye! Good-bye! Thank God to say Good-bye!

Now to feel like this about one's native land is terrible. I am sure I am exceptional, or at least an exaggerated case. Yet it seems to me most of my fellow-countrymen have the pinched, slightly pathetic look in their faces, the vague, wondering realization: It is dull! It is always essentially dull! My life is dull!

Of course, England is the easiest country in the world, easy, easy and nice. Everybody is nice, and everybody is easy. The English people on the whole are surely the *nicest* people in the world, and everybody makes everything so easy for everybody else, that there is almost nothing to resist at all. But this very easiness and this very niceness become at last a nightmare. It is as if the whole air were impregnated with chloroform or some other pervasive anaesthetic, that makes everything easy and nice, and takes the edge off everything, whether nice or nasty. As you inhale the drug of easiness and niceness, your vitality begins to sink. Perhaps not your physical vitality, but something else: the vivid flame of your individual life. England can afford to be so free and individual because no individual flame of life is sharp and vivid. It is just mildly warm and safe. You couldn't burn your fingers at it. Nice, safe, easy: the whole ideal. And yet under all the easiness is a gnawing uneasiness, as in a drug-taker.

It used not to be so. Twenty years ago London was to me thrilling, thrilling, thrilling, the vast and roaring heart of all adventure. It was not only the heart of the world, it was the heart of the world's living adventure. How wonderful the Strand, the Bank, Charing Cross at night, Hyde Park in the morning!

True, I am now twenty years older. Yet I have not lost my sense of adventure. But now all the adventure seems to me crushed out of London. The traffic is too heavy! It used to be going somewhere, on an adventure. Now it only rolls massively and overwhelmingly, going nowhere, only dully and enormously *going*. There is no adventure at the end of the 'buses' journey. The 'bus lapses into an inertia of dulness, then dully starts again. The traffic of London used to roar with the mystery of man's adventure on the seas of life, like a vast sea-shell, murmuring a thrilling, half-comprehensible story. Now it booms like monotonous, far-off guns, in a monotony of crushing something, crushing the earth, crushing out life, crushing everything dead.

And what does one do, in London? I, not having a job to attend to, lounge round and gaze in bleak wonder on the ceaseless dulness. Or I have luncheons and dinners with friends, and talk. Now my deepest private dread of London is my dread of this talk. I spend most of my days abroad, saying little, or with a bit of chatter and a silence again. But in London I feel like a spider whose thread has been caught by somebody, and is being drawn out of him, so he must spin, spin, spin, and all to no purpose. He is not even spinning his own web, for his own reasons.

So it is in London, at luncheon, dinner, or tea. I don't want to talk. I don't mean to talk. Yet the talk is drawn out of me, endlessly. And the others talk, endlessly also. It is ceaseless, it is intoxicating, it is the only real occupation of us who do not jazz. And it is purely futile. It is quite as bad as ever the Russians were: talk for talk's sake, without the very faintest intention of a result in action. Utter inaction and storms of talk. That again is London to me. And the sense of abject futility in it all only deepens the sense of abject dulness, so all there is to do is to go away.

ITALY

—

THE SPINNER AND THE MONKS

Written 1912–13. *Twilight in Italy*, 1916

THE Holy Spirit is a Dove, or an Eagle. In the Old Testament it was an Eagle; in the New Testament it is a Dove.

And there are, standing over the Christian world, the Churches of the Dove and the Churches of the Eagle. There are, moreover, the Churches which do not belong to the Holy Spirit at all, but which are built to pure fancy and logic; such as the Wren Churches in London.

The Churches of the Dove are shy and hidden: they nestle among trees, and their bells sound in the mellowness of Sunday; or they are gathered into a silence of their own in the very midst of the town, so that one passes them by without observing them; they are as if invisible, offering no resistance to the storming of the traffic.

But the Churches of the Eagle stand high, with their heads to the skies, as if they challenged the world below. They are the Churches of the Spirit of David, and their bells ring passionately, imperiously, imperiously, falling on the subservient world below.

The Church of San Francesco was a Church of the Dove. I passed it several times, in the dark, silent little square, without knowing it was a church. Its pink walls were blind, window-less, unnoticeable, it gave no sign, unless one caught sight of the tan curtain hanging in the door, and the slit of darkness beneath. Yet it was the chief church of the village.

But the Church of San Tommaso perched over the village. Coming down the cobbled, submerged street, many a time I looked up between the houses and saw the thin old church standing above in the light, as if it perched on the house-roofs. Its thin grey neck was held up stiffly, beyond was a vision of dark foliage, and the high hill-side.

I saw it often, and yet for a long time it never occurred to me that it actually existed. It was like a vision, a thing one does not expect to come close to. It was there standing away upon the house-tops, against a glamour of foliaged hill-side. It was submerged in the village, on the uneven, cobbled street, between old high walls and cavernous shops and the houses with flights of steps.

For a long time I knew how the day went, by the imperious clangour of midday and evening bells striking down upon the houses and the edge of the lake. Yet it did not occur to me to ask where these bells rang. Till at last my everyday trance was broken in upon, and I knew the ringing of the Church of San Tommaso. The church became a living connexion with me.

So I set out to find it, I wanted to go to it. It was very near. I could see it from the piazza by the lake. And the village itself had only a few hundreds of inhabitants. The church must be within a stone's-throw.

Yet I could not find it. I went out of the back door of the house, into the narrow gully of the back street. Women glanced down at me from the top of the flights of steps, old men stood, half-turning, half-crouching under the dark shadow of the walls, to stare. It was as if the strange creatures of the under-shadow were looking at me. I was of another element.

The Italian people are called 'Children of the Sun'. They might better be called 'Children of the Shadow'. Their souls are dark and nocturnal. If they are to be easy, they must be able to hide, to be hidden in lairs and caves of darkness. Going through these tiny, chaotic back-ways of the village was like venturing through the labyrinth made by furtive creatures, who watched from out of another element. And I was pale, and clear, and evanescent, like the light, and they were dark, and close, and constant, like the shadow.

So I was baffled by the tortuous, tiny, deep passages of the village. I could not find my way. I hurried towards the broken end of the street, where the sunshine and the olive-trees looked like a mirage before me. And there above me I saw the thin, stiff neck of old San Tommaso, grey and pale in the sun. Yet I could not get up to the church, I found myself again on the piazza.

Another day, however, I found a broken staircase where weeds grew in the gaps the steps had made in falling, and maidenhair hung on the darker side of the wall. I went up unwillingly, because the Italians used this old staircase as a privy, as they will any deep side-passage.

But I ran up the broken stairway, and came out suddenly, as by a miracle, clean on the platform of my San Tommaso, in the tremendous sunshine.

It was another world, the world of the eagle, the world of fierce abstraction. It was all clear, overwhelming sunshine, a platform hung in the light. Just below were the confused, tiled roofs of the village, and beyond them the pale-blue water, down below; and opposite, opposite my face and breast, the clear, luminous snow of the mountain across the lake, level with me apparently, though really much above.

I was in the skies now, looking down from my square terrace of cobbled pavement, that was worn like the threshold of the ancient church. Round the terrace ran a low, broad wall, the coping of the upper heaven where I had climbed.

There was a blood-red sail like a butterfly breathing down on the blue water, whilst the earth on the near side gave off a green-silver smoke of olive-trees, coming up and around the earth-coloured roofs.

It always remains to me that San Tommaso and its terrace hang suspended above the village, like the lowest step of heaven, of Jacob's ladder. Behind, the land rises in a high sweep. But the terrace of San Tommaso is let down from heaven, and does not touch the earth.

I went into the church. It was very dark, and impregnated with centuries of incense. It affected me like the lair of some enormous creature. My senses were aroused, they sprang awake in the hot, spiced darkness. My skin was expectant, as if it expected some contact, some embrace, as if it were aware of the contiguity of the physical world, the physical contact with the darkness and the heavy suggestive substance of the enclosure. It was a thick, fierce darkness of the senses. But my soul shrank.

I went out again. The pavement threshold was clear as a jewel, the marvellous clarity of sunshine that becomes blue in the height seemed to distil me into itself.

Across, the heavy mountain crouched along the side of the lake, the upper half brilliantly white, belonging to the sky, the lower half dark and grim. So, then, that is where heaven and earth are divided. From behind me, on the left, the headland swept down out of a great, pale-grey, arid height, through a rush of russet and crimson, to the olive smoke and the water like the level earth. And between, like a blade of the sky cleaving the earth asunder, went the pale-blue lake, cleaving mountain from mountain with the triumph of the sky.

Then I noticed that a big, blue-checked cloth was spread on the parapet before me, over the parapet of heaven. I wondered why it hung there.

Turning round, on the other side of the terrace, under a caper-bush that hung like a blood-stain from the grey wall above her, stood a little grey woman whose fingers were busy. Like the grey church, she made me feel as if I were not in existence. I was wandering by the parapet of heaven, looking down. But she stood back against the solid wall, under the caper-bush, unobserved and unobserving. She was like a fragment of earth, she was a living stone of the terrace, sunbleached. She took no notice of me, who was hesitating looking down at the earth beneath. She stood back under the sunbleached solid wall, like a stone rolled down and stayed in a crevice.

Her head was tied in a dark-red kerchief, but pieces of hair, like dirty snow, quite short, stuck out over her ears. And she was spinning. I wondered so much that I could not cross towards her. She was grey, and her apron, and her dress, and her kerchief, and her hands and her face, were all sun-bleached and sun-stained, greyey, bluey, browny, like stones and half-coloured leaves, sunny in their colourlessness. In my black coat, I felt myself wrong, false, an outsider.

She was spinning, spontaneously, like a little wind. Under

her arm she held a distaff of dark, ripe wood, just a straight stick with a clutch at the end, like a grasp of brown fingers full of a fluff of blackish, rusty fleece, held up near her shoulder. And her fingers were plucking spontaneously at the strands of wool drawn down from it. And hanging near her feet, spinning round upon a black thread, spinning busily, like a thing in a gay wind, was her shuttle, her bobbin wound fat with the coarse, blackish worsted she was making.

All the time, like motion without thought, her fingers teased out the fleece, drawing it down to a fairly uniform thickness: brown, old, natural fingers that worked as in a sleep, the thumb having a long grey nail; and from moment to moment there was a quick, downward rub, between thumb and forefinger, of the thread that hung in front of her apron, the heavy bobbin spun more briskly, and she felt again at the fleece as she drew it down, and she gave a twist to the thread that issued, and the bobbin spun swiftly.

Her eyes were clear as the sky, blue, empyrean, transcendent. They were clear, but they had no looking in them. Her face was like a sun-worn stone.

'You are spinning,' I said to her.

Her eyes glanced over me, making no effort of attention.

'Yes,' she said.

She saw merely a man's figure, a stranger, standing near. I was a bit of the outside, negligible. She remained as she was, clear and sustained like an old stone upon the hill-side. She stood short and sturdy, looking for the most part straight in front, unseeing, but glancing from time to time, with a little, unconscious attention, at the thread. She was slightly more animated than the sunshine and the stone and the motionless caper-bush above her. Still her fingers went along the strand of fleece near her breast.

'That is an old way of spinning,' I said.

'What?'

She looked up at me with eyes clear and transcendent as the heavens. But she was slightly roused. There was the slight motion of the eagle in her turning to look at me, a faint gleam of rapt light in her eyes. It was my unaccustomed Italian.

'That is an old way of spinning,' I repeated.

'Yes – an old way,' she repeated, as if to say the words so that they should be natural to her. And I became to her merely a transient circumstance, a man, part of the surroundings. We divided the gift of speech, that was all.

She glanced at me again, with her wonderful, unchanging eyes, that were like the visible heavens, unthinking, or like two flowers that are open in pure clear unconsciousness. To her I was a piece of the environment. That was all. Her world was clear and absolute, without consciousness of self. She was not self-conscious, because she was not aware that there was anything in the universe except *her* universe. In her universe I was a stranger, a foreign *signore*. That I had a world of my own, other than her own, was not conceived by her. She did not care.

So we conceive the stars. We are told that they are other worlds. But the stars are the clustered and single gleaming lights in the night-sky of our world. When I come home at night, there are the stars. When I cease to exist as the microcosm, when I begin to think of the cosmos, then the stars are other worlds. Then the macrocosm absorbs me. But the marcrocosm is not me. It is something which I, the microcosm am not.

So that there is something which is unknown to me and which nevertheless exists. I am finite, and my understanding has limits. The universe is bigger than I shall ever see, in mind or spirit. There is that which is not me.

If I say 'The planet Mars is inhabited', I do not know what I mean by 'inhabited', with reference to the planet Mars. I can only mean that that world is not my world. I can only know there is that which is not me. I am the microcosm, but the macrocosm is that also which I am not.

The old woman on the terrace in the sun did not know this. She was herself the core and centre to the world, the sun, and the single firmament. She knew that I was an inhabitant of lands which she had never seen. But what of that! There were parts of her own body which she had never seen, which physiologically she could never see. They were none the less her own because she had never seen them. The lands she had not seen were corporate parts of her own living body, the knowledge she had not attained was only the hidden knowledge of her own self. She *was* the substance of the knowledge, whether she had the knowledge in her mind or not. There was nothing which was not herself, ultimately. Even the man, the male, was part of herself. He was the mobile, separate part, but he was none the less herself because he was sometimes severed from her. If every apple in the world were cut in two, the apple would not be changed. The reality is the apple, which is just the same in the half-apple as in the whole.

And she, the old spinning-woman, was the apple, eternal, unchangeable, whole even in her partiality. It was this which gave the wonderful clear unconsciousness to her eyes. How could she be conscious of herself when all was herself?

She was talking to me of a sheep that had died, but I could not understand because of her dialect. It never occurred to her that I could not understand. She only thought me different, stupid. And she talked on. The ewes had lived under the house, and a part was divided off for the he-goat, because the other people brought their she-goats to be covered by the he-goat. But how the ewe came to die I could not make out.

Her fingers worked away all the time in a little, half-fretful movement, yet spontaneous as butterflies leaping here and there. She chattered rapidly on in her Italian that I could not understand, looking meanwhile into my face, because the story roused her somewhat. Yet not a feature moved. Her eyes remained candid and open and unconscious as the skies. Only a sharp will in them now and then seemed to gleam at me, as if to dominate me.

Her shuttle had caught in a dead chicory plant, and spun no more. She did not notice. I stooped and broke off the twigs. There was a glint of blue on them yet. Seeing what I was doing, she merely withdrew a few inches from the plant. Her bobbin hung free.

She went on with her tale, looking at me wonderfully. She seemed like the Creation, like the beginning of the world, the first morning. Her eyes were like the first morning of the world, so ageless.

Her thread broke. She seemed to take no notice, but mechanically picked up the shuttle, wound up a length of worsted, connecting the ends from her wool strand, set the bobbin spinning again, and went on talking, in her half-intimate, half-unconscious fashion, as if she were talking to her own world in me.

So she stood in the sunshine on the little platform, old and yet like the morning, erect and solitary, sun-coloured, sun-discoloured, whilst I at her elbow, like a piece of night and moonshine, stood smiling into her eyes, afraid lest she should deny me existence.

Which she did. She had stopped talking, did not look at me any more, but went on with her spinning, the brown shuttle twisting gaily. So she stood, belonging to the sunshine and the weather, taking no more notice of me than of the dark-stained caper-bush which hung from the wall above her head, whilst I, waiting at her side, was like the moon in the daytime sky, overshone, obliterated, in spite of my black clothes.

'How long has it taken you to do that much?' I asked.

She waited a minute, glanced at her bobbin.

'This much? I don't know. A day or two.'

'But you do it quickly.'

She looked at me, as if suspiciously and derisively. Then, quite suddenly, she started forward and went across the terrace to the great blue-and-white check cloth that was drying on the wall. I hesitated. She had cut off her consciousness from me. So I turned and ran away, taking the steps two at a time, to get away from her. In a moment I was between the walls, climbing upwards, hidden.

The school-mistress had told me I should find snowdrops behind San Tommaso. If she had not asserted such confident knowledge I should have doubted her translation of *perce-neige*. She meant Christmas roses all the while.

However, I went looking for snowdrops. The walls broke down suddenly, and I was out in a grassy olive orchard, following a track beside pieces of fallen overgrown masonry. So I came to skirt the brink of a steep little gorge at the bottom of which a stream was rushing down its steep slant to the lake. Here I stood to look for my snowdrops. The grassy, rocky bank went down steep from my feet. I heard water tittle-tattling away in deep shadow below. There were pale flecks in the dimness, but these, I knew, were primroses. So I scrambled down.

Looking up out of the heavy shadow that lay in the cleft, I could see, right in the sky, grey rocks shining transcendent in the pure empyrean. 'Are they so far up?' I thought. I did not dare to say, 'Am I so far down?' But I was uneasy. Nevertheless, it was a lovely place, in the cold shadow, complete; when one forgot the shining rocks far above, it was a complete, shadowless world of shadow. Primroses were everywhere in nests of pale bloom upon the dark, steep face of the cleft, and tongues of fern hanging out, and here and there under the rods and twigs of bushes were tufts of wrecked Christmas roses, nearly over, but still, in the coldest corners, the lovely buds like handfuls of snow. There had been such crowded sumptuous tufts of Christmas roses everywhere in the stream-gullies, during the shadow of winter, that these few remaining flowers were hardly noticeable.

I gathered instead the primroses, that smelled of earth and of the weather. There were no snowdrops. I had found the day before a bank of crocuses, pale, fragile, lilac-coloured flowers with dark veins, pricking up keenly like myriad little lilac-coloured flames among the grass, under the olive-trees. And I wanted very much to find the snowdrops hanging in the gloom. But there were not any.

I gathered a handful of primroses, then I climbed suddenly, quickly out of the deep watercourse, anxious to get back to the sunshine before the evening fell. Up above I saw the olive-trees in their sunny golden grass, and sunlit grey rocks immensely high up. I was afraid lest the evening would fail whilst I was groping about like an otter in the damp and the darkness, that the day of sunshine would be over.

Soon I was up in the sunshine again, on the turf under the olive-trees, reassured. It was the upper world of glowing light, and I was safe again.

All the olives were gathered, and the mills were going

night and day, making a great, acrid scent of olive oil in preparation, by the lake. The little stream rattled down. A mule-driver 'Hued!' to his mules on the Strada Vecchia. High up, on the Strada Nuova, the beautiful, new, military high-road, which winds with beautiful curves up the mountain-side, crossing the same stream several times in clear-leaping bridges, travelling cut out of sheer slope high above the lake, winding beautifully and gracefully forward to the Austrian frontier, where it ends: high up on the lovely swinging road, in the strong evening sunshine, I saw a bullock wagon moving like a vision, though the clanking of the wagon and the crack of the bullock-whip resounded close in my ears.

Everything was clear and sun-coloured up there, clear-grey rocks partaking of the sky, tawny grass and scrub, browny-green spires of cypresses, and then the mist of grey-green olives fuming down to the lake-side. There was no shadow, only clear sun-substance built up to the sky, a bullock wagon moving slowly in the high sunlight, along the uppermost terrace of the military road. I sat in the warm stillness of the transcendent afternoon.

The four o'clock steamer was creeping down the lake from the Austrian end, creeping under the cliffs. Far away, the Verona side, beyond the Island, lay fused in dim gold. The mountain opposite was so still, that my heart seemed to fade in its beatings, as if it too would be still. All was perfectly still, pure substance. The little steamer on the floor of the world below, the mules down the road cast no shadow. They too were pure sun-substance travelling on the surface of the sun-made world.

A cricket hopped near me. Then I remembered that it was Saturday afternoon, when a strange suspension comes over the world. And then, just below me, I saw two monks walking in their garden between the naked, bony vines, walking in their wintry garden of bony vines and olive-trees, their brown cassocks passing between the brown vine-stocks, their heads bare to the sunshine, sometimes a glint of light as their feet strode from under their skirts.

It was so still, everything so perfectly suspended, that I felt them talking. They marched with the peculiar march of monks, a long, loping stride, their heads together, their skirts swaying slowly, two brown monks with hidden hands, sliding under the bony vines and beside the cabbages, their heads always together in hidden converse. It was as if I were attending with my dark soul to their inaudible undertone. All the time I sat still in silence, I was one with them, a partaker, though I could hear no sound of their voices. I went with the long stride of their skirted feet, that slid springless and noiseless from end to end of the garden, and back again. Their hands were kept down at their sides, hidden in the long sleeves and the skirts of their robes. They did not touch each other, nor gesticulate as they walked. There was no motion save the long, furtive stride and the heads leaning together. Yet there was an eagerness in their conversation. Almost like shadow-creatures ventured out of their cold, obscure element, they went backwards and forwards in their wintry garden, thinking nobody could see them.

Across, above them, was the faint rousing dazzle of snow. They never looked up. But the dazzle of snow began to glow as they walked, the wonderful, faint, ethereal flush of the long range of snow in the heavens, at evening, began to kindle. Another world was coming to pass, the cold, rare night. It was dawning in exquisite, icy rose upon the long mountain-summit opposite. The monks walked backwards and forwards, talking, in the first undershadow.

And I noticed that up above the snow, frail in the bluish sky, a frail moon had put forth, like a thin, scalloped film of ice floated out on the slow current of the coming night. And a bell sounded.

And still the monks were pacing backwards and forwards, backwards and forwards, with a strange, neutral regularity.

The shadows were coming across everything, because of the mountains in the west. Already the olive wood where I sat was extinguished. This was the world of the monks, the rim of pallor between night and day. Here they paced, backwards and forwards, backwards and forwards, in the neutral, shadowless light of shadow.

Neither the flare of day nor the completeness of night reached them, they paced the narrow path of the twilight, treading in the neutrality of the law. Neither the blood nor the spirit spoke in them, only the law, the abstraction of the average. The infinite is positive and negative. But the average is only neutral. And the monks trod backward and forward down the line of neutrality.

Meanwhile, on the length of mountain-ridge, the snow grew rosy-incandescent, like heaven breaking into blossom. After all, eternal not-being and eternal being are the same. In the rosy snow that shone in heaven over a darkened earth was the ecstasy of consummation. Night and day are one, light and dark are one, both the same in the origin and in the issue, both the same in the moment of ecstasy, light fused in darkness and darkness fused in light, as in the rosy snow above the twilight.

But in the monks it was not ecstasy, in them it was neutrality, the under earth. Transcendent, above the shadowed, twilit earth was the rosy snow of ecstasy. But spreading far over us, down below, was the neutrality of the twilight, of the monks. The flesh neutralizing the spirit, the spirit neutralizing the flesh, the law of the average asserted, this was the monks as they paced backward and forward.

The moon climbed higher, away from the snowy, fading ridge, she became gradually herself. Between the roots of the olive-tree was a rosy-tipped daisy just going to sleep. I gathered it and put it among the frail, moony little bunch of primroses, so that its sleep should warm the rest. Also I put in some little periwinkles, that were very blue, reminding me of the eyes of the old woman.

The day was gone, the twilight was gone, and the snow was invisible as I came down to the side of the lake. Only the moon, white and shining, was in the sky, like a woman glorying in her own loveliness as she loiters superbly to the gaze of all the world, looking sometimes through the fringe of dark olive leaves, sometimes looking at her own superb, quivering body, wholly naked in the water of the lake.

My little old woman was gone. She, all day-sunshine, would

have none of the moon. Always she must live like a bird, looking down on all the world at once, so that it lay all subsidiary to herself, herself the wakeful consciousness hovering over the world like a hawk, like a sleep of wakefulness. And, like a bird, she went to sleep as the shadows came.

She did not know the yielding up of the senses and the possession of the unknown, through the senses, which happens under a superb moon. The all-glorious sun knows none of these yieldings up. He takes his way. And the daisies at once go to sleep. And the soul of the old spinning-woman also closed up at sunset, the rest was a sleep, a cessation.

It is all so strange and varied: the dark-skinned Italians ecstatic in the night and the moon, the blue-eyed old woman ecstatic in the busy sunshine, the monks in the garden below, who are supposed to unite both, passing only in the neutrality of the average. Where, then, is the meeting-point: where in mankind is the ecstasy of light and dark together, the supreme transcendence of the afterglow, day hovering in the embrace of the coming night like two angels embracing in the heavens, like Eurydice in the arms of Orpheus, or Persephone embraced by Pluto?

Where is the supreme ecstasy in mankind, which makes day a delight and night a delight, purpose an ecstasy and a concourse in ecstasy, and single abandon of the single body and soul also an ecstasy under the moon? Where is the transcendent knowledge in our hearts, uniting sun and darkness, day and night, spirit and senses? Why do we not know that the two in consummation are one; that each is only part; partial and alone for ever; but that the two in consummation are perfect, beyond the range of loneliness or solitude?

FLOWERY TUSCANY

Written 1926–7. *New Criterion*, October-December, 1927. *Phoenix*, 1936

I

EACH country has its own flowers, that shine out specially there. In England it is daisies and buttercups, hawthorn and cowslips. In America, it is goldenrod, stargrass, June daisies, Mayapple and asters, that we call Michaelmas daisies. In India, hibiscus and datura and champa flowers, and in Australia mimosa, that they call wattle, and sharp-tongued strange heath flowers. In Mexico it is cactus flowers, that they call roses of the desert, lovely and crystalline among many thorns: and also the dangling yard-long clusters of the cream bells of the yucca, like dropping froth.

But by the Mediterranean, now as in the days of the Argosy, and, we hope, for ever, it is narcissus and anemone, asphodel and myrtle. Narcissus and anemone, asphodel, crocus, myrtle, and parsley, they leave their sheer significance only by the Mediterranean. There are daisies in Italy too: at Paestum there are white little carpets of daisies, in March, and Tuscany is spangled with celandine. But for all that, the daisy and the celandine are English flowers, their best significance is for us and for the North.

The Mediterranean has narcissus and anemone, myrtle and asphodel and grape hyacinth. These are the flowers that speak and are understood in the sun round the Middle Sea.

Tuscany is especially flowery, being wetter than Sicily and more homely than the Roman hills. Tuscany manages to remain so remote, and secretly smiling to itself in its many sleeves. There are so many hills popping up, and they take no notice of one another. There are so many little deep valleys with streams that seem to go their own little way entirely, regardless of river and sea. There are thousands, millions of utterly secluded little nooks, though the land has been under cultivation these thousands of years. But the intensive culture of vine and olive and wheat, by the ceaseless industry of naked human hands and winter-shod feet, and slow-stepping, soft-eyed oxen does not devastate a country, does not denude it, does not lay it bare, does not uncover its nakedness, does not drive away either Pan or his children. The streams run and rattle over wild rocks of secret places, and murmur through blackthorn thickets where the nightingales sing all together, unruffled and undaunted.

It is queer that a country so perfectly cultivated as Tuscany, where half the produce of five acres of land will have to support ten human mouths, still has so much room for the wild flowers and the nightingale. When little hills heave themselves suddenly up, and shake themselves free of neighbours, man has to build his garden and his vineyard, and sculp his landscape. Talk of hanging gardens of Babylon, all Italy, apart from the plains, is a hanging garden. For centuries upon centuries man has been patiently modelling the surface of the Mediterranean countries, gently rounding the hills, and graduating the big slopes and the little slopes into the almost invisible levels of terraces. Thousands of square miles of Italy have been lifted in human hands, piled and laid back in tiny little flats, held up by the drystone walls, whose stones came from the lifted earth. It is a work of many, many centuries. It is the gentle sensitive sculpture of all the landscape. And it is the achieving of the peculiar Italian beauty which is so exquisitely natural, because man, feeling his way sensitively to the fruitfulness of the earth, has moulded the earth to his necessity without violating it.

Which shows that it *can* be done. Man *can* live on the earth and by the earth without disfiguring the earth. It has been done here, on all these sculptured hills and softly, sensitively terraced slopes.

But, of course, you can't drive a steam plough on terraces four yards wide, terraces that dwindle and broaden and sink and rise a little, all according to the pitch and the breaking outline of the mother hill. Corn has got to grow on these little shelves of earth, where already the grey olive stands semi-invisible, and the grape-vine twists upon its own scars. If oxen can step with that lovely pause at every little stride, they can plough the narrow field. But they will have to leave a tiny fringe, a grassy lip over the drystone wall below. And if the terraces are too narrow to plough, the peasant digging them will still leave the grassy lip, because it helps to hold the surface in the rains.

And here the flowers take refuge. Over and over and over and over has this soil been turned, twice a year, sometimes three times a year, for several thousands of years. Yet the flowers have never been driven out. There is a very rigorous digging and sifting, the little bulbs and tubers are flung away into perdition, not a weed shall remain.

Yet spring returns, and on the terrace lips, and in the stony nooks between terraces, up rise the aconites, the crocuses, the narcissus and the asphodel, the inextinguishable wild tulips. There they are, for ever hanging on the precarious brink of an existence, but for ever triumphant, never quite losing their footing. In England, in America, the flowers get rooted out, driven back. They become fugitive. But in the intensive cultivation of ancient Italian terraces, they dance round and hold their own.

Spring begins with the first narcissus, rather cold and shy and wintry. They are the little bunchy, creamy narcissus with the yellow cup like the yolk of the flower. The natives call these flowers *tazzette*, little cups. They grow on the grassy banks rather sparse, or push up among thorns.

To me they are winter flowers, and their scent is winter. Spring starts in February, with the winter aconite. Some icy day, when the wind is down from the snow of the mountains, early in February, you will notice on a bit of fallow land, under the olive trees, tight, pale-gold little balls, clenched tight as nuts, and resting on round ruffs of green near the ground. It is winter aconite suddenly come.

The winter aconite is one of the most charming flowers. Like all the early blossoms, once her little flower emerges it is quite naked. No shutting a little green sheath over herself, like the daisy or the dandelion. Her bubble of frail, pale, pure gold rests on the round frill of her green collar, with the snowy wind trying to blow it away.

But without success. The *tramontana* ceases, comes a day of wild February sunshine. The clenched little nuggets of the aconite puff out, they become like bubbles, like small balloons, on a green base. The sun blazes on, with February splendour. And by noon, all under the olives are wide-open little suns, the aconites spreading all their rays; and there is an exquisitely sweet scent, honey-sweet, not narcissus-frosty; and there is a February humming of little brown bees.

Till afternoon, when the sun slopes, and the touch of snow comes back into the air.

But at evening, under the lamp on the table, the aconites are wide and excited, and there is a perfume of sweet spring that makes one almost start humming and trying to be a bee.

Aconites don't last very long. But they turn up in all odd places – on clods of dug earth, and in land where the broad-beans are thrusting up, and along the lips of terraces. But they like best land left fallow for one winter. There they throng, showing how quick they are to seize on an opportunity to live and shine forth.

In a fortnight, before February is over, the yellow bubbles of the aconite are crumpling to nothingness. But already in a cosy nook the violets are dark purple, and there is a new little perfume in the air.

Like the debris of winter stand the hellebores, in all the wild places, and the butcher's broom is flaunting its last bright red berry. Hellebore is Christmas roses, but in Tuscany the flowers never come white. They emerge out of the grass towards the end of December, flowers wintry of winter, and they are delicately pale green, and of a lovely shape, with yellowish stamens. They have a peculiar wintry quality of invisibility, so lonely rising from the sere grass, and pallid green, held up like a little hand-mirror that reflects nothing. At first they are single upon a stem, short and lovely, and very wintry-beautiful, with a will not to be touched, not to be noticed. One instinctively leaves them alone. But as January draws towards February, these hellebores, these greenish

Christmas roses become more assertive. Their pallid water-green becomes yellower, pale sulphur-yellow-green, and they rise up, they are in tufts, in throngs, in veritable bushes of greenish open flowers, assertive, bowing their faces with a hellebore assertiveness. In some places they throng among the bushes and above the water of the stream, giving the peculiar pale glimmer almost of primroses, as you walk among them. Almost of primroses, yet with a coarse hellebore leaf and an uprearing hellebore assertiveness, like snakes in winter.

And as one walks among them, one brushes the last scarlet off the butcher's broom. This low little shrub is the Christmas holly of Tuscany, only a foot or so high, with a vivid red berry stuck on in the middle of its sharp hard leaf. In February the last red ball rolls off the prickly plume, and winter rolls with it. The violets already are emerging from the moisture.

But before the violets make any show, there are the crocuses. If you walk up through the pine-wood, that lifts its umbrellas of pine so high, up till you come to the brow of the hill at the top, you can look south, due south, and see snow on the Apennines, and on a blue afternoon, seven layers of blue-hilled distance.

Then you sit down on that southern slope, out of the wind, and there it is warm, whether it be January or February, *tramontana* or not. There the earth has been baked by innumerable suns, baked and baked again; moistened by many rains, but never wetted for long. Because it is rocky, and full to the south, and sheering steep in the slope.

And there, in February, in the sunny baked desert of that crumbly slope, you will find the first crocuses. On the sheer aridity of crumbled stone you see a queer, alert little star, very sharp and quite small. It has opened out rather flat, and looks like a tiny freesia flower, creamy, with a smear of yellow yolk. It has no stem, seems to have been just lightly dropped on the crumbled, baked rock. It is the first hill-crocus.

II

North of the Alps, the everlasting winter is interrupted by summers that struggle and soon yield; south of the Alps, the everlasting summer is interrupted by spasmodic and spiteful winters that never get a real hold, but that are mean and dogged. North of the Alps, you may have a pure winter's day in June. South of the Alps, you may have a midsummer day in December or January or even February. The in-between, in either case, is just as it may be. But the lands of the sun are south of the Alps, for ever.

Yet things, the flowers especially, that belong to both sides of the Alps, are not much earlier south than north of the mountains. Through all the winter there are roses in the garden, lovely creamy roses, more pure and mysterious than those of summer, leaning perfect from the stem. And the narcissus in the garden are out by the end of January, and the little simple hyacinths early in February.

But out in the fields, the flowers are hardly any sooner than English flowers. It is mid-February before the first violets, the first crocus, the first primrose. And in mid-February one may find a violet, a primrose, a crocus in England, in the hedgerows and the garden corner.

And still there is a difference. There are several kinds of wild crocus in this region of Tuscany: being little spiky mauve ones, and spiky little creamy ones, that grow among the pine-trees of the bare slopes. But the beautiful ones are those of a meadow in the corner of the woods, the low hollow meadow below the steep, shadowy pine-slopes, the secretive grassy dip where the water seeps through the turf all winter, where the stream runs between thick bushes, where the nightingale sings his mightiest in May, and where the wild thyme is rosy and full of bees, in summer.

Here the lavender crocuses are most at home – here sticking out of the deep grass, in a hollow like a cup, a bowl of grass, come the lilac-coloured crocuses, like an innumerable encampment. You may see them at twilight, with all the buds shut, in the mysterious stillness of the grassy underworld, palely glimmering like myriad folded tents. So the apaches still camp, and close their tepees, in the hollows of the great hills of the West, at night.

But in the morning it is quite different. Then the sun shines strong on the horizontal green cloud-puffs of the pines, the sky is clear and full of life, the water runs hastily, still browned by the last juice of crushed olives. And there the earth's bowl of crocuses is amazing. You cannot believe that the flowers are really still. They are open with such delight, and their pistil-thrust is so red-orange, and they are so many, all reaching out wide and marvellous, that it suggests a perfect ecstasy of radiant, thronging movement, lit-up violet and orange, and surging in some invisible rhythm of concerted, delightful movement. You cannot believe they do not move, and make some sort of crystalline sound of delight. If you sit still and watch, you begin to move with them, like moving with the stars, and you feel the sound of their radiance. All the little cells of the flowers must be leaping with flowery life and utterance.

And the small brown honey-bees hop from flower to flower, dive down, try, and off again. The flowers have been already rifled, most of them. Only sometimes a bee stands on his head, kicking slowly inside the flower, for some time. He has found something. And all the bees have little loaves of pollen, bee-bread, in their elbow-joints.

The crocuses last in their beauty for a week or so, and as they begin to lower their tents and abandon camp, the violets begin to thicken. It is already March. The violets have been showing like tiny dark hounds for some weeks. But now the whole pack comes forth, among the grass and the tangle of wild thyme, till the air all sways subtly scented with violets, and the banks above where the crocuses had their tents are now swarming brilliant purple with violets. They are the sweet violets of early spring, but numbers have made them bold, for they flaunt and ruffle till the slopes are a bright blue-purple blaze of them, full in the sun, with an odd late crocus still standing wondering and erect amongst them.

And now that it is March, there is a rush of flowers. Down by the other stream, which turns sideways to the sun, and has tangles of brier and bramble, down where the hellebore has stood so wan and dignified all winter, there are now white tufts of primroses, suddenly come. Among the tangle and near the water-lip, tufts and bunches of primroses, in abundance. Yet they look more wan, more pallid, more flimsy than English primroses. They lack some of the full wonder of the northern flowers. One tends to overlook them, to turn to the great, solemn-faced purple violets that rear up from the bank, and above all, to the wonderful little towers of the grape-hyacinth.

I know no flower that is more fascinating, when it first appears, than the blue grape-hyacinth. And yet, because it lasts so long, and keeps on coming so repeatedly, for at least two months, one tends later on to ignore it, even to despise it a little. Yet that is very unjust.

The first grape-hyacinths are flowers of blue, thick and rich and meaningful, above the unrenewed grass. The upper buds are pure blue, shut tight; round balls of pure, perfect warm blue, blue, blue; while the lower bells are darkish blue-purple, with the spark of white at the mouth. As yet, none of the lower bells has withered, to leave the greenish, separate sparseness of fruiting that spoils the grape-hyacinth later on, and makes it seem naked and functional. All hyacinths are like that in the seeding.

But, at first, you have only a compact tower of night-blue clearing to dawn, and extremely beautiful. If we were tiny as fairies, and lived only a summer, how lovely these great trees of bells would be to us, towers of night and dawn-blue globes. They would rise above us thick and succulent, and the purple globes would push the blue ones up, with white sparks of ripples, and we should see a god in them.

As a matter of fact, someone once told me they were the flowers of the many-breasted Artemis; and it is true, the Cybele of Ephesus, with her clustered breasts, was like a grape-hyacinth at the bosom.

This is the time, in March, when the sloe is white and misty in the hedge-tangle by the stream, and on the slope of land the peach tree stands pink and alone. The almond blossom, silvery pink, is passing, but the peach, deep-toned, bluey, not at all ethereal, this reveals itself like flesh, and the trees are like isolated individuals, the peach and the apricot.

A man said this spring: 'Oh, I *don't* care for peach blossom! It is such a vulgar pink!' One wonders what anybody means by a 'vulgar' pink. I think pink flannelette is rather vulgar. But probably it's the flannelette's fault, not the pink. And peach blossom has a beautiful sensual pink, far from vulgar, most rare and private. And pink is so beautiful in a landscape, pink houses, pink almond, pink peach, and purply apricot, pink asphodels.

It is so conspicuous and so individual, that pink among the coming green of spring, because the first flowers that emerge from winter seem always white or yellow or purple. Now the celandines are out, and along the edges of the *podere*, the big, sturdy, black-purple anemones, with black hearts.

They are curious, these great, dark-violet anemones. You may pass them on a grey day, or at evening or early morning, and never see them. But as you come along in the full sunshine, they seem to be baying at you with all their throats, baying deep purple into the air. It is because they are hot and wide open now, gulping the sun. Whereas when they are shut, they have a silkiness and a curved head, like the curve of an umbrella handle, and a peculiar outward colourlessness, that makes them quite invisible. They may be under your feet, and you will not see them.

Altogether anemones are odd flowers. On these last hills above the plain, we have only the big black-purple ones, in tufts here and there, not many. But two hills away, the young green corn is blue with the lilac-blue kind, still the broad-petalled sort with the darker heart. But these flowers are smaller than our dark-purple, and frailer, more silky. Ours are substantial, thickly vegetable flowers, and not abundant. The others are lovely and silky-delicate, and the whole corn is blue with them. And they have a sweet, sweet scent, when they are warm.

Then on the priest's *podere* there are the scarlet, Adonis-blood anemones: only in one place, in one long fringe under a terrace, and there by a path below. These flowers above all you will never find unless you look for them in the sun. Their silver silk outside makes them quite invisible, when they are shut up.

Yet, if you are passing in the sun, a sudden scarlet faces on to the air, one of the loveliest scarlet apparitions in the world. The inner surface of the Adonis-blood anemone is as fine as velvet, and yet there is no suggestion of pile, not as much as on a velvet rose. And from this inner smoothness issues the red colour, perfectly pure and unknown of earth, no earthiness, and yet solid, not transparent. How a colour manages to be perfectly strong and impervious, yet of a purity that suggests condensed light, yet not luminous, at least, not transparent, is a problem. The poppy in her radiance is translucent, and the tulip in her utter redness has a touch of opaque earth. But the Adonis-blood anemone is neither translucent nor opaque. It is just pure condensed red, of a velvetiness without velvet, and a scarlet without glow.

This red seems to me the perfect premonition of summer – like the red on the outside of apple blossom – and later, the red of the apple. It is the premonition in redness of summer and of autumn.

The red flowers are coming now. The wild tulips are in bud, hanging their grey leaves like flags. They come up in myriads, wherever they get a chance. But they are holding back their redness till the last days of March, the early days of April.

Still, the year is warming up. By the high ditch the common magenta anemone is hanging its silky tassels, or opening its great magenta daisy-shape to the hot sun. It is much nearer to red than the big-petalled anemones are; except the Adonis-blood. They say these anemones spring from the tears of Venus, which fell as she went looking for Adonis. At that rate, how the poor lady must have wept, for the anemones by the Mediterranean are common as daisies in England.

The daisies are out here too, in sheets, and they too are red-mouthed. The first ones are big and handsome. But as March goes on, they dwindle to bright little things, like tiny buttons, clouds of them together. That means summer is nearly here.

The red tulips open in the corn like poppies, only with a heavier red. And they pass quickly, without repeating themselves. There is little lingering in a tulip.

In some places there are odd yellow tulips, slender, spiky, and Chinese-looking. They are very lovely, pricking out their dulled yellow in slim spikes. But they too soon lean, expand beyond themselves, and are gone like an illusion.

And when the tulips are gone, there is a moment's pause, before summer. Summer is the next move.

III

In the pause towards the end of April, when the flowers seem to hesitate, the leaves make up their minds to come out. For some time, at the very ends of the bare boughs of fig trees, spurts of pure green have been burning like little cloven tongues of green fire vivid on the tips of the candelabrum. Now these spurts of green spread out, and begin to take the shape of hands, feeling for the air of summer. And tiny green figs are below them, like glands on the throat of a goat.

For some time, the long stiff whips of the vine have had knobby pink buds, like flower buds. Now these pink buds begin to unfold into greenish, half-shut fans of leaves with red in the veins, and tiny spikes of flower, like seed-pearls. Then, in all its down and pinky dawn, the vine-rosette has a frail, delicious scent of a new year.

Now the aspens on the hill are all remarkable with the translucent membranes of blood-veined leaves. They are gold-brown, but not like autumn, rather like the thin wings of bats when like birds – call them birds – they wheel in clouds against the setting sun, and the sun glows through the stretched membrane of their wings, as through thin, brown-red stained glass. This is the red sap of summer, not the red dust of autumn. And in the distance the aspens have the tender panting glow of living membrane just come awake. This is the beauty of the frailty of spring.

The cherry tree is something the same, but more sturdy. Now, in the last week of April, the cherry blossom is still white, but waning and passing away: it is late this year; and the leaves are clustering thick and softly copper in their dark blood-filled glow. It is queer about fruit trees in this district. The pear and the peach were out together. But now the pear tree is a lovely thick softness of new and glossy green, vivid with a tender fullness of apple-green leaves, gleaming among all the other green of the landscape, the half-high wheat, emerald, and the grey olive, half-invisible, the browning green of the dark cypress, the black of the evergreen oak, the rolling, heavy green puffs of the stone-pines, the flimsy green of small peach and almond trees, the sturdy young green of horse-chestnut. So many greens, all in flakes and shelves and tilted tables and round shoulders and plumes and shaggles and uprisen bushes, of greens and greens, sometimes blindingly brilliant at evening, when the landscape looks as if it were on fire from inside, with greenness and with gold.

The pear is perhaps the greenest thing in the landscape. The wheat may shine lit-up yellow, or glow bluish, but the pear tree is green in itself. The cherry has white, half-absorbed flowers, so has the apple. But the plum is rough with her new foliage, and inconspicuous, inconspicuous as the almond, the peach, the apricot, which one can no longer find in the landscape, though twenty days ago they were the distinguished pink individuals of the whole countryside. Now they are gone. It is the time of green, pre-eminent green, in ruffles and flakes and slabs.

In the wood, the scrub-oak is only just coming uncrumpled, and the pines keep their hold on winter. They are wintry things, stone-pines. At Christmas, their heavy green clouds are richly beautiful. When the cypresses raise their tall and naked bodies of dark green, and the osiers are vivid red-orange, on the still blue air, and the land is lavender; then, in mid-winter, the landscape is most beautiful in colour, surging with colour.

But now, when the nightingale is still drawing out his long, wistful, yearning, teasing plaint-note, and following it up with a rich and joyful burble, the pines and the cypresses seem hard and rusty, and the wood has lost its subtlety and its mysteriousness. It still seems wintry in spite of the yellowing young oaks, and the heath in flower. But hard, dull pines above, and hard, dull, tall heath below, all stiff and resistant, this is out of the mood of spring.

In spite of the fact that the stone-white heath is in full flower, and very lovely when you look at it, it does not, casually, give the impression of blossom. More the impression of haivng its tips and crests all dipped in hoarfrost; or in a whitish dust. It has a peculiar ghostly colourlessness amid the darkish colourlessness of the wood altogether, which completely takes away the sense of spring.

Yet the tall white heath is very lovely, in its invisibility. It grows sometimes as tall as a man, lifting up its spires and its shadowy-white fingers with a ghostly fullness, amid the dark, rusty green of its lower bushiness; and it gives off a sweet honeyed scent in the sun, and a cloud of fine white stone-dust, if you touch it. Looked at closely, its little bells are most beautiful, delicate and white, with the brown-purple inner eye and the dainty pin-head of the pistil. And out in the sun at the edge of the wood, where the heath grows tall and thrusts up its spires of dim white next a brilliant, yellow-flowering vetch-bush, under a blue sky, the effect has a real magic.

And yet, in spite of all, the dim whiteness of all the flowering heath-fingers only adds to the hoariness and out-of-date quality of the pine-woods, now in the pause between spring and summer. It is the ghost of the interval.

Not that this week is flowerless. But the flowers are little lonely things, here and there: the early purple orchid, ruddy and very much alive, you come across occasionally, then the little groups of bee-orchid, with their ragged concerted indifference to their appearance. Also there are the huge bud-spikes of the stout, thick-flowering pink orchid, huge buds like fat ears of wheat, hard-purple and splendid. But already odd grains of the wheat-ear are open, and out of the purple hangs the delicate pink rag of a floweret. Also there are very lovely and choice cream-coloured orchids with brown spots on the long and delicate lip. These grow in the more moist places, and have exotic tender spikes, very rare-seeming. Another orchid is a little, pretty yellow one.

But orchids, somehow, do not make a summer. They are too aloof and individual. The little slate-blue scabious is out, but not enough to raise an appearance. Later on, under the real hot sun, he will bob into notice. And by the edges of the paths there are odd rose cushions of wild thyme. Yet these, too, are rather samples than the genuine thing. Wait another month, for wild thyme.

The same with the irises. Here and there, in fringes along the upper edge of terraces, and in odd bunches among the stones, the dark-purple iris sticks up. It is beautiful, but it hardly counts. There is not enough of it, and it is torn and buffeted by too many winds. First the wind blows with all its might from the Mediterranean, not cold, but infinitely wearying, with its rude and insistent pushing. Then, after a moment of calm, back comes a hard wind from the Adriatic, cold and disheartening. Between the two of them, the dark-purple iris flutters and tatters and curls as if it were burnt: while the yellow rock-rose streams at the end of its thin stalk, and wishes it had not been in such a hurry to come out.

There is really no hurry. By May, the great winds will drop, and the great sun will shake off his harassments. Then the nightingale will sing an unbroken song, and the discreet, barely audible Tuscan cuckoo will be a little more audible. Then the lovely pale-lilac irises will come out in all their showering abundance of tender, proud, spiky bloom, till the air will gleam with mauve, and a new crystalline lightness will be everywhere.

The iris is half-wild, half-cultivated. The peasants sometimes dig up the roots, iris root, orris root (orris powder, the perfume that is still used). So, in May, you will find ledges and terraces, fields just lit up with the mauve light of irises, and so much scent in the air, you do not notice it, you do not even know it. It is all the flowers of iris, before the olive invisibly blooms.

There will be tufts of iris everywhere, rising up proud and tender. When the rose-coloured wild gladiolus is mingled in the corn, and the love-in-the-mist opens blue: in May and June, before the corn is cut.

But as yet it is neither May nor June, but the end of April, the pause between spring and summer, the nightingale singing interruptedly, the bean-flowers dying in the bean-fields, the bean-perfume passing with spring, the little birds hatching in the nests, the olives pruned, and the vines, the last bit of late ploughing finished, and not much work to hand, now, not until the peas are ready to pick, in another two weeks or so. Then all the peasants will be crouching between the pea-rows, endlessly, endlessly gathering peas, in the long pea-harvest which lasts two months.

So the change, the endless and rapid change. In the sunny countries, the change seems more vivid, and more complete than in the grey countries. In the grey countries, there is a grey or dark permanency, over whose surface passes change ephemeral, leaving no real mark. In England, winters and summers shadowily give place to one another. But underneath lies the grey substratum, the permanency of cold, dark reality where bulbs live, and reality is bulbous, a thing of endurance and stored-up, starchy energy.

But in the sunny countries, change is the reality and permanence is artificial and a condition of imprisonment. In the North, man tends instinctively to imagine, to conceive that the sun is lighted like a candle, in an everlasting darkness, and that one day the candle will go out, the sun will be exhausted, and the everlasting dark will resume uninterrupted sway. Hence, to the northerner, the phenomenal world is essentially tragical, because it is temporal and must cease to exist. Its very existence implies ceasing to exist, and this is the root of the feeling of tragedy.

But to the southerner, the sun is so dominant that, if every phenomenal body disappeared out of the universe, nothing would remain but bright luminousness, sunniness. The absolute is sunniness; and shadow, or dark, is only merely relative: merely the result of something getting between one and the sun.

This is the instinctive feeling of the ordinary southerner. Of course, if you start to *reason*, you may argue that the sun is a phenomenal body. Therefore it came into existence, therefore it will pass out of existence, therefore the very sun is tragic in its nature.

But this is just argument. We think, because we have to

light a candle in the dark, therefore some First Cause had to kindle the sun in the infinite darkness of the beginning.

The argument is entirely shortsighted and specious. We do not know in the least whether the sun ever came into existence, and we have not the slightest possible ground for conjecturing that the sun will ever pass out of existence. All that we do know, by actual experience, is that shadow comes into being when some material object intervenes between us and the sun, and that shadow ceases to exist when the intervening object is removed. So that, of all temporal or transitory or bound-to-cease things that haunt our existence, shadow, or darkness. is the one which is purely and simply temporal. We can think of death, if we like, as of something permanently intervening between us and the sun: and this is at the root of the southern, under-world idea of death. But this doesn't alter the sun at all. As far as experience goes, in the human race, the one thing that is always there is the shining sun, and dark shadow is an accident of intervention.

Hence, strictly, there is no tragedy. The universe contains no tragedy, and man is only tragical because he is afraid of death. For my part, if the sun always shines, and always will shine, in spite of millions of clouds of words, then death, somehow, does not have many terrors. In the sunshine, even death is sunny. And there is no end to the sunshine.

That is why the rapid change of the Tuscan spring is utterly free, for me, of any sense of tragedy. 'Where are the snows of yesteryear?' Why, precisely where they ought to be. Where are the little yellow aconites of eight weeks ago? I neither know nor care. They were sunny and the sun shines, and sunniness means change, and petals passing and coming. The winter aconites sunnily came, and sunnily went. What more? The sun always shines. It is our fault if we don't think so.

MAN IS A HUNTER

Written 1926–7. *Phoenix*, 1936

It is a very nice law which forbids shooting in England on Sundays. Here in Italy, on the contrary, you would think there was a law ordering every Italian to let off a gun as often as possible. Before the eyelids of dawn have come apart, long before the bells of the tiny church jangle to announce daybreak, there is a sputter and crackle as of irritating fireworks, scattering from the olive gardens and from the woods. You sigh in your bed. The Holy Day has started: the huntsmen are abroad; they will keep at it till heaven sends the night, and the little birds are no more.

The very word *cacciatore*, which means hunter, stirs one's bile. Oh, Nimrod, oh, Bahram, put by your arrows:

> And Bahram, the great hunter, the wild ass
> Stamps o'er his bed, but cannot wake his sleep.

Here, an infinite number of tame asses shoot over my head, if I happen to walk in the wood to look at the arbutus berries, and they never fail to rouse my ire, no matter how fast asleep it may have been.

Man is a hunter! *L'uomo è cacciatore:* the Italians are rather fond of saying it. It sounds so virile. One sees Nimrod surging through the underbrush, with his spear, in the wake of a bleeding lion. And if it is a question of a man who has got a girl into trouble. '*L'uomo è cacciatore*' – 'man is a hunter' – what can you expect? It behoves the 'game' to look out for itself. Man is a hunter!

There used to be a vulgar song: 'If the Missis wants to go for a row, let 'er go'. Here it should be: 'If the master wants to run, with a gun, let him run'. For the pine-wood is full of them, as a dog's back with fleas in summer. They crouch, they lurk, they stand erect, motionless as virile statues, with gun on the alert. Then *bang!* they have shot something, with an astonishing amount of noise. And then they run, with fierce and predatory strides, to the spot.

There is nothing! Nothing! The game! *La caccia!* – where is it? If they had been shooting at the ghost of Hamlet's father, there could not be a blanker and more spooky emptiness. One expects to see a wounded elephant lying on its side, writhing its trunk; at the very least, a wild boar ploughing the earth in his death-agony. But no! There is nothing, just nothing at all. Man, being a hunter, is, fortunately for the rest of creation, a very bad shot.

Nimrod, in velveteen corduroys, bandolier, cartridges, game-bag over his shoulder and gun in his hand, stands with feet apart, *virilissimo*, on the spot where the wild boar should be, and gazes downwards at some imaginary point in underworld space. So! Man is a hunter. He casts a furtive glance around, under the arbutus bush, and a tail of his eye in my direction, knowing I am looking on in raillery. Then he hitches his game-bag more determinedly over his shoulder, grips his gun, and strides off uphill, large strides, virile as Hector. Perhaps even he is a Hector, Italianized into Ettore. Anyhow, he's going to be the death of something or somebody, if only he can shoot straight.

A Tuscan pine-wood is by no means a jungle. The trees are umbrella-pines, with the umbrellas open, and bare handles. They are rather parsimoniously scattered. The undergrowth, moreover, is allowed to grow only for a couple of years or so; then it is most assiduously reaped, gleaned, gathered, cleaned up clean as a lawn, for cooking Nimrod's macaroni. So that, in a *pineta*, you have a piny roof over your head, and for the rest a pretty clear run for your money. So where can the game lurk? There is hardly cover for a bumble-bee. Where can the game be that is worth all this powder? The lions and wolves and boars that must prowl perilously round all these Nimrods?

You will never know. Or not until you are going home, between the olive-trees. The hunters have been burning powder in the open, as well as in the wood: a proper fusillade. Then, on the path between the olives, you may pick up a warm, dead bullfinch, with a bit of blood on it. The little grey bird lies on its side, with its frail feet closed, and its red breast ruffled. Nimrod, having hit for once, has failed to find his quarry.

So you will know better when the servant comes excitedly and asks: 'Signore, do you want any game?' Game! Splendid idea! A couple of partridges? a hare? even a wild rabbit? Why, of course! So she arrives in triumph with a knotted red handkerchief, and the not very bulky game inside it. Untie the knots! Aha! – Alas! There, in a little heap on the table, three robins, two finches, four hedge-sparrows, and two starlings, in a fluffy, coloured, feathery little heap, all the small heads rolling limp. 'Take them away,' you say. 'We don't eat little birds.' 'But these,' she says, tipping up the starlings roughly, 'these are big ones.' 'Not these, either, do we eat.' 'No?' she exclaims, in a tone which means: '*More fools you!*' And, disgusted, disappointed at not having sold the goods, she departs with the game.

You will know best of all if you go to the market, and see whole yard-lengths of robins, like coral and onyx necklaces, and strings of bullfinches, goldfinches, larks, sparrows, nightingales, starlings, temptingly offered along with strings of sausages, these last looking like the strings of pearls in the show. If one bought the birds to wear as ornament, barbaric necklaces, it would be more conceivable. You can get quite a string of different-coloured ones for tenpence. But imagine the small mouthful of little bones each of these tiny carcasses must make!

But, after all, a partridge and a pheasant are only a bit bigger than a sparrow and a finch. And compared to a flea, a robin is big game. It is all a question of dimensions. Man is a hunter. 'If the master wants to hunt, don't you grunt; let him hunt!'

GERMANY

—

THE CRUCIFIX ACROSS THE MOUNTAINS

Written in 1912. *Westminster Gazette*, 22 March, 1913.
Twilight in Italy, 1916

THE imperial road to Italy goes from Munich across the Tyrol, through Innsbruck and Bozen to Verona, over the mountains. Here the great processions passed as the emperors went south, or came home again from rosy Italy to their own Germany.

And how much has that old imperial vanity clung to the German soul? Did not the German kings inherit the empire of bygone Rome? It was not a very real empire, perhaps, but the sound was high and splendid.

Maybe a certain Grössenwahn is inherent in the German nature. If only nations would realize that they have certain natural characteristics, if only they could understand and agree to each other's particular nature, how much simpler it would all be.

The imperial procession no longer crosses the mountains, going south. That is almost forgotten, the road has almost passed out of mind. But still it is there, and its signs are standing.

The crucifixes are there, not mere attributes of the road, yet still having something to do with it. The imperial processions, blessed by the Pope and accompanied by the great bishops, must have planted the holy idol like a new plant among the mountains, there where it multiplied and grew according to the soil, and the race that received it.

As one goes among the Bavarian uplands and foothills, soon one realizes here is another land, a strange religion. It is a strange country, remote, out of contact. Perhaps it belongs to the forgotten, imperial processions.

Coming along the clear, open roads that lead to the mountains, one scarcely notices the crucifixes and the shrines.

Perhaps one's interest is dead. The crucifix itself is nothing, a factory-made piece of sentimentalism. The soul ignores it.

But gradually, one after another looming shadowily under their hoods, the crucifixes seem to create a new atmosphere over the whole of the countryside, a darkness, a weight in the air that is so unnaturally bright and rare with the reflection from the snows above, a darkness hovering just over the earth. So rare and unearthly the light is, from the mountains, full of strange radiance. Then every now and again recurs the crucifix, at the turning of an open, grassy road, holding a shadow and a mystery under its pointed hood.

I was startled into consciousness one evening, going alone over a marshy place at the foot of the mountains, when the sky was pale and unearthly, invisible, and the hills were nearly black. At a meeting of the tracks was a crucifix, and between the feet of the Christ a handful of withered poppies. It was the poppies I saw, then the Christ.

It was an old shrine, the wood-sculpture of a Bavarian peasant. The Christ was a peasant of the foot of the Alps. He had broad cheek-bones and sturdy limbs. His plain rudimentary face stared fixedly at the hills, his neck was stiffened, as if in resistance to the fact of the nails and the cross, which he could not escape. It was a man nailed down in spirit, but set stubbornly against the bondage and the disgrace. He was a man of middle-age, plain, crude, with some of the meanness of the peasant, but also with a kind of dogged nobility that does not yield its soul to the circumstance. Plain, almost blank in his soul, the middle-aged peasant of the crucifix resisted unmoving the misery of his position. He did not yield. His soul was set, his will was fixed. He was himself, let his circumstances be what they would, his life fixed down.

Across the marsh was a tiny square of orange-coloured light, from the farm-house with the low, spreading roof. I remembered how the man and his wife and the children worked on till dark, silent and intent, carrying the hay in their arms out of the streaming thunder-rain into the shed, working silent in the soaking rain.

The body bent forward towards the earth, closing round on

itself; the arms clasped full of hay, clasped round the hay that presses soft and close to the breast and the body, that pricks heat into the arms and the skin of the breast, and fills the lungs with the sleepy scent of dried herbs: the rain that falls heavily and wets the shoulders, so that the shirt clings to the hot, firm skin and the rain comes with heavy, pleasant coldness on the active flesh, running in a trickle down towards the loins, secretly; this is the peasant, this hot welter of physical sensation. And it is all intoxicating. It is intoxicating almost like a soporific, like a sensuous drug, to gather the burden to one's body in the rain, to stumble across the living grass to the shed, to relieve one's arms of the weight, to throw down the hay on to the heap, to feel light and free in the dry shed, then to return again into the chill, hard rain, to stoop again under the rain, and rise to return again with the burden.

It is this, this endless heat and rousedness of physical sensation which keeps the body full and potent, and flushes the mind with a blood heat, a blood sleep. And this sleep, this heat of physical experience, becomes at length a bondage, at last a crucifixion. It is the life and the fulfilment of the peasant, this flow of sensuous experience. But at last it drives him almost mad, because he cannot escape.

For overhead there is always the strange radiance of the mountains, there is the mystery of the icy river rushing through its pink shoals into the darkness of the pine-woods, there is always the faint tang of ice on the air, and the rush of hoarse-sounding water.

And the ice and the upper radiance of snow are brilliant with timeless immunity from the flux and the warmth of life. Overhead they transcend all life, all the soft, moist fire of the blood. So that a man must needs live under the radiance of his own negation.

There is a strange, clear beauty of form about the men of the Bavarian highlands, about both men and women. They are large and clear and handsome in form, with blue eyes very keen, the pupil small, tightened, the iris keen, like sharp light shining on blue ice. Their large, full-moulded limbs and erect bodies are distinct, separate, as if they were perfectly chiselled out of the stuff of life, static, cut off. Where they are everything is set back, as in a clear frosty air.

Their beauty is almost this, this strange, clean-cut isolation, as if each one of them would isolate himself still farther and for ever from the rest of his fellows.

Yet they are convivial, they are almost the only race with the souls of artists. Still they act the mystery plays with instinctive fullness of interpretation, they sing strangely in the mountain fields, they love make-belief and mummery, their processions and religious festivals are profoundly impressive, solemn, and rapt.

It is a race that moves on the poles of mystic sensual delight. Every gesture is a gesture from the blood, every expression is a symbolic utterance.

For learning there is sensuous experience, for thought there is myth and drama and dancing and singing. Everything is of the blood, of the senses. There is no mind. The mind is a suffusion of physical heat, it is not separated, it is kept submerged.

At the same time, always, overhead, there is the eternal, negative radiance of the snows. Beneath is life, the hot jet of the blood playing elaborately. But above is the radiance of changeless not-being. And life passes away into this changeless radiance. Summer and the prolific blue-and-white flowering of the earth goes by, with the labour and the ecstasy of man, disappears, and is gone into brilliance that hovers overhead, the radiant cold which waits to receive back again all that which has passed for the moment into being.

The issue is too much revealed. It leaves the peasant no choice. The fate gleams transcendent above him, the brightness of eternal, unthinkable not-being. And this our life, this admixture of labour and of warm experience in the flesh, all the time it is steaming up to the changeless brilliance above, the light of the everlasting snows. This is the eternal issue.

Whether it is singing or dancing or play-acting or physical transport of love, or vengeance or cruelty, or whether it is work or sorrow or religion, the issue is always the same at last, into the radiant negation of eternity. Hence the beauty and completeness, the finality of the highland peasant. His figure, his limbs, his face, his motion, it is all formed in beauty, and it is all completed. There is no flux nor hope nor becoming, all *is*, once and for all. The issue is eternal, timeless, and changeless. All being and all passing away is part of the issue, which is eternal and changeless. Therefore there is no becoming and no passing away. Everything *is*, now and for ever. Hence the strange beauty and finality and isolation of the Bavarian peasant.

It is plain in the crucifixes. Here is the essence rendered in sculpture of wood. The face is blank and stiff, almost expressionless. One realizes with a start how unchanging and conventionalized is the face of the living man and woman of these parts, handsome, but motionless as pure form. There is also an underlying meanness, secretive, cruel. It is all part of the beauty, the pure, plastic beauty. The body also of the Christus is stiff and conventionalized, yet curiously beautiful in proportion, and in the static tension which makes it unified into one clear thing. There is no movement, no possible movement. The being is fixed, finally. The whole body is locked in one knowledge, beautiful, complete. It is one with the nails. Not that it is languishing or dead. It is stubborn, knowing its own undeniable being, sure of the absolute reality of the sensuous experience. Though he is nailed down upon an irrevocable fate, yet within that fate he has the power and the delight of all sensuous experience. So he accepts the fate and the mystic delight of the senses with one will, he is complete and final. His sensuous experience is supreme, a consummation of life and death at once.

It is the same at all times, whether it is the mowing with the scythe on the hill-slopes, or hewing the timber, or steering the raft down the river which is all effervescent with ice; whether it is drinking in the Gasthaus, or making love, or playing some mummer's part, or hating steadily and cruelly, or whether it is kneeling in spellbound subjection in the incense-filled church, or walking in the strange, dark, subject-procession to bless the fields, or cutting the young birch-trees for the feast of Frohenleichnam, it is always the same, the dark, powerful, mystic, sensuous experience is the whole of him, he is mindless and bound within the absoluteness of the issue, the unchangeability of the great icy not-being which holds good for ever, and is supreme.

Passing farther away, towards Austria, travelling up the Isar, till the stream becomes smaller and whiter and the air is colder, the full glamour of the northern hills, which are so marvellously luminous and gleaming with flowers, wanes and gives way to a darkness, a sense of ominousness. Up there I saw another little Christ, who seemed the very soul of the place. The road went beside the river, that was seething with snowy ice-bubbles, under the rocks and the high, wolf-like pine-trees, between the pinkish shoals. The air was cold and hard and high, everything was cold and separate. And in a little glass case beside the road sat a small, hewn Christ, the head resting on the hand; and he meditates, half-wearily, doggedly, the eyebrows lifted in strange abstraction, the elbow resting on the knee. Detached he sits and dreams and broods, wearing his little golden crown of thorns, and his little cloak of red flannel that some peasant woman has stitched for him.

No doubt he still sits there, the small, blank-faced Christ in the cloak of red flannel, dreaming, brooding, enduring, persisting. There is a wistfulness about him, as if he knew that the whole of things was too much for him. There was no solution, either, in death. Death did not give the answer to the soul's anxiety. That which is, is. It does not cease to be when it is cut. Death cannot create nor destroy. What is, is.

The little brooding Christ knows this. What is he brooding, then? His static patience and endurance is wistful. What is it that he secretly yearns for, amid all the placidity of fate? 'To be, or not to be', this may be the question, but it is not a question for death to answer. It is not a question of living or not-living. It is a question of being – to be or not to be. To persist or not to persist, that is not the question; neither is it to endure or not to endure. The issue, is it eternal not-being? If not, what, then, is being? For overhead the eternal radiance of the snow gleams unfailing, it receives the efflorescence of all life and is unchanged, the issue is bright and immortal, the snowy not-being. What, then, is being?

As one draws nearer to the turning-point of the Alps, towards the culmination and the southern slope, the influence of the educated world is felt once more. Bavaria is remote in spirit, as yet unattached. Its crucifixes are old and grey and abstract, small like the kernel of the truth. Farther into Austria they become new, they are painted white, they are larger, more obtrusive. They are the expressions of a later, newer phase, more introspective and self-conscious. But still they are genuine expressions of the people's soul.

Often, one can distinguish the work of a particular artist here and there in a district. In the Zemm valley, in the heart of the Tyrol, behind Innsbruck, there are five or six crucifixes by one sculptor. He is no longer a peasant working out an idea, conveying a dogma. He is an artist, trained and conscious, probably working in Vienna. He is consciously trying to convey a *feeling*, he is no longer striving awkwardly to render a truth, a religious fact.

The chief of his crucifixes stands deep in the Klamm, in the dank gorge where it is always half-night. The road runs under the rock and the trees, half-way up the one side of the pass. Below, the stream rushes ceaselessly, embroiled among great stones, making an endless loud noise. The rock face opposite rises high overhead, with the sky far up. So that one is walking in a half-night, an underworld. And just below the path, where the pack-horses go climbing to the remote, infolded villages, in the cold gloom of the pass hangs the large, pale Christ. He is larger than life-size. He has fallen forward, just dead, and the weight of the full-grown, mature body hangs on the nails of the hands. So the dead, heavy body drops forward, sags, as if it would tear away and fall under its own weight.

It is the end. The face is barren with a dead expression of weariness, and brutalized with pain and bitterness. The rather ugly. passionate mouth is set for ever in the disillusionment of death. Death is the complete disillusionment, set like a seal over the whole body and being, over the suffering and weariness and the bodily passion.

The pass is gloomy and damp, the water roars unceasingly, till it is almost like a constant pain. The driver of the pack-horses, as he comes up the narrow path in the side of the gorge, cringes his sturdy cheerfulness as if to obliterate himself, drawing near to the large, pale Christ, and he takes his hat off as he passes, though he does not look up, but keeps his face averted from the crucifix. He hurries by in the gloom, climbing the steep path after his horses, and the large, white Christ hangs extended above.

The driver of the pack-horses is afraid. The fear is always there in him, in spite of his sturdy, healthy robustness. His soul is not sturdy. It is blenched and whitened with fear. The mountains are dark overhead, the water roars in the gloom below. His heart is ground between the mill-stones of dread. When he passes the extended body of the dead Christ he takes off his hat to the Lord of Death. Christ is the Deathly One, He is Death incarnate.

And the driver of the pack-horses acknowledges this deathly Christ as supreme Lord. The mountain peasant seems grounded upon fear, the fear of death, of physical death. Beyond this he knows nothing. His supreme sensation is in physical pain, and in its culmination. His great climax, his consummation, is death. Therefore he worships it, bows down before it, and is fascinated by it all the while. It is his fulfilment, death, and his approach to fulfilment is through physical pain.

And so these monuments to physical death are found everywhere in the valleys. By the same hand that carved the big Christ, a little farther on, at the end of a bridge, was another crucifix, a small one. This Christ had a fair beard, and was thin, and his body was hanging almost lightly, whereas the other Christ was large and dark and handsome. But in this, as well as in the other, was the same neutral triumph of death, complete, negative death, so complete as to be abstract, beyond cynicism in its completeness of leaving off.

Everywhere is the same obsession with the fact of physical pain, accident, and sudden death. Wherever a misfortune has befallen a man, there is nailed up a little memorial of the event, in propitiation of the God of hurt and death. A man is standing up to his waist in water, drowning in full stream, his arms in the air. The little painting in its wooden frame is nailed to the tree, the spot is sacred to the accident. Again, another little crude picture fastened to a rock: a tree, falling on a man's leg, smashes it like a stalk, while the blood flies up. Always there is the strange ejaculation of anguish and fear, perpetuated in the little paintings nailed up in the place of the disaster.

This is the worship, then, the worship of death and the approaches to death, physical violence, and pain. There is something crude and sinister about it, almost like depravity, a form of reverting, turning back along the course of blood by which we have come.

Turning the ridge on the great road to the south, the imperial road to Rome, a decisive change takes place. The Christs have been taking on various different characters, all of them more or less realistically conveyed. One Christus is very elegant, combed and brushed and foppish on his cross, as Gabriele D'Annunzio's son posing as a martyred saint. The martyrdom of this Christ is according to the most polite convention. The elegance is very important, and very Austrian. One might almost imagine the young man had taken up this striking and original position to create a delightful sensation among the ladies. It is quite in the Viennese spirit. There is something brave and keen in it, too. The individual pride of body triumphs over every difficulty in the situation. The pride and satisfaction in the clean, elegant form, the perfectly trimmed hair, the exquisite bearing, are more important than the fact of death or pain. This may be foolish, it is at the same time admirable.

But this tendency of the crucifix, as it nears the ridge to the south, is to become weak and sentimental. The carved Christs turn up their faces and roll back their eyes very piteously, in the approved Guido Reni fashion. They are overdoing the pathetic turn. They are looking to heaven and thinking about themselves, in self-commiseration. Others again are beautiful as elegies. It is dead Hyacinth lifted and extended to view, in all his beautiful, dead youth. The young male body droops forward on the cross, like a dead flower. It looks as if its only true nature were to be dead. How lovely is death, how poignant, real, and satisfying! It is the true elegiac spirit.

Then there are the ordinary, factory-made Christs, which are not very significant. They are as null as the Christs we see represented in England, just vulgar nothingness. But these figures have gashes of red, a red paint of blood, which is sensational.

Beyond the Brenner, I have only seen vulgar or sensational crucifixes. There are great gashes on the breast and the knees of the Christ-figure, and the scarlet flows out and trickles down, till the crucified body has become a ghastly striped thing of red and white, just a sickly thing of striped red.

They paint the rocks at the corners of the tracks, among the mountains: a blue and white ring for the road to Ginzling, a red smear for the way to St Jakob. So one follows the blue and white ring, or the three stripes of blue and white, or the red smear, as the case may be. And the red on the rocks, the dabs of red paint, are of just the same colour as the red upon the crucifixes; so that the red upon the crucifixes is paint, and the signs on the rocks are sensational, like blood.

I remember the little brooding Christ of the Isar, in his little cloak of red flannel and his crown of gilded thorns, and he remains real and dear to me, among all this violence of representation.

'*Couvre-toi de gloire. Tartarin - couvre-toi de flanelle.*' Why should it please me so that his cloak is of red flannel?

In a valley near St Jakob, just over the ridge, a long way from the railway, there is a very big, important shrine by the roadside. It is a chapel built in the baroque manner, florid pink and cream outside, with opulent small arches. And inside is the most startlingly sensational Christus I have ever seen. He is a big, powerful man, seated after the crucifixion, perhaps after the resurrection, sitting by the grave. He sits sideways, as if the extremity were over, finished, the agitation done with, only the result of the experience remaining. There is some blood on his powerful, naked, defeated body, that sits rather hulked. But it is the face which is so terrifying. It is slightly turned over the hulked, crucified shoulder, to look. And the look of this face, of which the body has been killed, is beyond all expectation horrible. The eyes look at one, yet have no seeing in them, they seem to see only their own blood. For they are bloodshot till the whites are scarlet, the iris is purpled. These red, bloody eyes with their stained pupils, glancing awfully at all who enter the shrine, looking as if to see through the blood of the late brutal death, are terrible. The naked, strong body has known death, and sits in utter dejection, finished, hulked, a weight of shame. And what remains of life is in the face, whose expression is sinister and gruesome, like that of an unrelenting criminal violated by torture. The criminal look of misery and hatred on the fixed, violated face and in the bloodshot eyes is almost impossible. He is conquered, beaten, broken, his body is a mass of torture, an unthinkable shame. Yet his will remains obstinate and ugly, integral with utter hatred.

It is a great shock to find this figure sitting in a handsome, baroque, pink-washed shrine in one of those Alpine valleys which to our thinking are all flowers and romance, like the picture in the Tate Gallery. 'Spring in the Austrian Tyrol' is to our minds a vision of pristine loveliness. It contains also this Christ of the heavy body defiled by torture and death, the strong, virile life overcome by physical violence, the eyes still looking back bloodshot in consummate hate and misery.

The shrine was well kept and evidently much used. It was hung with ex-voto limbs and with many gifts. It was a centre of worship, of a sort of almost obscene worship. Afterwards the black pine-trees and the river of the valley seemed unclean, as if an unclean spirit lived there. The very flowers seemed unnatural and the white gleam on the mountain-tops was a glisten of supreme, cynical horror.

After this, in the populous valleys, all the crucifixes were more or less tainted and vulgar. Only high up, where the crucifix becomes smaller and smaller, is there left any of the old beauty and religion. Higher and higher, the monument becomes smaller and smaller, till in the snows it stands out like a post, or a thick arrow stuck barb upwards. The crucifix itself is a small thing under the pointed hood, the barb of the arrow. The snow blows under the tiny shed, upon the little exposed Christ. All round is the solid whiteness of snow, the awful curves and concaves of pure whiteness of the mountain-top, the hollow whiteness between the peaks, where the path crosses the high, extreme ridge of the pass. And here stands the last crucifix, half buried, small and tufted with snow. The guides tramp slowly, heavily past, not observing the presence of the symbol, making no salute. Farther down, every mountain peasant lifted his hat. But the guide tramps by without concern. His is a professional importance now.

On a small mountain track on the Jaufen, not far from Meran, was a fallen Christus. I was hurrying downhill to escape from an icy wind which almost took away my consciousness, and I was looking up at the gleaming, unchanging snow-peaks all round. They seemed like blades immortal in the sky. So I almost ran into a very old Martertafel. It leaned on the cold, stony hill-side surrounded by the white peaks in the upper air.

The wooden hood was silver-grey with age, and covered, on the top, with a thicket of lichen, which stuck up in hoary tufts. But on the rock at the foot of the post was the fallen Christ, armless, who had tumbled down and lay in an unnatural posture, the naked, ancient wooden sculpture of the body on the naked, living rock. It was one of the old uncouth Christs hewn out of bare wood, having the long wedge-shaped limbs and thin, flat legs that are significant of the true spirit, the desire to convey a religious truth, not a sensational experience.

The arms of the fallen Christ had broken off at the shoulders, and they hung on their nails, as ex-voto limbs hang in the shrines. But these arms dangled from the palms, one at each end of the cross, the muscles, carved sparely in the old wood, looking all wrong, upside down. And the icy wind blew them backwards and forwards, so that they gave a painful impression, there in the stark, sterile place of rock and cold. Yet I dared not touch the fallen body of the Christ, that lay on its back in so grotesque a posture at the foot of the post. I wondered who would come and take the broken thing away, and for what purpose.

MERCURY

Written 1926. *Atlantic Monthly*, February, 1927.
Nation and Athenaeum, 5 February, 1927.
Phoenix, 1936

It was Sunday, and very hot. The holiday-makers flocked to the hill of Mercury, to rise two thousand feet above the steamy haze of the valleys. For the summer had been very wet, and the sudden heat covered the land in hot steam.

Every time it made the ascent, the funicular was crowded. It hauled itself up the steep incline, that towards the top looked almost perpendicular, the steel thread of the rails in the gulf of pine-trees hanging like an iron rope against a wall. The women held their breath, and didn't look. Or they looked back towards the sinking levels of the river, steamed and dim, far-stretching over the frontier.

When you arrived at the top there was nothing to do. The hill was a pine-covered cone; paths wound between the high tree-trunks, and you could walk round and see the glimpses of the world all round, all round: the dim, far river-plain, with a dull glint of the great stream, to westwards; southwards, the black, forest-covered, agile-looking hills, with emerald-green clearings and a white house or two; east, the inner valley, with two villages, factory chimneys, pointed churches, and hills beyond; and north, the steep hills of forest, with reddish crags and reddish castle ruins. The hot sun burned overhead, and all was in steam.

Only on the very summit of the hill there was a tower, an outlook tower; a long restaurant with its beer-garden, all the little yellow tables standing their round disks under the horse-chestnut trees; then a bit of rock-garden on the slope. But the great trees began again in wilderness a few yards off.

The Sunday crowd came up in waves from the funicular. In waves they ebbed through the beer-garden. But not many sat down to drink. Nobody was spending any money. Some paid to go up the outlook tower, to look down on a world of vapours and black, agile-crouching hills, and half-crooked towns. Then everybody dispersed along the paths, to sit among the trees in the cool air.

There was not a breath of wind. Lying and looking upwards at the shaggy, barbaric middle-world of the pine-trees, it was difficult to decide whether the pure high trunks supported the upper thicket of darkness, or whether they descended from it like great cords stretched downwards. Anyhow, in between the tree-top world and the earth-world went the wonderful clean cords of innumerable proud tree-trunks, clear as rain. And as you watched, you saw that the upper world was faintly moving, faintly, most faintly swaying, with a circular movement, though the lower trunks were utterly motionless and monolithic.

There was nothing to do. In all the world, there was nothing to do, and nothing to be done. Why have we all come to the top of the Merkur? There is nothing for us to do.

What matter? We have come a stride beyond the world. Let it steam and cook its half-baked reality below there. On the hill of Mercury we take no notice. Even we do not trouble to wander and pick the fat, blue, sourish bilberries. Just lie and see the rain-pure tree-trunks like chords of music between two worlds.

The hours pass by: people wander and disappear and reappear. All is hot and quiet. Humanity is rarely boisterous any more. You go for a drink: finches run among the few people at the tables: everybody glances at everybody, but with remoteness.

There is nothing to do but to return and lie down under the pine trees. Nothing to do. But why do anything, anyhow? The desire to do anything has gone. The tree-trunks, living like rain, they are quite active enough.

At the foot of the obsolete tower there is an old tablet-stone with a very much battered Mercury, in relief. There is also an altar, or votive stone, both from the Roman times. The Romans are supposed to have worshipped Mercury on the summit. The battered god, with his round sun-head, looks very hollow-eyed and unimpressive in the purplish-red sandstone of the district. And no one any more will throw grains of offering in the hollow of the votive stone: also common, purplish-red sandstone, very local and un-Roman.

The Sunday people do not even look. Why should they? They keep passing on into the pine-trees. And many sit on the benches; many lie upon the long chairs. It is very hot, in the afternoon, and very still.

Till there seems a faint whistling in the tops of the pine-trees, and out of the universal semi-consciousness of the afternoon arouses a bristling uneasiness. The crowd is astir, looking at the sky. And sure enough, there is a great flat blackness reared up in the western sky, curled with white wisps and loose breast-feathers. It looks very sinister, as only the elements still can look. Under the sudden weird whistling of the upper pine trees, there is a subdued babble and calling of frightened voices.

They want to get down; the crowd want to get off the hill of Mercury, before the storm comes. At any price to get off the hill! They stream towards the funicular, while the sky blackens with incredible rapidity. And as the crowd presses down towards the little station, the first blaze of lightning opens out, followed immediately by a crash of thunder, and great darkness. In one strange movement, the crowd takes refuge in the deep veranda of the restaurant, pressing among the little tables in silence. There is no rain, and no definite wind, only a sudden coldness which makes the crowd press closer.

They press closer, in the darkness and the suspense. They have become curiously unified, the crowd, as if they had fused into one body. As the air sends a chill waft under the veranda the voices murmur plaintively, like birds under leaves, the bodies press closer together, seeking shelter in contact.

The gloom, dark as night, seems to continue a long time. Then suddenly the lightning dances white on the floor, dances and shakes upon the ground, up and down, and lights up the white striding of a man, lights him up only to the hips, white and naked and striding, with fire on his heels. He seems to be hurrying, this fiery man whose upper half is invisible, and at his naked heels white little flames seem to flutter. His flat, powerful thighs, his legs white as fire stride rapidly across the open, in front of the veranda, dragging little white flames at the ankles, with the movement. He is going somewhere, swiftly.

In the great bang of the thunder the apparition disappears. The earth moves, and the house jumps in complete darkness. A faint whimpering of terror comes from the crowd, as the cold air swirls in. But still, upon the darkness, there is no rain. There is no relief: a long wait.

Brilliant and blinding, the lightning falls again; a strange bruising thud comes from the forest, as all the little tables and secret tree-trunks stand for one unnatural second exposed. Then the blow of the thunder, under which the house and the crowd reel as under an explosion. The storm is playing directly upon the Merkur. A belated sound of tearing branches comes out of the forest.

And again the white splash of the lightning on the ground: but nothing moves. And again the long, rattling, instantaneous volleying of the thunder, in the darkness. The crowd is panting with fear, as the lightning again strikes white, and something again seems to burst, in the forest, as the thunder crashes.

At last, into the motionlessness of the storm, in rushes the wind, with the fiery flying of bits of ice, and the sudden sea-like roaring of the pine trees. The crowd winces and draws back, as the bits of ice hit in the faces like fire. The roar of the trees is so great, it becomes like another silence. And through it is heard the crashing and splintering of timber, as the hurricane concentrates upon the hill.

Down comes the hail, in a roar that covers every other sound, threshing ponderously upon the ground and the roofs and the trees. And as the crowd surges irresistibly into the interior of the building, from the crushing of this ice-fall, still amid the sombre hoarseness sounds the tinkle and crackle of things breaking.

After an eternity of dread, it ends suddenly. Outside is a faint gleam of yellow light, over the snow and the endless debris of twigs and things broken. It is very cold, with the atmosphere of ice and deep winter. The forest looks wan, above the white earth, where the ice-balls lie in their myriads, six inches deep, littered with all the twigs and things they have broken.

'Yes! Yes!' said the men, taking sudden courage as the yellow light comes into the air. 'Now we can go!'

The first brave ones emerge, picking up the big hailstones, pointing to the overthrown tables. Some, however, do not linger. They hurry to the funicular station, to see if the apparatus is still working.

The funicular station is on the north side of the hill. The men come back, saying there is no one there. The crowd begins to emerge upon the wet, crunching whiteness of the hail, spreading around in curiosity, waiting for the men who operate the funicular.

On the south side of the outlook tower two bodies lay in the cold but thawing hail. The dark-blue of the uniforms showed blackish. Both men were dead. But the lightning had completely removed the clothing from the legs of one man, so that he was naked from the hips down. There he lay, his face sideways on the snow, and two drops of blood running from his nose into his big, blond, military moustache. He lay there near the votive stone of the Mercury. His companion, a young man, lay face downwards, a few yards behind him.

The sun began to emerge. The crowd gazed in dread, afraid to touch the bodies of the men. Why had they, the dead funicular men, come round to this side of the hill, anyhow?

The funicular would not work. Something had happened to it in the storm. The crowd began to wind down the bare hill, on the sloppy ice. Everywhere the earth bristled with broken pine boughs and twigs. But the bushes and the leafy trees were stripped absolutely bare, to a miracle. The lower earth was leafless and naked as in winter.

'Absolute winter!' murmured the crowd, as they hurried, frightened, down the steep, winding descent, extricating themselves from the fallen pine-branches.

Meanwhile the sun began to steam in great heat.

A LETTER FROM GERMANY

Written 19 February, 1924. *New Statesman*, 13 October, 1934. *Phoenix*, 1936

WE are going back to Paris to-morrow, so this is the last moment to write a letter from Germany. Only from the fringe of Germany, too.

It is a miserable journey from Paris to Nancy, through that Marne country, where the country still seems to have had the soul blasted out of it, though the dreary fields are ploughed and level, and the pale wire trees stand up. But it is all void and null. And in the villages, the smashed houses in the street rows, like rotten teeth between good teeth.

You come to Strasbourg, and the people still talk Alsatian German, as ever, in spite of French shop-signs. The place feels dead. And full of cotton goods, white goods, from Mülhausen, from the factories that once were German. Such cheap white cotton goods, in a glut.

The cathedral front rearing up high and flat and fanciful, a sort of darkness in the dark, with round rose windows and long, long prisons of stone. Queer, that men should have ever wanted to put stone upon fanciful stone to such a height, without having it fall down. The Gothic! I was always glad when my card-castle fell. But these Goths and Alemans seemed to have a craze for peaky heights.

The Rhine is still the Rhine, the great divider. You feel it as you cross. The flat, frozen, watery places. Then the cold and curving river. Then the other side, seeming so cold, so empty, so frozen, so forsaken. The train stands and steams fiercely. Then it draws through the flat Rhine plain, past frozen pools of flood-water, and frozen fields, in the emptiness of this bit of occupied territory.

Immediately you are over the Rhine, the spirit of place has changed. There is no more attempt at the bluff of geniality.

The marshy places are frozen. The fields are vacant. There seems nobody in the world.

It is as if the life had retreated eastwards. As if the Germanic life were slowly ebbing away from contact with western Europe, ebbing to the deserts of the east. And there stand the heavy, ponderous, round hills of the Black Forest, black with an inky blackness of Germanic trees, and patched with a whiteness of snow. They are like a series of huge, involved black mounds, obstructing the vision eastwards. You look at them from the Rhine plain, and know that you stand on an actual border, up against something.

The moment you are in Germany, you know. It feels empty, and, somehow, menacing. So must the Roman soldiers have watched those black, massive round hills: with a certain fear, and with the knowledge that they were at their own limit. A fear of the invisible natives. A fear of the invisible life lurking among the woods. A fear of their own opposite.

So it is with the French: this almost mystic fear. But one should not insult even one's fears.

Germany, this bit of Germany, is very different from what it was two-and-a-half years ago, when I was here. Then it was still open to Europe. Then it still looked to western Europe for a reunion – for a sort of reconciliation. Now that is over. The inevitable, mysterious barrier has fallen again, and the great leaning of the Germanic spirit is once more eastwards, towards Russia, towards Tartary. The strange vortex of Tartary has become the positive centre again, the positivity of western Europe is broken. The positivity of our civilization has broken. The influences that come, come invisibly out of Tartary. So that all Germany reads *Beasts, Men, and Gods* with a kind of fascination. Returning again to the fascination of the destructive East, that produced Attila.

So it is at night. Baden-Baden is a little quiet place, all its guests gone. No more Turgenievs or Dostoievskys or Grand Dukes or King Edwards coming to drink the waters. All the outward effect of a world-famous watering place. But empty now, a mere Black Forest village with the wagon-loads of timber going through, to the French.

The Rentenmark, the new gold mark of Germany, is abominably dear. Prices are high in England, but English money buys less in Baden than it buys in London, by a long chalk. And there is no work – consequently no money. Nobody buys anything, except absolute necessities. The shopkeepers are in despair. And there is less and less work.

Everybody gives up the telephone – can't afford it. The tram-cars don't run, except about three times a day to the station. Up to the Annaberg, the suburb, the lines are rusty, no trams ever go. The people can't afford the ten pfennigs for the fare. Ten pfennigs is an important sum now: one penny. It is really a hundred milliards of marks.

Money becomes insane, and people with it.

At night the place is almost dark, economizing light. Economy, economy, economy – that too becomes an insanity. Luckily the government keeps bread fairly cheap.

But at night you feel strange things stirring in the darkness, strange feelings stirring out of this still-unconquered Black Forest. You stiffen your backbone and you listen to the night. There is a sense of danger. It is not the people. They don't seem dangerous. Out of the very air comes a sense of danger, a queer, *bristling* feeling of uncanny danger.

Something has happened. Something has happened which has not yet eventuated. The old spell of the old world has broken, and the old, bristling, savage spirit has set in. The war did not break the old peace-and-production hope of the world, though it gave it a severe wrench. Yet the old peace-and-production hope still governs, at least the consciousness. Even in Germany it has not quite gone.

But it feels as if, virtually, it were gone. The last two years have done it. The hope in peace-and-production is broken. The old flow, the old adherence is ruptured. And a still older flow has set in. Back, back to the savage polarity of Tartary, and away from the polarity of civilized Christian Europe. This, it seems to me, has already happened. And it is a happening of far more profound import than any actual *event*. It is the father of the next phase of events.

And the feeling never relaxes. As you travel up the Rhine

valley, still the same latent sense of danger, of silence, of suspension. Not that the people are actually planning or plotting or preparing. I don't believe it for a minute. But something has happened to the human soul, beyond all help. The human soul recoiling now from unison, and making itself strong elsewhere. The ancient spirit of prehistoric Germany coming back, at the end of history.

The same in Heidelberg. Heidelberg full, full, full of people. Students the same, youths with rucksacks the same, boys and maidens in gangs come down from the hills. The same, and not the same. These queer gangs of *Young Socialists*, youths and girls, with their non-materialistic professions, their half-mystic assertions, they strike one as strange. Something primitive, like loose, roving gangs of broken, scattered tribes, so they affect one. And the swarms of people somehow produce an impression of silence, of secrecy, of stealth. It is as if everything and everybody recoiled away from the old unison, as barbarians lurking in a wood recoil out of sight. The old habits remain. But the bulk of the people have no money. And the whole stream of feeling is reversed.

So you stand in the woods above the town and see the Neckar flowing green and swift and slippery out of the gulf of Germany, to the Rhine. And the sun sets slow and scarlet into the haze of the Rhine valley. And the old, pinkish stone of the ruined castle across looks sultry, the marshalry is in shadow below, the peaked roofs of old, tight Heidelberg compressed in its river gateway glimmer and glimmer out. There is a blue haze.

And it all looks as if the years were wheeling swiftly backwards, no more onwards. Like a spring that is broken, and whirls swiftly back, so time seems to be whirling with mysterious swiftness to a sort of death. Whirling to the ghost of the Middle Ages of Germany, then to the Roman days, then to the days of the silent forest and the dangerous, lurking barbarians.

Something about the Germanic races is unalterable. White-skinned, elemental, and dangerous. Our civilization has come from the fusion of the dark-eyes with the blue. The meeting and mixing and mingling of the two races has been the joy of our ages. And the Celt has been there, alien, but necessary as some chemical re-agent to the fusion. So the civilization of Europe rose up. So these cathedrals and these thoughts.

But now the Celt is the disintegrating agent. And the Latin and southern races are falling out of association with the northern races, the northern Germanic impulse is recoiling towards Tartary, the destructive vortex of Tartary.

It is a fate; nobody now can alter it. It is a fate. The very blood changes. Within the last three years, the very constituency of the blood has changed, in European veins. But particularly in Germanic veins.

At the same time, we have brought it about ourselves – by a Ruhr occupation, by an English nullity, and by a German false will. We have done it ourselves. But apparently it was not to be helped.

Quos vult perdere Deus, dementat prius.

MEXICO AND NEW MEXICO

—

NEW MEXICO

Written December, 1928. *Survey Graphic*, May, 1931. *Phoenix*, 1936

SUPERFICIALLY, the world has become small and known. Poor little globe of earth, the tourists trot round you as easily as they trot round the Bois or round Central Park. There is no mystery left, we've been there, we've seen it, we know all about it. We've done the globe, and the globe is done.

This is quite true, superficially. On the superficies, horizontally, we've been everywhere and done everything, we know all about it. Yet the more we know, superficially, the less we penetrate, vertically. It's all very well skimming across the surface of the ocean, and saying you know all about the sea. There still remain the terrifying under-deeps, of which we have utterly no experience.

The same is true of land travel. We skim along, we get there, we see it all, we've done it all. And as a rule, we never once go through the curious film which railroads, ships, motor-cars, and hotels stretch over the surface of the whole earth. Peking is just the same as New York, with a few different things to look at; rather more Chinese about, etc. Poor creatures that we are, we crave for experience, yet we are like flies that crawl on the pure and transparent mucous-paper in which the world like a bon-bon is wrapped so carefully that we can never get at it, though we see it there all the time as we move about it, apparently in contact, yet actually as far removed as if it were the moon.

As a matter of fact, our great-grandfathers, who never went anywhere, in actuality had more experience of the world than we have, who have seen everything. When they listened to a lecture with lantern-slides, they really held their breath before the unknown, as they sat in the village school-room. We, bowling along in a rickshaw in Ceylon, say to ourselves: 'It's very much what you'd expect.' We really know it all.

We are mistaken. The know-it-all state of mind is just the result of being outside the mucous-paper wrapping of civilization. Underneath is everything we don't know and are afraid of knowing.

I realized this with shattering force when I went to New Mexico.

New Mexico, one of the United States, part of the U.S.A. New Mexico, the picturesque reservation and playground of the eastern states, very romantic, old Spanish, Red Indian, desert mesas, pueblos, cowboys, penitentes, all that film-stuff. Very nice, the great South-West, put on a sombrero and knot a red kerchief round your neck, to go out in the great free spaces!

That is New Mexico wrapped in the absolutely hygienic and shiny mucous-paper of our trite civilization. That is the New Mexico known to most of the Americans who know it at all. But break through the shiny sterilized wrapping, and actually *touch* the country, and you will never be the same again.

I think New Mexico was the greatest experience from the outside world that I have ever had. It certainly changed me for ever. Curious as it may sound, it was New Mexico that liberated me from the present era of civilization, the great era of material and mechanical development. Months spent in holy Kandy, in Ceylon, the holy of holies of southern Buddhism, had not touched the great psyche of materialism and idealism which dominated me. And years, even in the exquisite beauty of Sicily, right among the old Greek paganism that still lives there, had not shattered the essential Christianity on which my character was established. Australia was a sort of dream or trance, like being under a spell, the self remaining unchanged, so long as the trance did not last too long. Tahiti, in a mere glimpse, repelled me: and so did California, after a stay of a few weeks. There seemed a strange brutality in the spirit of the western coast and I felt: O, let me get away!

But the moment I saw the brilliant, proud morning shine high up over the deserts of Santa Fe, something stood still in my soul, and I started to attend. There was a certain magnificence in the high-up day, a certain eagle-like royalty, so different from the equally pure, equally pristine and lovely morning of Australia, which is so soft, so utterly pure in its softness, and betrayed by green parrots flying. But in the lovely morning of Australia one went into a dream. In the magnificent fierce morning of New Mexico one sprang awake, a new part of the soul woke up suddenly and the old world gave way to a new.

There are all kinds of beauty in the world, thank God, though ugliness is homogeneous. How lovely is Sicily, with Calabria across the sea like an opal, and Etna with her snow in a world above and beyond! How lovely is Tuscany, with little red tulips wild among the corn: or bluebells at dusk in England, or mimosa in clouds of pure yellow among the grey-green dun foliage of Australia, under a soft, blue, unbreathed sky! But for a *greatness* of beauty I have never experienced anything like New Mexico. All those mornings when I went with a hoe along the ditch to the Cañon, at the ranch, and stood, in the fierce, proud silence of the Rockies, on their foothills, to look far over the desert to the blue mountains away in Arizona, blue as chalcedony, with the sage-brush desert sweeping grey-blue in between, dotted with tiny cube-crystals of houses, the vast amphitheatre of lofty, indomitable desert, sweeping round to the ponderous Sangre de Cristo mountains on the east, and coming up flush at the pine-dotted foot-hills of the Rockies! What splendour! Only the tawny eagle could really sail out into the splendour of it all. Leo Stein once wrote to me: It is the most aesthetically-satisfying landscape I know. To me it was much more than that. It had a splendid silent terror, and a vast far-and-wide magnificence which made it way beyond mere aesthetic appreciation. Never is the light more pure and overweening than there, arching with a royalty almost cruel over the hollow, uptilted world. For it is curious that the land which has produced modern political democracy at its highest pitch should give one the greatest sense of overweening, terrible proudness and mercilessness: but so beautiful, God! so beautiful! Those that have spent morning after morning alone there pitched among the pines above the great proud world of desert will know, almost unbearably how beautiful it is, how clear and unquestioned is the might of the day. Just day itself is tremendous there. It is so easy to understand that the Aztecs gave hearts of men to the sun. For the sun is not merely hot or scorching, not at all. It is of a brilliant and unchallengeable purity and haughty serenity which would make one sacrifice the heart to it. Ah, yes, in New Mexico the heart is sacrificed to the sun, and the human being is left stark, heartless, but undauntedly religious.

And that was the second revelation out there. I had looked over all the world for something that would strike *me* as religious. The simple piety of some English people, the semi-pagan mystery of some Catholics in southern Italy, the intensity of some Bavarian peasants, the semi-ecstasy of Buddhists or Brahmins: all this had seemed religious all right, as far as the parties concerned were involved, but it didn't involve me. I looked on at their religiousness from the outside. For it is still harder to feel religion at will than to love at will.

I had seen what I felt was a hint of wild religion in the so-called devil dances of a group of naked villagers from the far-remote jungle in Ceylon, dancing at midnight under the torches, glittering wet with sweat on their dark bodies as if they had been gilded, at the celebration of the Pera-hera, in Kandy, given to the Prince of Wales. And the utter dark absorption of these naked men, as they danced with their knees wide apart, suddenly affected me with a *sense* of religion. I *felt* religion for a moment. For religion is an experience, an uncontrollable sensual experience, even more so than love: I use sensual to mean an experience deep down in the senses, inexplicable and inscrutable.

But this experience was fleeting, gone in the curious turmoil of the Pera-hera, and I had no permanent feeling of religion till I came to New Mexico and penetrated into the old human race-experience there. It is curious that it should be in

America, of all places, that a European should really experience religion, after touching the old Mediterranean and the East. It is curious that one should get a sense of living religion from the Red Indians, having failed to get it from Hindus or Sicilian Catholics or Cingalese.

Let me make a reservation. I don't stand up to praise the Red Indian as he reveals himself in contact with white civilization. From that angle, I am forced to admit that he *may* be thoroughly objectionable. Even my small experience knows it. But also I know he *may* be thoroughly nice, even in his dealings with white men. It's a question of individuals, a good deal, on both sides.

But in this article, I don't want to deal with the everyday or superficial aspect of New Mexico, outside the mucous-paper wrapping. I *want* to go beneath the surface. But therefore the American Indian in his behaviour as an American citizen doesn't really concern me. What concerns me is what he is – or what he seems to me to be, in his ancient, ancient race-self and religious-self.

For the Red Indian seems to me much older than Greeks or Hindus or any Europeans or even Egyptians. The Red Indian, as a civilized and truly religious man, civilized beyond taboo and totem, as he is in the south, is religious in perhaps the oldest sense, and deepest, of the word. That is to say, he is a remnant of the most deeply religious race still living. So it seems to me.

But again let me protect myself. The Indian who sells you baskets on Albuquerque station or who slinks around Taos plaza may be an utter waster and an indescribably low dog. Personally he may be even less religious than a New York sneak-thief. He may have broken with his tribe, or his tribe itself may have collapsed finally from its old religious integrity, and ceased, really, to exist. Then he is only fit for rapid absorption into white civilization, which must make the best of him.

But while a tribe retains its religion and keeps up its religious practices, and while any member of the tribe shares in those practices, then there is a tribal integrity and a living tradition going back far beyond the birth of Christ, beyond the pyramids, beyond Moses. A vast old religion which once swayed the earth lingers in unbroken practice there in New Mexico, older, perhaps, than anything in the world save Australian aboriginal taboo and totem, and that is not yet religion.

You can feel it, the atmosphere of it, around the pueblos. Not, of course, when the place is crowded with sight-seers and motor-cars. But go to Taos pueblo on some brilliant snowy morning and see the white figure on the roof: or come riding through at dusk on some windy evening, when the black skirts of the silent women blow around the white wide boots, and you will feel the old, old roots of human consciousness still reaching down to depths we know nothing of: and of which, only too often, we are jealous. It seems it will not be long before the pueblos are uprooted.

But never shall I forget watching the dancers, the men with the fox-skin swaying down from their buttocks, file out at San Geronimo, and the women with seed rattles following. The long, streaming, glistening black hair of the men. Even in ancient Crete long hair was sacred in a man, as it is still in the Indians. Never shall I forget the utter absorption of the dance, so quiet, so steadily, timelessly rhythmic, and silent, with the ceaseless down-tread, always to the earth's centre, the very reverse of the upflow of Dionysiac or Christian ecstasy. Never shall I forget the deep singing of the men at the drum, swelling and sinking, the deepest sound I have heard in all my life, deeper than thunder, deeper than the sound of the Pacific Ocean, deeper than the roar of a deep waterfall: the wonderful deep sound of men calling to the unspeakable depths.

Never shall I forget coming into the little pueblo of San Felipe one sunny morning in spring, unexpectedly, when bloom was on the trees in the perfect little pueblo more old, more utterly peaceful and idyllic than anything in Theocritus, and seeing a little casual dance. Not impressive as a spectacle, only, to me, profoundly moving because of the truly terrifying religious absorption of it.

Never shall I forget the Christmas dances at Taos, twilight, snow, the darkness coming over the great wintry mountains and the lonely pueblo, then suddenly, again, like dark calling to dark, the deep Indian cluster-singing around the drum, wild and awful, suddenly rousing on the last dusk as the procession starts. And then the bonfires leaping suddenly in pure spurts of high flame, columns of sudden flame forming an alley for the procession.

Never shall I forget the kiva of birch-trees, away in the Apache country, in Arizona this time, the tepees and flickering fires, the neighing of horses unseen under the huge dark night, and the Apaches all abroad, in their silent moccasined feet: and in the kiva, beyond a little fire, the old man reciting, reciting in the unknown Apache speech, in the strange wild Indian voice that re-echoes away back to before the Flood, reciting apparently the traditions and legends of the tribes, going on and on, while the young men, the *braves* of to-day wandered in, listened, and wandered away again, overcome with the power and majesty of that utterly old tribal voice, yet uneasy with their half-adherence to the modern civilization, the two things in contact. And one of these *braves* shoved his face under my hat, in the night, and stared with his glittering eyes close to mine. He'd have killed me then and there, had he dared. He didn't dare: and I knew it: and he knew it.

Never shall I forget the Indian races, when the young men, even the boys, run naked, smeared with white earth and stuck with bits of eagle fluff for the swiftness of the heavens, and the old men brush them with eagle feathers, to give them power. And they run in the strange hurling fashion of the primitive world, hurled forward, not making speed deliberately. And the race is not for victory. It is not a contest. There is no competition. It is a great cumulative effort. The tribe this day is adding up its male energy and exerting it to the utmost – for what? To get power, to get strength: to come, by sheer cumulative, hurling effort of the bodies of men, into contact with the great cosmic source of vitality which gives strength, power, energy to the men who can grasp it, energy for the zeal of attainment.

It was a vast old religion, greater than anything we know: more starkly and nakedly religious. There is no God, no conception of a god. All is god. But it is not the pantheism we are accustomed to, which expresses itself as 'God is everywhere, God is in everything'. In the oldest religion, everything was alive, not supernaturally but naturally alive. There were only deeper and deeper streams of life, vibrations of life more and more vast. So rocks were alive, but a mountain had a deeper, vaster life than a rock, and it was much harder for a man to bring his spirit, or his energy, into contact with the life of the mountain, and so draw strength from the mountain, as from a great standing well of life, than it was to come into contact with the rock. And he had to put forth a great religious effort. For the whole life-effort of man was to get his life into contact with the elemental life of the cosmos, mountain-life, cloud-life, thunder-life, air-life, earth-life, sun-life. To come into immediate *felt* contact, and so derive energy, power, and a dark sort of joy. This effort into sheer naked contact, *without an intermediary or mediator*, is the root meaning of religion, and at the sacred races the runners hurled themselves in a terrible cumulative effort, through the air, to come at last into naked contact with the very life of the air, which is the life of the clouds, and so of the rain.

It was a vast and pure religion, without idols or images, even mental ones. It is the oldest religion, a cosmic religion the same for all peoples, not broken up into specific gods or saviours or systems. It is the religion which precedes the god-concept, and is therefore greater and deeper than any god-religion.

And it lingers still, for a little while, in New Mexico: but long enough to have been a revelation to me. And the Indian, however objectionable he may be on occasion, has still some of the strange beauty and pathos of the religion that brought him forth and is now shedding him away into oblivion. When Trinidad, the Indian boy, and I planted corn at the ranch, my soul paused to see his brown hands softly moving the earth over the maize in pure ritual. He was back in his old religious self, and the ages stood still. Ten minutes later he was making a fool of himself with the horses. Horses were never part of the Indian's religious life, never would be. He hasn't a tithe of the feeling for them that he has for a bear, for example. So horses don't like Indians.

But there it is: the newest democracy ousting the oldest religion! And once the oldest religion is ousted, one feels the democracy and all its paraphernalia will collapse, and the oldest religion, which comes down to us from man's pre-war days, will start again. The sky-scraper will scatter on the winds like thistledown, and the genuine America, the America of New Mexico, will start on its course again. This is an interregnum.

INDIANS AND AN ENGLISHMAN

Written autumn, 1922. *Dial*, February, 1923.
***Phoenix*, 1936**

SUPPOSING one fell on to the moon, and found them talking English, it would be something the same as falling out of the open world plump down here in the middle of America. 'Here' means New Mexico, the Southwest, wild and woolly and artistic and sage-brush desert.

It is all rather like comic opera played with solemn intensity. All the wildness and woolliness and westernity and motor-cars and art and sage and savage are so mixed up, so incongruous, that it is a farce, and everybody knows it. But they refuse to play it as farce. The wild and woolly section insists on being heavily dramatic, bold and bad on purpose; the art insists on being real American and artistic; motor-cars insist on being thrilled, moved to the marrow; highbrows insist on being ecstatic; Mexicans insist on being Mexicans, squeezing the last black drop of macabre joy out of life; and Indians wind themselves in white cotton sheets like Hamlet's father's ghost, with a lurking smile.

And here am I, a lone lorn Englishman, tumbled out of the known world of the British Empire on to this stage: for it persists in seeming like a stage to me, and not like the proper world.

Whatever makes a proper world, I don't know. But surely two elements are necessary: a common purpose and a common sympathy. I can't see any common purpose. The Indians and Mexicans don't even seem very keen on dollars. That full moon of a silver dollar doesn't strike me as overwhelmingly hypnotic out here. As for a common sympathy or understanding, that's beyond imagining. West is wild and woolly and bad-on-purpose; commerce is a little self-conscious about its own pioneering importance – Pioneers! O Pioneers! – highbrow is bent on getting to the bottom of everything and saving the lost soul down there in the depths; Mexican is bent on being Mexican and not gringo; and the Indian is all the things that all the others aren't. And so everybody smirks at everybody else, and says tacitly: 'Go on; you do your little stunt, and I'll do mine,' and they're like the various troupes in a circus, all performing at once, with nobody for Master of Ceremonies.

It seems to me, in this country, everything is taken so damn seriously that nothing remains serious. Nothing is so farcical as insistent drama. Everybody is lurkingly conscious of this. Each section or troupe is quite willing to admit that all the other sections are buffoon stunts. But it itself is the real thing, solemnly bad in its badness, good in its goodness, wild in its wildness, woolly in its woolliness, arty in its artiness, deep in its depths – in a word, earnest.

In such a masquerade of earnestness, a bewildered straggler out of the far-flung British Empire, myself! Don't let me for a moment pretend to *know* anything. I know less than nothing. I simply gasp like a bumpkin in a circus ring, with the horse-lady leaping over my head, the Apache war-whooping in my ear, the Mexican staggering under crosses and bumping me as he goes by, the artist whirling colours across my dazzled vision, the highbrows solemnly declaiming at me from all the cross-roads. If, dear reader, you, being the audience who has paid to come in, feel that you must take up an attitude to me, let it be one of amused pity.

One has to take sides. First, one must be either pro-Mexican or pro-Indian; then, either art or intellect; then, Republican or Democrat; and so on. But as for me, poor lamb, if I bleat at all in the circus ring, it will be my own shorn lonely bleat of a lamb who's lost his mother.

The first Indians I really saw were the Apaches in the Apache Reservation of this state. We drove in a motor-car, across desert and mesa, down cañons and up divides and along arroyos and so forth, two days, till at afternoon our two Indian men ran the car aside from the trail and sat under the pine tree to comb their long black hair and roll it into the two roll-plaits that hang in front of their shoulders, and put on all their silver-and-turquoise jewellery and their best blankets: because we were nearly there. On the trail were horsemen passing, and wagons with Ute Indians and Navajos.

'*De donde viene Usted?*' . . .

We came at dusk from the high shallows and saw on a low crest the points of Indian tents, the tepees, and smoke, and silhouettes of tethered horses and blanketed figures moving. In the shadow a rider was following a flock of white goats that flowed like water. The car ran to the top of the crest, and there was a hollow basin with a lake in the distance, pale in the dying light. And this shallow upland basin, dotted with Indian tents, and the fires flickering in front, and crouching blanketed figures, and horsemen crossing the dusk from tent to tent, horsemen in big steeple hats sitting glued on their ponies, and bells tinkling, and dogs yapping, and tilted wagons trailing in on the trail below, and a smell of wood-smoke and of cooking, and wagons coming in from far off, and tents pricking on the ridge of the round *vallum*, and horsemen dipping down and emerging again, and more red sparks of fires glittering, and crouching bundles of women's figures squatting at a fire before a little tent made of boughs, and little girls in full petticoats hovering, and wild barefoot boys throwing bones at thin-tailed dogs, and tents away in the distance, in the growing dark, on the slopes, and the trail crossing the floor of the hollows in the low dusk.

There you had it all, as in the hollow of your hand. And to my heart, born in England and kindled with Fenimore Cooper, it wasn't the wild and woolly West, it was the nomad nations gathering still in the continent of hemlock trees and prairies. The Apaches came and talked to us, in their steeple black hats and plaits wrapped with beaver fur, and their silver and beads and turquoise. Some talked strong American, and some talked only Spanish. And they had strange lines in their faces.

The two kivas, the rings of cut aspen trees stuck in the ground like the walls of a big hut of living trees, were on the plain, at either end of the race-track. And as the sun went down, the drums began to beat, the drums with their strong-weak, strong-weak pulse that beat on the plasm of one's tissue. The car slid down to the south kiva. Two elderly men held the drum, and danced the pàt-pat, pàt-pat quick beat on flat feet, like birds that move from the feet only, and sang with wide mouths: Hie! Hie! Hie! Hy-a! Hy-a! Hy-a! Hie! Hie! Ay-away-away-a! Strange dark faces with wide, shouting mouths and rows of small, close-set teeth, and strange lines on the faces, part ecstasy, part mockery, part humorous, part devilish, and the strange, calling, summoning sound in a wild song-shout, to the thud-thud of the drum. Answer of the same from the other kiva, as of a challenge accepted. And from the gathering darkness around, men drifting slowly in, each carrying an aspen twig, each joining to cluster close in two rows upon the drum, holding each his aspen twig inwards, their faces all together, mouths all open in the song-shout, and all of them all the time going on the two feet, pàt-pat, pàt-pat, to the thud-thud of the drum and the strange, plangent yell of the chant, edging inch by inch, pàt-pat, pàt-pat, pàt-pat, sideways in a cluster along the track, towards the distant cluster of the challengers from the other kiva, who were sing-shouting and edging onwards, sideways, in the dusk, their faces all together, their leaves all inwards, towards the drum, and their feet going pàt-pat, pàt-pat on the dust, with their buttocks stuck out a little, faces all inwards, shouting open-mouthed to the drum, and half laughing, half mocking, half devilment, half fun. *Hie! Hie! Hie! Hie-away-awaya!* The strange yell, song, shout rising so lonely in the dusk, as if pine trees could suddenly, shaggily sing. Almost a pre-animal sound, full of triumph in life, and devilment against other life, and mockery, and humorousness, and the pàt-pat, pàt-pat of the rhythm. Sometimes more youths coming up, and as they draw near laughing, they give the war-whoop, like a turkey giving a startled shriek and then gobble-gobbling with laughter – Ugh! – the shriek half laughter, then the gobble-gobble-gobble like a great demoniac chuckle. Then chuckle in the war-whoop. – They produce the gobble from the deeps of the stomach, and say it makes them feel good.

Listening, an acute sadness, and a nostalgia, unbearably

yearning for something, and a sickness of the soul came over me. The gobble-gobble chuckle in the whoop surprised me in my very tissues. Then I got used to it, and could hear in it the humanness, the playfulness, and then, beyond that, the mockery and the diabolical, pre-human, pine-tree fun of cutting dusky throats and letting the blood spurt out unconfined. Gobble-agobble-agobble, the unconfined loose blood, gobble, agobble, the dead, mutilated lump, gobble-agobble-agobble, the fun, the greatest man-fun. The war-whoop!

So I felt. I may have been all wrong, and other folk may feel much more natural and reasonable things. But so I felt. And the sadness and the nostalgia of the song-calling, and the resinous continent of pine trees and turkeys, the feet of birds treading a dance, far off, when man was dusky and not individualized.

I am no ethnologist. The point is, what is the feeling that passes from an Indian to me, when we meet? We are both men, but how do we feel together? I shall never forget that first evening when I first came into contact with Red Men, away in the Apache country. It was not what I had thought it would be. It was something of a shock. Again something in my soul broke down, letting in a bitterer dark, a pungent awakening to the lost past, old darkness, new terror, new root-griefs, old root-richnesses.

The Apaches have a cult of water-hatred; they never wash flesh or rag. So never in my life have I smelt such an unbearable sulphur-human smell as comes from them when they cluster; a smell that takes the breath from the nostrils.

We drove the car away half a mile or more, back from the Apache hollow, to a lonely ridge, where we pitched camp under pine trees. Our two Indians made the fire, dragged in wood, then wrapped themselves in their best blankets and went off to the tepees of their friends. The night was cold and starry.

After supper I wrapped myself in a red serape up to the nose, and went down alone to the Apache encampment. It is good, on a chilly night in a strange country, to be wrapped almost to the eyes in a good Navajo blanket. Then you feel warm inside yourself, and as good as invisible, and the dark air thick with enemies. So I stumbled on, startling the hobbled horses that jerked aside from me. Reaching the rim-crest one saw many fires burning in red spots round the slopes of the hollow, and against the fires many crouching figures. Dogs barked, a baby cried from a bough shelter, there was a queer low crackle of voices. So I stumbled alone over the ditches and past the tents, down to the kiva. Just near was a shelter with a big fire in front, and a man, an Indian, selling drinks, no doubt Budweiser beer and grape-juice, non-intoxicants. Cowboys in chaps and big hats were drinking too, and one screechy, ungentle cowgirl in khaki. So I went on in the dark up the opposite slope. The dark Indians passing in the night peered at me. The air was full of a sort of sportiveness, playfulness, that had a jeering, malevolent vibration in it, to my fancy. As if this play were another kind of harmless-harmful welfare, overbearing. Just the antithesis of what I understand by jolliness: ridicule. Comic sort of bullying. No jolly, free laughter. Yet a great deal of laughter. But with a sort of gibe in it.

This, of course, may just be the limitation of my European fancy. But that was my feeling. One felt a stress of will, of human wills, in the dark air, gibing even in the comic laughter. And a sort of unconscious animosity.

Again a sound of a drum down below, so again I stumbled down to the kiva. A bunch of young men were clustered – seven or eight round a drum, and standing with their faces together, loudly and mockingly singing the song-yells, some of them treading the pàt-pat, some not bothering. Just behind was the blazing fire and the open shelter of the drink-tent, with Indians in tall black hats and long plaits in front of their shoulders, and bead-braided waistcoats, and hands in their pockets; some swathed in sheets, some in brilliant blankets, and all grinning, laughing. The cowboys with big spurs still there, horses' bridles trailing, and cowgirl screeching her laugh. One felt an inevitable silent gibing, animosity in each group, one for the other. At the same time, an absolute avoidance of any evidence of this.

The young men round the drum died out and started again. As they died out, the strange uplifted voice in the kiva was heard. It seemed to me the outside drumming and singing served to cover the voice within the kiva.

The kiva of young green trees was just near, two paces only. On the ground outside, boughs and twigs were strewn round to prevent anyone's coming close to the enclosure. Within was the firelight. And one could see through the green of the leaf-screen, men round a fire inside there, and one old man, the same old man always facing the open entrance, the fire between him and it. Other Indians sat in a circle, of which he was the key. The old man had his dark face lifted, his head bare, his two plaits falling on his shoulders. His close-shutting Indian lips were drawn open, his eyes were as if half-veiled, as he went on and on, on and on, in a distinct, plangent, recitative voice, male and yet strangely far-off and plaintive, reciting, reciting, reciting like a somnambulist, telling, no doubt, the history of the tribe interwoven with the gods. Other Apaches sat round the fire. Those nearest the old teller were stationary, though one chewed gum all the time and one ate bread-cake and others lit cigarettes. Those nearer the entrance rose after a time, restless. At first some strolled in, stood a minute, then strolled out, desultory. But as the night went on, the ring round the fire inside the wall of green young trees was complete, all squatting on the ground, the old man with the lifted face and parted lips and half-unseeing eyes going on and on, across the fire. Some men stood lounging with the half self-conscious ease of the Indian behind the seated men. They lit cigarettes. Some drifted out. Another filtered in. I stood wrapped in my blanket in the cold night, at some little distance from the entrance, looking on.

A big young Indian came and pushed his face under my hat to see who or what I was.

'*Buenos!*'

'*Buenos!*'

'*Qué quiere?*'

'*No hablo español.*'

'Oh, only English, eh? You can't come in here.'

'I don't want to.'

'This Indian church.'

'Is it?'

'I don't let people come, only Apache, only Indian.'

'You keep watch?'

'I keep watch, yes; Indian Church, eh?'

'And the old man preaches?'

'Yes, he preaches.'

After which I stood quite still and uncommunicative. He waited for a further development. There was none. So, after giving me another look, he went to talk to other Indians, *sotto voce*, by the door. The circle was complete; groups stood behind the squatting ring, some men were huddled in blankets, some sitting just in trousers and shirt, in the warmth near the fire, some wrapped close in white cotton sheets. The firelight shone on the dark, unconcerned faces of the listeners, as they chewed gum, or ate bread, or smoked a cigarette. Some had big silver ear-rings swinging, and necklaces of turquoise. Some had waistcoats all bead braids. Some wore store shirts and store trousers, like Americans. From time to time some man pushed another piece of wood on the fire.

They seemed to be paying no attention; it all had a very perfunctory appearance. But they kept silent, and the voice of the old reciter went on blindly, from his lifted, bronze mask of a face with its wide-opened lips. They furl back their teeth as they speak, and they use a sort of resonant tenor voice that has a plangent, half-sad twanging sound, vibrating deep from the chest. The old man went on and on, for hours, in that urgent, far-off voice. His hair was grey, and parted, and his two round plaits hung in front of his shoulders on his shirt. From his ears dangled pieces of blue turquoise, tied with string. An old green blanket was wrapped round above his waist, and his feet in old moccasins were crossed before the fire. There was a deep pathos, for me, in the old, mask-like, virile figure, with its metallic courage of persistence, old memory, and its twanging male voice. So far, so great a memory. So dauntless a persistence in the piece of living red earth seated on the naked earth, before the fire; this old, bronze-resonant man with his eyes as if glazed in old memory, and his voice issuing in endless plangent monotony from the wide, unfurled mouth.

And the young men, who chewed chewing-gum and listened without listening. The voice no doubt registered on their under-consciousness, as they looked around, and lit a cigarette, and spat sometimes aside. With their day-consciousness they hardly attended.

As for me, standing outside, beyond the open entrance, I was no enemy of theirs; far from it. The voice out of the far-off was not for my ears. Its language was unknown to me. And I did not wish to know. It was enough to hear the sound issuing plangent from the bristling darkness of the far past, to see the bronze mask of the face lifted, the white, small, close-packed teeth showing all the time. It was not for me, and I knew it. Nor had I any curiosity to understand it. The soul is as old as the oldest day, and has its own hushed echoes, its far-off tribal understandings sunk and incorporated. We do not need to live the past over again. Our darkest tissues are twisted in this old tribal experience, our warmest blood came out of the old tribal fire. And they vibrate still in answer, our blood, our tissue. But me, the conscious me, I have gone a long road since then. And as I look back, like memory terrible as bloodshed, the dark faces round the fire in the night, and one blood beating in me and them. But I don't want to go back to them, ah, never. I never want to deny them or break with them. But there is no going back. Always onward, still further. The great devious onward-flowing stream of conscious human blood. From them to me, and from me on.

I don't want to live again the tribal mysteries my blood has lived long since. I don't want to know as I have known, in the tribal exclusiveness. But every drop of me trembles still alive to the old sound, every thread in my body quivers to the frenzy of the old mystery. I know my derivation. I was born of no virgin, of no Holy Ghost. Ah, no, these old men telling the tribal tale were my fathers. I have a dark-faced, bronze-voiced father far back in the resinous ages. My mother was no virgin. She lay in her hour with this dusky-lipped tribe-father. And I have not forgotten him. But he, like many an old father with a changeling son, he would like to deny me. But I stand on the far edge of their firelight, and am neither denied nor accepted. My way is my own, old red father: I can't cluster at the drum any more.

JUST BACK FROM THE SNAKE DANCE – TIRED OUT

Written August, 1924. *The Laughing Horse*, September, 1924. *Letters*, 1932

ONE wonders what one came for – what all those people went for. The Hopi country is hideous – a clayey pale-grey desert with death-grey *mesas* sticking up like broken pieces of ancient dry grey bread. And the hell of a lumpy trail for forty miles. Yet car after car lurched and bobbed and ducked across the dismalness, on Sunday afternoon.

The Hopi country is some forty miles across, and three stale *mesas* jut up in its desert. The dance was on the last *mesa*, and on the furthest brim of the last *mesa*, in Hotevilla. The various Hopi villages are like broken edges of bread crust, utterly grey and arid, on top of these *mesas*: and so you pass them: first Walpi: then unseen Chimopova: then Oraibi on the last *mesa*: and beyond Oraibi, on the same *mesa*, but on a still higher level of grey rag-rock, and away at the western brim, is Hotevilla.

The *pueblos* of little grey houses are largely in ruin, dry raggy bits of disheartening ruin. One wonders what dire necessity or what Cain-like stubbornness drove the Hopis to these dismal grey heights and extremities. Anyhow, once they got there, there was evidently no going back. But the *pueblos* are mostly ruin. And even then, very small.

Hotevilla is a scrap of a place with a plaza no bigger than a fair-sized back-yard: and the chief house on the square a ruin. But into this plaza finally three thousand onlookers piled. A mile from the village was improvised the official camping ground, like a corral with hundreds of black motor cars. Across the death-grey desert, bump and lurch, came strings of more black cars, like a funeral *cortège*. Till everybody had come – about three thousand bodies.

And all these bodies piled in the oblong plaza, on the roofs, in the ruined windows, and thick around on the sandy floor, under the old walls: a great crowd. There were Americans of all sorts, wild west and tame west, American women in pants, an extraordinary assortment of female breeches: and at least two women in skirts, relics of the last era. There were Navajo women in full skirts and velvet bodices: there were Hopi women in bright shawls: a negress in a low-cut black blouse and a black sailor hat: various half-breeds: and all the men to match. The ruined house had two wide square window-holes: in the one was forced an apparently naked young lady with a little black hat on. She laid her naked handsome arm like a white anaconda along the sill, and posed as Queen Semiramis seated and waiting. Behind her, the heads of various Americans to match: perhaps movie people. In the next window-hole, a poppy-show of Indian women in coloured shawls and glistening long black fringe above their conventionally demure eyes. Two windows to the west!

And what had they all come to see? come so far, over so weary a way to camp uncomfortably? To see a little bit of a snake dance in a plaza no bigger than a back-yard? Light grey-daubed antelope priests (so called) and a dozen black-daubed snake-priests (so called). No drums, no pageantry. A hollow muttering. And then one of the snake-priests hopping slowly round with the neck of a pale, bird-like snake nipped between his teeth, while six elder priests dusted the six younger, snake-adorned priests with prayer feathers on the shoulders, hopping behind like a children's game. Like a children's game – Old Roger is dead and is low in his grave! After a few little rounds, the man set his snake on the sand, and away it steered, towards the massed spectators sitting around: and after it came a snake priest with a snake stick, picked it up with a flourish from the shrinking crowd, and handed it to an antelope priest in the background. The six young men renewed their snake as the eagle his youth – sometimes the youngest, a boy of fourteen or so, had a rattlesnake ornamentally dropping from his teeth, sometimes a racer, a thin whip snake, sometimes a heavier bull-snake, which wrapped its long end round his knee like a garter – till he calmly undid it. More snakes, till the priests at the back had little armfuls, like armfuls of silk stockings that were going to hang on the line to dry.

When all the snakes had had their little ride in a man's mouth, and had made their little excursion towards the crowd, they were all gathered, like a real lot of wet silk stockings – say forty – or thirty – and left to wriggle all together for a minute in meal, corn-meal, that the women of the *pueblo* had laid down on the sand of the plaza. Then, hey presto! – they were snatched up like fallen washing, and the two priests ran away with them westward, down the *mesa*, to set them free among the rocks, at the snake-shrine (so called).

And it was over. Navajos began to ride to the sunset, black motor-cars began to scuttle with their backs to the light. It was over.

And what had we come to see, all of us? Men with snakes in their mouths, like a circus? Nice clean snakes, all washed and cold-creamed by the priests (so called). Like wet pale silk stockings. Snakes with little bird-like heads, that bit nobody, but looked more harmless than doves? And funny men with blackened faces and whitened jaws, like a corpse band?

A show? But it was a tiny little show, for all that distance.

Just a show! The south-west is the great playground of the white American. The desert isn't good for anything else. But it does make a fine national playground. And the Indian, with his long hair and his bits of pottery and blankets and clumsy home-made trinkets, he's a wonderful live toy to play with. More fun than keeping rabbits, and just as harmless. Wonderful, really, hopping round with a snake in his mouth. Lots of fun! Oh, the wild west is lots of fun: the Land of Enchantment. Like being right inside the circus-ring: lots of sand, and painted savages jabbering, and snakes and all that. Come on, boys! Lots of fun! The great south-west, the national circus-ground. Come on, boys; we've every bit as much right to it as anybody else. Lots of fun!

As for the hopping Indian with his queer muttering gibberish and his dangling snake – why, he sure is cute! He says he's dancing to make his corn grow. What price irrigation, Jimmy? He says the snakes are emissaries to his rain god, to tell him to send rain to the corn on the Hopi Reservation, so the Hopis will have lots of corn-meal. What price a spell of work on the railway, Jimmy? Get all the corn-meal you want with two dollars a day, anyhow.

But oh, dry up! Let every man have his own religion. And if there wasn't any snake dance we couldn't come to see it. Miss lots of fun. Good old Hopi, he sure is cute with a rattler between his teeth. You sure should see him, boy. If you don't, you miss a lot.

CORASMIN AND THE PARROTS

Written late 1924. *Adelphi*, 1925. *Mornings in Mexico*, 1927

ONE says Mexico: one means, after all, one little town away South in the Republic: and in this little town, one rather crumbly adobe house built round two sides of a garden *patio*: and of this house, one spot on the deep, shady verandah facing inwards to the trees, where there are an onyx table and three rocking-chairs and one little wooden chair, a pot with carnations, and a person with a pen. We talk so grandly, in capital letters, about Morning in Mexico. All it amounts to is one little individual looking at a bit of sky and trees, then looking down at the page of his exercise book.

It is a pity we don't always remember this. When books come out with grand titles, like *The Future of America* or *The European Situation*, it's a pity we don't immediately visualize a thin or a fat person, in a chair or in bed, dictating to a bob-haired stenographer or making little marks on paper with a fountain pen.

Still, it is morning, and it is Mexico. The sun shines. But then, during the winter, it always shines. It is pleasant to sit out of doors and write, just fresh enough, and just warm enough. But then it is Christmas next week, so it ought to be just right.

There is a little smell of carnations, because they are the nearest thing. And there is a resinous smell of ocote wood, and a smell of coffee, and a faint smell of leaves, and of Morning, and even of Mexico. Because when all is said and done, Mexico has a faint, physical scent of her own, as each human being has. And this is a curious, inexplicable scent, in which there are resin and perspiration and sun-burned earth and urine among other things.

And cocks are still crowing. The little mill where the natives have their corn ground is puffing rather languidly. And because some women are talking in the entrance-way, the two tame parrots in the trees have started to whistle.

The parrots, even when I don't listen to them, have an extraordinary effect on me. They make my diaphragm convulse with little laughs, almost mechanically. They are a quite commonplace pair of green birds, with bits of bluey red, and round, disillusioned eyes, and heavy, overhanging noses. But they listen intently. And they reproduce. The pair whistle now like Rosalino, who is sweeping the *patio* with a twig broom; and yet it is so unlike him to be whistling full vent, when any of us is around, that one looks at him to see. And the moment one sees him, with his black head bent rather drooping and hidden as he sweeps, one laughs.

The parrots whistle exactly like Rosalino, only a little more so. And this little-more-so is extremely, sardonically funny. With their sad old long-jowled faces and their flat disillusioned eyes, they reproduce Rosalino and a little-more-so without moving a muscle. And Rosalino, sweeping the *patio* with his twig broom, scraping the tittering leaves into little heaps, covers himself more and more with the cloud of his own obscurity. He doesn't rebel. He is powerless. Up goes the wild, sliding Indian whistle into the morning, very powerful, with an immense energy seeming to drive behind it. And always, always a little more than lifelike.

Then they break off into a cackling chatter, and one knows they are shifting their clumsy legs, perhaps hanging on with their beaks and clutching with their cold, slow claws, to climb to a higher bough, like rather raggedy green buds climbing to the sun. And suddenly, the penetrating, demonish mocking voices:

'*Perro!* Oh, *Perro! Perr-rro!* Oh, *Perr-rro! Perro!*'

They are imitating somebody calling the dog. *Perro* means dog. But that any creature should be able to pour such a suave prussic-acid sarcasm over the voice of a human being calling a dog, is incredible. One's diaphragm chuckles involuntarily. And one thinks: *Is it possible?* Is it possible that we are so absolutely, so innocently, so *ab ovo* ridiculous?

And not only is it possible, it is patent. We cover our heads in confusion.

Now they are yapping like a dog: exactly like Corasmin. Corasmin is a little fat, curly white dog who was lying in the sun a minute ago, and has now come into the verandah shade, walking with slow resignation, to lie against the wall near by my chair. 'Yap-yap-yap! Wouf! Wouf! Yap-yapyapyap!!' go the parrots, exactly like Corasmin when some stranger comes into the *zaguan*, Corasmin and a little-more-so.

With a grin on my face I look down at Corasmin. And with a silent, abashed resignation in his yellow eyes, Corasmin looks up at me, with a touch of reproach. His little white nose is sharp, and under his eyes there are dark marks, as under the eyes of one who has known much trouble. All day he does nothing but walk resignedly out of the sun, when the sun gets too hot, and out of the shade, when the shade gets too cool. And bite ineffectually in the region of his fleas.

Poor old Corasmin: he is only about six, but resigned, unspeakably resigned. Only not humble. He does not kiss the rod. He rises in spirit above it, letting his body lie.

'*Perro!* Oh, *Perr-rro! Perr-rro! Perr-rr-rro!*' shriek the parrots, with the strange penetrating, antediluvian malevolence that seems to make even the trees prick their ears. It is a sound that penetrates one straight at the diaphragm, belonging to the ages before brains were invented. And Corasmin pushes his sharp little nose into his bushy tail, closes his eyes because I am grinning, feigns to sleep; and then, in an orgasm of self-consciousness, starts up to bite in the region of his fleas.

'*Perr-ro! Perr-rro!*' And then a restrained, withheld sort of yapping. The fiendish rolling of the Spanish 'r', malevolence rippling out of all the vanished, spiteful aeons. And following it, the small, little-curly-dog sort of yapping. They can make their voices so devilishly small and futile, like a little curly dog. And follow it up with that ringing malevolence that swoops up the ladders of the sunbeams right to the stars, rolling the Spanish 'r'.

Corasmin slowly walks away from the verandah, his head drooped, and flings himself down in the sun. No! He gets up again, in an agony of self-control, and scratches the earth loose a little, to soften his lie. Then flings himself down again.

Invictus! The still-unconquered Corasmin! The sad little white curly pendulum oscillating ever slower between the shadow and the sun.

In the fell clutch of circumstance
I have not winced nor cried aloud
Under the bludgeonings of chance
My head is bloody, but unbowed.

But that is human bombast, and a little too ridiculous even for Corasmin. Poor old Corasmin's clear yellow eyes! He is going to be master of his own soul, under all the vitriol those parrots pour over him. But he's not going to throw out his chest in a real lust of self-pity. That belongs to the next cycle of evolution.

I wait for the day when the parrots will start throwing English at us, in the pit of our stomachs. They cock their heads and listen to our gabble. But so far they haven't got it. It puzzles them. Castilian, and Corasmin, and Rosalino come more natural.

Myself, I don't believe in evolution, like a long string hooked on to a First Cause, and being slowly twisted in unbroken continuity through the ages. I prefer to believe in what the Aztecs called Suns: that is, Worlds successively created and destroyed. The sun itself convulses, and the worlds go out like so many candles when somebody coughs in the middle of them. Then subtly, mysteriously, the sun convulses again, and a new set of worlds begins to flicker alight.

This pleases my fancy better than the long and weary twisting of the rope of Time and Evolution, hitched on to the revolving hook of a First Cause. I like to think of the whole show going bust, *bang!* – and nothing but bits of chaos flying about. Then out of the dark, new little twinklings reviving from nowhere, nohow.

I like to think of the world going pop! when the lizards had grown too unwieldy, and it was time they were taken down a peg or two. Then the little humming birds beginning to spark in the darkness, and a whole succession of birds shaking themselves clean of the dark matrix, flamingoes rising upon one leg like dawn commencing, parrots shrieking about midday, *almost* able to talk, then peacocks unfolding at evening like the night with stars. And apart from these little, pure birds, a lot of unwieldy skinny-necked monsters bigger than crocodiles, barging through the mosses; till it was time to put a stop to them. When someone mysteriously touched the button, and the sun went bang, with smithereens of birds bursting in all directions. Only a few parrots' eggs and peacocks' eggs and eggs of flamingoes snuggling in some safe nook, to hatch on the next Day, when the animals arose.

Up reared the elephant, and shook the mud off his back. The birds watched him in sheer stupefaction. What? *What in heaven's name is this wingless, beakless old perambulator?*

No good, oh birds! Curly, little white Corasmin ran yapping out of the undergrowth, the new undergrowth, till parrots, going white at the gills, flew off into the ancientest recesses. Then the terrific neighing of the wild horse was heard in the twilight for the first time, and the bellowing of lions through the night.

And the birds were sad. What is this? they said. A whole vast gamut of new noises. A universe of new voices.

Then the birds under the leaves hung their heads and were dumb. No good our making a sound, they said. We are superseded.

The great big, booming, half-naked birds were blown to smithereens. Only the real little feathery individuals hatched out again and remained. This was a consolation. The larks and warblers cheered up, and began to say their little say, out of the old 'Sun', to the new sun. But the peacock, and the turkey, and the raven, and the parrot above all, they could not get over it. Because, in the old days of the Sun of Birds, they had been the big guns. The parrot had been the old boss of the flock. He was so clever.

Now he was, so to speak, up a tree. Nor dare he come down, because of the toddling littly curly white Corasmin, and suchlike, down below. He felt absolutely bitter. That wingless, beakless, featherless, curly misshapen bird's nest of a Corasmin had usurped the face of the earth, waddling about, whereas his Grace, the heavy-nosed old Duke of a parrot, was forced to sit out of reach up a tree, dispossessed.

So, like the riff-raff up in the gallery at the theatre, aloft in the Paradiso of the vanished Sun, he began to whistle and jeer.

'*Yap-yap!*' said his new little lordship of a Corasmin. 'Ye Gods!' cried the parrot. 'Hear him forsooth! *Yap-yap!* he says! Could anything be more imbecile? Yap-yap! Oh, Sun of the Birds, hark at that! *Yap-yap-yap!* Perro! *Perro! Perr-rro!* Oh, *Perr-rr-rro!*'

The parrot had found his cue. Stiff-nosed, heavy-nosed old duke of the birds, he wasn't going to give in and sing a new song, like those fool brown thrushes and nightingales. Let them twitter and warble. The parrot was a gentleman of the old school. He was going to jeer now! Like an ineffectual old aristocrat.

'*Oh! Perr-rro! Perr-rro-o-o-o!*'

The Aztecs say there have been four Suns, and ours is the fifth. The first Sun, a tiger, or a jaguar, a night-spotted monster of rage, rose out of nowhere and swallowed it, with all its huge, mercifully forgotten insects along with it. The second Sun blew up in a great wind, that was when the big lizards must have collapsed. The third Sun burst in water, and drowned all the aimals that were considered unnecessary, together with the first attempts at animal men.

Out of the floods rose our own Sun, and little naked man.

'Hello!' said the old elephant. 'What's that noise?' And he pricked his ears, listening to a new voice on the face of the earth. The sound of man, and *words* for the first time. Terrible, unheard-of sound! The elephant dropped his tail and ran into the deep jungle, and there stood looking down his nose.

But little white curly Corasmin was fascinated. '*Come on! Perro! Perro!*' called the naked two-legged one. And Corasmin, fascinated, said to himself: 'Can't hold out against that name. Shall have to go!' so off he trotted, at the heels of the naked one. Then came the horse, then the elephant, spell-bound at being given a name. The other animals ran for their lives, and stood quaking.

In the dust, however, the snake, the oldest dethroned king of all, bit his tail once more and said to himself: *'Here's another! No end to these new lords of creation! But I'll bruise his heel! Just as I swallow the eggs of the parrot! and lick up the little Corasmin-pups.'*

And in the branches, the parrot said to himself: *'Hello! What's this new sort of half-bird? Why! he's got Corasmin trotting at his heels! Must be a new sort of boss! Let's listen to him! and see if I can't take him off.'*

Perr-rro! Perr-rr-rro-oo! Oh, *Perro!*

The parrot had hit it.

And the monkey, cleverest of creatures, cried with rage when he heard men speaking. '*Oh why couldn't I do it!*' he chattered. But no good, he belonged to the old Sun. So he sat and gibbered across the invisible gulf in time, which is the 'other dimension' that clever people gas about: calling it 'fourth dimension', as if you could measure it with a foot-rule, the same as the obedient other three dimensions.

If you come to think of it, when you look at the monkey you are looking straight into the other dimension. He's got length and breadth and height all right, and he's in the same universe of Space and Time as you are. But there's another dimension. He's different. There's no rope of evolution linking him to you, like a navel string. No! Between you and him there's a cataclysm and another dimension. It's no good. You can't link him up. Never will. It's the other dimension.

He mocks at you and gibes at you and imitates you. Sometimes he is even more *like* you than you are yourself. It's funny, and you laugh just a bit on the wrong side of your face. It's the other dimension.

He stands in one Sun, you in another. He whisks his tail in one Day, you scratch your head in another. He jeers at you, and is afraid of you. You laugh at him and are frightened of him.

What's the length and the breadth, what's the height and the depths between you and me? says the monkey.

You get out a tape-measure, and he flies into an obscene mockery of you.

It's the other dimension, put the tape-measure away, it won't serve.

'*Perro!* Oh, *Perr-rro!*' shrieks the parrot.

Corasmin looks up at me, as much as to say:

'It's the other dimension. There's no help for it. Let us agree about it.'

And I look down into his yellow eyes, and say:

'You're quite right, Corasmin, it's the other dimension. You and I, we admit it. But the parrot won't, and the monkey won't, and the crocodile won't, neither the earwig. They all wind themselves up and wriggle inside the cage of the other dimension, hating it. And those that have voices jeer, and those that have mouths bite, and the insects that haven't even mouths, they turn up their tails and nip with them, or sting. Just behaving according to their own dimension: which, for me, is the other dimension.'

And Corasmin wags his tail mildly, and looks at me with real wisdom in his eyes. He and I, we understand each other in the wisdom of the other dimension.

But the flat, saucer-eyed parrot won't have it. Just won't have it.

'*Oh Perro! Perr-rro! Perr-rro-o-o-o!* Yap-yap-yap!'

And Rosalino, the Indian *mozo*, looks up at me with his eyes veiled by their own blackness. We won't have it either: he is hiding and repudiating. Between us also is the gulf of the other dimension, and he wants to bridge it with the foot-rule of the three-dimensional space. He knows it can't be done. So do I. Each of us knows the other knows.

But he can imitate me, even more than life-like. As the parrot can him. And I have to laugh at his *me*, a bit on the wrong side of my face, as he has to grin on the wrong side of his face when I catch his eye as the parrot is whistling *him*. With a grin, with a laugh we pay tribute to the other dimension. But Corasmin is wiser. In his clear, yellow eyes is the self-possession of full admission.

The Aztecs said this world, our Sun, would blow up from inside, in earthquakes. Then what will come, in the other dimension, when we are superseded?

A LITTLE MOONSHINE WITH LEMON

Written December, 1925. *The Laughing Horse*, April, 1926. *Mornings in Mexico*, 1927

'Ye Gods. he doth bestride the narrow world
Like a Colossus . . .!'

THERE is a bright moon, so that even the vines make a shadow, and the Mediterranean has a broad white shimmer between its dimness. By the shore, the lights of the old houses twinkle quietly, and out of the wall of the headland advances the glare of a locomotive's lamps. It is a feast day, St Catherine's Day, and the men are all sitting round the little tables, down below, drinking wine or vermouth.

And what about the ranch, the little ranch in New Mexico? The time is different there: but I too have drunk my glass to St Catherine, so I can't be bothered to reckon. I consider that there, too, the moon is in the south-east, standing, as it were, over Santa Fe, beyond the bend of those mountains of Picoris.

Sono io! say the Italians. I am I! Which sounds simpler than it is.

Because which I am I, after all, now that I have drunk a glass also to St Catherine, and the moon shines over the sea, and my thoughts, just because they are fleetingly occupied by the moon on the Mediterranean, and ringing with the last farewell: *Dunque! Signore! di nuovo!* – must needs follow the moon-track south-west, to the great South-west, where the ranch is.

They say: *in vino veritas*. Bah! They say so much! But in the wine of St Catherine, my little ranch, and the three horses down among the timber. Or if it has snowed, the horses are gone away, and it is snow, and the moon shines on the alfalfa slope, between the pines, and the cabins are blind. There is nobody there. Everything shut up. Only the big pine-tree in front of the house, standing still and unconcerned, alive.

Perhaps when I have a *Weh* at all, my Heimweh is for the

tree in front of the house, the overshadowing tree whose green top one never looks at. But on the trunk one hangs the various odds and ends of iron things. It is so near. One goes out of the door, and the tree-trunk is there, like a guardian angel.

The tree-trunk, and the long work table, and the fence! Then beyond, since it is night, and the moon shines, for me at least, away beyond is a light, at Taos, or at Ranchos de Taos. Here, the castle of Noli is on the western skyline. But there, no doubt it has snowed, since even here the wind is cold. There it has snowed, and the nearly full moon blazes wolf-like, as here it never blazes: risen like a were-wolf over the mountains. So there is a faint hoar shagginess of pine-trees, away at the foot of the alfalfa field, and a grey gleam of snow in the night, on the level desert, and a ruddy point of human light, in Ranchos de Taos.

And beyond, you see them even if you don't see them, the circling mountains, since there is a moon.

So, one hurries indoors, and throws more logs on the fire.

One doesn't either. One hears Giovanni calling from below, to say good night! He is going down to the village for a spell. *Vado giú! Signor Lorenzo! Buona notte!*

And the Mediterranean whispers in the distance, a sound like in a shell. And save that somebody is whistling, the night is very bright and still. The Mediterranean, so eternally young, the very symbol of youth! And Italy, so reputedly old, yet forever so child-like and naïve! Never, never for a moment able to comprehend the wonderful, hoary age of America, the continent of the afterwards.

I wonder if I am here, or if I am just going to bed at the ranch. Perhaps looking in Montgomery Ward's catalogue for something for Christmas, and drinking moonshine and hot water, since it is cold. Go out and look if the chickens are shut up warm: if the horses are in sight: if Susan, the black cow, has gone to her nest among the trees, for the night. Cows don't eat much at night. But Susan will wander in the moon. The moon makes her uneasy. And the horses stamp around the cabins.

In a cold like this, the stars snap like distant coyotes, beyond the moon. And you'll see the shadow of actual coyotes, going across the alfalfa field. And the pine-trees make little noises, sudden and stealthy, as if they were walking about. And the place heaves with ghosts. That place, the ranch, heaves with ghosts. But when one has got used to one's own home ghosts, be they never so many, and so potent, they are like one's own family, but nearer than the blood. It is the ghosts one misses most, the ghosts there, of the Rocky Mountains, that never go beyond the timber and that linger, like the animals, round the water-spring. I know them, they know me: we go well together. But they reproach me for going away. They are resentful too.

Perhaps the snow is in tufts on the greasewood bushes. Perhaps the blue jays fall in a blue, metallic cloud out of the pine-trees in front of the house, at dawn, in the terrific cold, when the dangerous light comes watchful over the mountains, and touches the desert far-off, far-off, beyond the Rio Grande.

And I, I give it up. There is a choice of vermouth, Marsala, red wine or white. At the ranch, to-night, because it is cold, I should have moonshine, not very good moonshine, but still warming: with hot water and lemon, and sugar, and a bit of cinnamon from one of those little red Schilling's tins. And I should light my little stove in the bedroom, and let it roar a bit, sucking the wind. Then dart to bed, with all the ghosts of the ranch cosily round me, and sleep till the very coldness of my emerged nose wakes me. Waking, I shall look at once through the glass panels of the bedroom door, and see the trunk of the great pine-tree, like a person on guard, and a low star just coming over the mountain, very brilliant, like someone swinging an electric lantern.

Si vedrà la primavera
Fiorann' i mandorlini –

Ah, well, let it be vermouth, since there's no moonshine with lemon and cinnamon. Supposing I called Giovanni, and told him I wanted:

'Un poco di chiar' di luna, con canella e limone ...'

Writing and Painting

JOHN GALSWORTHY

Written February, 1927. *Scrutinies*, 1928.
Phoenix, 1936

LITERARY criticism can be no more than a reasoned account of the feeling produced upon the critic by the book he is criticizing. Criticism can never be a science: it is, in the first place, much too personal, and in the second, it is concerned with values that science ignores. The touchstone is emotion, not reason. We judge a work of art by its effect on our sincere and vital emotion, and nothing else. All the critical twiddle-twaddle about style and form, all this pseudo-scientific classifying and analysing of books in an imitation-botanical fashion, is mere impertinence and mostly dull jargon.

A critic must be able to *feel* the impact of a work of art in all its complexity and its force. To do so, he must be a man of force and complexity himself, which few critics are. A man with a paltry, impudent nature will never write anything but paltry, impudent criticism. And a man who is *emotionally* educated is rare as a phoenix. The more scholastically educated a man is generally, the more he is an emotional boor.

More than this, even an artistically and emotionally educated man must be a man of good faith. He must have the courage to admit what he feels, as well as the flexibility to *know* what he feels. So Sainte-Beuve remains, to me, a great critic. And a man like Macaulay, brilliant as he is, is unsatisfactory, because he is not honest. He is emotionally very alive – but he juggles his feelings. He prefers a fine effect to the sincere statement of the aesthetic and emotional reaction. He is quite intellectually capable of giving us a true account of what he feels. But not morally. A critic must be emotionally alive in every fibre, intellectually capable and skilful in essential logic, and then morally very honest.

Then it seems to me a good critic should give his reader a few standards to go by. He can change the standards for every new critical attempt, so long as he keeps good faith. But it is just as well to say: This and this is the standard we judge by.

Sainte-Beuve, on the whole, set up the standard of the 'good man'. He sincerely believed that the great man was essentially the good man in the widest range of human sympathy. This remained his universal standard. Pater's standard was the lonely philosopher of pure thought and pure aesthetic truth. Macaulay's standard was tainted by a political or democratic bias, he must be on the side of the weak. Gibbon tried a purely moral standard, individual morality.

Reading Galsworthy again – or most of him, for all is too much – one feels oneself in need of a standard, some conception of a real man and a real woman, by which to judge all these Forsytes and their contemporaries. One cannot judge them by the standard of the good man, nor of the man of pure thought, nor of the treasured humble nor the moral individual. One would like to judge them by the standard of the human being, but what, after all, is that? That is the trouble with the Forsytes. They are human enough, since anything in humanity is human, just as anything in nature is natural. Yet not one of them seems to be a really vivid human being. They are social beings. And what do we mean by that?

It remains to define, just for the purpose of this criticism, what we mean by a social being as distinct from a human being. The necessity arises from the sense of dissatisfaction which these Forsytes give us. Why can't we admit them as human beings? Why can't we have them in the same category as Sairey Gamp for example, who is satirically conceived, or as Jane Austen's people, who are social enough? We can accept Mrs Gamp or Jane Austen's characters or even George Meredith's Egoist as human beings in the same category as ourselves. Whence arises this repulsion from the Forsytes, this refusal, this emotional refusal, to have them identified with our common humanity? Why do we feel so instinctively that they are inferiors?

It is because they seem to us to have lost caste as human beings, and to have sunk to the level of the social being, that peculiar creature that takes the place in our civilization of the slave in the old civilizations. The human individual is a queer animal, always changing. But the fatal change today is the collapse from the psychology of the free human individual into the psychology of the social being, just as the fatal change in the past was a collapse from the freeman's psyche to the psyche of the slave. The free moral and the slave moral, the human moral and the social moral: these are the abiding antitheses.

While a man remains a man, a true human individual, there is at the core of him a certain innocence or *naïveté* which defies all analysis, and which you cannot bargain with, you can only deal with it in good faith from your own corresponding innocence or *naïveté*. This does not mean that the human being is nothing but naïve or innocent. He is Mr Worldly Wiseman also to his own degree. But in his essential core he is naïve, and money does not touch him. Money, of course, with every man living goes a long way. With the alive human being it may go as far as his penultimate feeling. But in the last naked him it does not enter.

With the social being it goes right through the centre and is the controlling principle no matter how much he may pretend, nor how much bluff he may put up. He may give away all he has to the poor and still reveal himself as a social being swayed finally and helplessly by the money-sway, and by the social moral, which is inhuman.

It seems to me that when the human being becomes too much divided between his subjective and objective consciousness, at last something splits in him and becomes a social being. When he becomes too much aware of objective reality, and of his own isolation in the face of the universe of objective reality, the core of his identity splits, his nucleus collapses, his innocence or his *naïveté* perishes, and he becomes only a subjective-objective reality, a divided thing hinged together but not strictly individual.

While a man remains a man, before he falls and becomes a social individual, he innocently feels himself altogether within the great continuum of the universe. He is not divided nor cut off. Men may be against him, the tide of affairs may be rising to sweep him away. But he is one with the living continuum of the universe. From this he cannot be swept away. Hamlet and Lear feel it, as does Oedipus or Phaedra. It is the last and the deepest feeling that is in man while he remains a man. It is there the same in a deist like Voltaire or a scientist like Darwin: it is there, imperishable, in every great man: in Napoleon the same, till material things piled too much on him and he lost it and was doomed. It is the essential innocence and *naïveté* of the human being, the sense of being at one with the great universe-continuum of space-time-life, which is vivid in a great man, and a pure nuclear spark in every man who is still free.

But if man loses his mysterious naïve assurance, which is his innocence; if he gives *too* much importance to the external objective reality and so collapses in his natural innocent pride, then he becomes obsessed with the idea of objectives or material assurance; he wants to *insure* himself, and perhaps everybody else: universal insurance. The impulse rests on fear. Once the individual loses his naïve at-one-ness with the living universe he falls into a state of fear and tries to insure himself with wealth. If he is an altruist he wants to insure everybody, and feels it is the tragedy of tragedies if this can't be done. But the whole necessity for thus materially insuring oneself with wealth, money, arises from the state of fear into which a man falls who has lost his at-one-ness with the living universe, lost his peculiar nuclear innocence and fallen into fragmentariness. Money, material salvation is the only salvation. What is salvation is God. Hence money is God. The social being may rebel even against this god, as do many of Galsworthy's characters. But that does not give them back their innocence. They are only anti-materialists instead of positive materialists. And the anti-materialist is a social being just the same as the materialist, neither more or less. He is castrated just the same, made a neuter by having lost his innocence, the bright little individual spark of his at-oneness.

When one reads Mr Galsworthy's books it seems as if there were not on earth one single human individual. They are all these social beings, positive and negative. There is not a free soul among them, not even Pendyce, or June Forsyte. If money does not actively determine their being, it does negatively. Money, or property, which is the same thing. Mrs Pendyce, lovable as she is, is utterly circumscribed by property. Ultimately, she is not lovable at all, she is part of the fraud, she is prostituted to property. And there is nobody else. Old Jolyon is merely a sentimental materialist. Only for one moment do we see a man, and that is the road-sweeper in *Fraternity* after he comes out of prison and covers his face. But even *his* manhood has to be explained away by a wound in the head: an abnormality.

Now it looks as if Mr Galsworthy set out to make that very point: to show that the Forsytes were not full human individuals, but social beings fallen to a lower level of life. They have lost that bit of free manhood and free womanhood which makes men and women. *The Man of Property* has the elements of a very great novel, a very great satire. It sets out to reveal the social being in all his strength and inferiority. But the author has not the courage to carry it through. The greatness of the book rests in its new and sincere and amazingly profound satire. It is the ultimate satire on modern humanity, and done from the inside, with really consummate skill and sincere creative passion, something quite new. It seems to be a real effort to show up the social being in all his weirdness. And then it fizzles out.

Then, in the love affair of Irene and Bosinney, and in the sentimentalizing of old Jolyon Forsyte, the thing is fatally blemished. Galsworthy had not quite enough of the superb courage of his satire. He faltered, and gave in to the Forsytes. It is a thousand pities. He might have been the surgeon the modern soul needs so badly, to cut away the proud flesh of our Forsytes from the living body of men who are fully alive. Instead, he put down the knife and laid on a soft sentimental poultice, and helped to make the corruption worse.

Satire exists for the very purpose of killing the social being, showing him what an inferior he is and, with all his parade of social honesty, how subtly and corruptly debased. Dishonest to life, dishonest to the living universe on which he is parasitic as a louse. By ridiculing the social being, the satirist helps the true individual, the real human being, to rise to his feet again and go on with the battle. For it is always a battle, and always will be.

Not that the majority are necessarily social beings. But the majority is only *conscious* socially: humanly, mankind is helpless and unconscious, unaware even of the thing most precious to any human being, that core of manhood or womanhood, naïve, innocent at-one-ness with the living universe-continuum, which alone makes a man individual and, as an individual, *essentially* happy, even if he be driven mad like Lear. Lear was essentially happy, even in his greatest misery. A happiness from which Goneril and Regan were excluded as lice and bugs are excluded from happiness, being social beings, and, as such, parasites, fallen from true freedom and independence.

But the tragedy to-day is that men are only materially and socially conscious. They are unconscious of their own manhood, and so they let it be destroyed. Out of free men we produce social beings by the thousand every week.

The Forsytes are all parasites, and Mr Galsworthy set out, in a really magnificent attempt, to let us see it. They are parasites upon the thought, the feelings, the whole body of life of really living individuals who have gone before them and who exist alongside with them. All they can do, having no individual life of their own, is out of fear to rake together property, and to feed upon the life that has been given by living men to mankind. They have no life, and so they live for ever, in perpetual fear of death, accumulating property to ward off death. They keep up convention, but they cannot carry on a tradition. There is a tremendous difference between the two things. To carry on a tradition you must add something to the tradition. But to keep up a convention needs only the monotonous persistency of a parasite, the endless endurance of the craven, those who fear life because they are not alive, and who cannot die because they cannot live – the social beings.

As far as I can see, there is nothing but Forsyte in Galsworthy's books: Forsyte positive or Forsyte negative, Forsyte successful or Forsyte *manqué*. That is, every single character is determined by money: either the getting it, or the having it, or the wanting it, or the utter lacking it. Getting it are the Forsytes as such; having it are the Pendyces and the patricians and Hilarys and Biancas and all that lot; wanting it are the Irenes and Bosinneys and the young Jolyons; and utterly lacking it are all the charwomen and squalid poor who form the background – the shadows of the 'having' ones, as old Mr Stone says. This is the whole Galsworthy gamut, all absolutely determined by money, and not an individual soul among them. They are all fallen, all social beings, a castrated lot.

Perhaps the overwhelming numerousness of the Forsytes frightened Mr Galsworthy from utterly damning them. Or perhaps it was something else, something more serious in him. Perhaps it was his utter failure to see what you were when you *weren't* a Forsyte. What was there *besides* Forsytes in all the wide human world? Mr Galsworthy looked, and found nothing. Strictly and truly, after his frightened search, he had found nothing. But he came back with Irene and Bosinney, and offered us that. Here! he seems to say. Here is the anti-Forsyte! Here! Here you have it! Love! Pa-assion! PASSION.

We look at this love, this PASSION, and we see nothing but a doggish amorousness and a sort of anti-Forsytism. They are the *anti* half of the show. Runaway dogs of these Forsytes, running in the back garden and furtively and ignominiously copulating – this is the effect, on me, of Mr Galsworthy's grand love affairs, Dark Flowers or Bosinneys, or Apple Trees or George Pendyce – whatever they be. About every one of them something ignominious and doggish, like dogs copulating in the street, and looking round to see if the Forsytes are watching.

Alas! this is the Forsyte trying to be freely sensual. He can't do it; he's lost it. He can only be doggishly messy. Bosinney is not only a Forsyte, but an anti-Forsyte, with a vast grudge against property. And the thing a man has a vast grudge against is the man's determinant. Bosinney is a property hound, but he has run away from the kennels, or been born outside the kennels, so he is a rebel. So he goes sniffing round the property bitches, to get even with the successful property hounds that way. One cannot help preferring Soames Forsyte, in a choice of evils.

Just as one prefers June or any of the old aunts to Irene. Irene seems to me a sneaking, creeping, spiteful sort of bitch, an anti-Forsyte, absolutely living off the Forsytes – yes, to the very end; absolutely living off their money and trying to do them dirt. She is like Bosinney, a property mongrel doing dirt in the property kennels. But she is a real property prostitute, like the little model in *Fraternity*. Only she is *anti*! It is a type recurring again and again in Galsworthy: the parasite upon the parasites, 'Big fleas have little fleas, etc.' And Bosinney and Irene, as well as the vagabond in *The Island Pharisees*, are among the little fleas. And as a tramp loves his own vermin, so the Forsytes and the Hilarys love these, their own particular body parasites, their *antis*.

It is when he comes to sex that Mr Galsworthy collapses finally. He becomes nastily sentimental. He wants to make sex important, and he only makes it repulsive. Sentimentalism is the working off on yourself of feelings you haven't really got. We all *want* to have certain feelings: feelings of love, of passionate sex, of kindliness, and so forth. Very few people really feel love, or sex passion, or kindliness, or anything else that goes at all deep. So the mass just fake these feelings inside themselves. Faked feelings! The world is all gummy with them. They are better than real feelings, because you can spit them out when you brush your teeth; and then to-morrow you can fake them afresh.

Shelton, in *The Island Pharisees*, is the first of Mr Galsworthy's lovers, and he might as well be the last. He is almost comical. All we know of his passion for Antonia is that he feels at the beginning a 'hunger' for her, as if she were a beefsteak. And towards the end he once kisses her, and expects her, no doubt, to fall instantly at his feet overwhelmed. He never for a second feels a moment of gentle sympathy with her. She is class-bound, but she doesn't seem to have been inhuman. The inhuman one was the lover. He can gloat over her in the distance, as if she were a dish of pig's trotters, *pieds truffés*: she can be an angelic *vision* to him a little way off, but when the poor thing has to be just a rather ordinary middle-class girl to him, quite near, he hates her with a comical, rancorous hate. It is most queer. He is helplessly *anti*. He hates her for even existing as a woman of her own class, for even having her own existence. Apparently she should just be a floating female sex-organ, hovering round to satisfy his little 'hungers', and then *basta*. Anything of the real meaning of sex, which involves the whole of a human being, never occurs to him. It is a function, and the female is a sort of sexual appliance, no more.

And so we have it again and again, on this low and bastard level, all the human correspondence lacking. The sexual level is extraordinarily low, like dogs. The Galsworthy heroes are all weirdly in love with themselves, when we know them better, afflicted with chronic narcissism. They know just three types of women: the Pendyce mother, prostitute to property; the Irene, the essential *anti* prostitute, the floating, flaunting female organ; and the social woman, the mere lady. All three are loved and hated in turn by the recurrent heroes. But it is all on the debased level of property, positive or *anti*. It is all a doggy form of prostitution. Be quick and have done.

One of the funniest stories is *The Apple Tree*. The young man finds, at a lonely Devon farm, a little Welsh farm-girl, who being a Celt and not a Saxon, at once falls for the Galsworthian hero. This young gentleman in the throes of narcissistic love for his marvellous self, falls for the maid because she has fallen so utterly and abjectly for him. She doesn't call him 'My King', not being Wellsian; she only says: 'I can't live away from you. Do what you like with me. Only let me come with you!' The proper prostitutional announcement!

For this, of course, a narcissistic young gentleman just down from Oxford falls at once. Ensues a grand pa-assion. He goes to buy her a proper frock to be carried away in, meets a college friend with a young lady sister, has jam for tea and stays the night, and the grand pa-assion has died a natural death by the time he spreads the marmalade on his bread. He has returned to his own class, and nothing else exists. He marries the young lady, true to his class. But to fill the cup of his vanity, the maid drowns herself. It is funny that maids only seem to do it for these narcissistic young gentlemen who, looking in the pool for their own image, desire the added satisfaction of seeing the face of drowned Ophelia there as well; saving them the necessity of taking the narcissus plunge in person. We have gone one better than the myth. Narcissus, in Mr Galsworthy, doesn't drown himself. He asks Ophelia, or Megan, kindly to drown herself instead. And in this fiction she actually does. And he feels so *wonderful* about it!

Mr Galsworthy's treatment of passion is really rather shameful. The whole thing is doggy to a degree. The man has a temporary 'hunger'; he is 'on the heat' as they say of dogs. The heat passes. It's done. Trot away, if you're not tangled. Trot off, looking shame-faced over your shoulder. People have been watching! Damn them! But never mind, it'll blow over. Thank God, the bitch is trotting in the other direction. She'll soon have another trail of dogs after her. That'll wipe out my traces. Good for that! Next time I'll get properly married and do my doggishness in my own house.

With the fall of the individual, sex falls into a dog's heat. Oh, if only Mr Galsworthy had had the strength to satirize this too, instead of pouring a sauce of sentimental savouriness over it. Of course, if he had done so he would never have been a popular writer, but he would have been a great one.

However, he chose to sentimentalize and glorify the most doggy sort of sex. Setting out to satirize the Forsytes, he glorifies the *anti*, who is one worse. While the individual remains real and unfallen, sex remains a vital and supremely important thing. But once you have the fall into social beings, sex becomes disgusting, like dogs on the heat. Dogs are social beings, with no true canine individuality. Wolves and foxes don't copulate on the pavement. Their sex is wild and in act utterly private. Howls you may hear, but you will never see anything. But the dog is tame – and he makes excrement and he copulates on the pavement, as if to spite you. He is the Forsyte *anti*.

The same with human beings. Once they become tame they become in a measure, exhibitionists, as if to spite everything. They have no real feelings of their own. Unless somebody 'catches them at it' they don't really feel they've felt anything at all. And this is how the mob is today. It is Forsyte *anti*. It is the social being spiting society.

Oh, if only Mr Galsworthy had satirized *this* side of Forsytism, the anti-Forsyte posturing of the 'rebel', the narcissus and the exhibitionist, the dogs copulating on the pavement! Instead of that, he glorified it, to the eternal shame of English literature.

The satire, which in *The Man of Property* really had a certain noble touch, soon fizzles out, and we get that series of Galsworthian 'rebels', who are, like all the rest of the modern middle-class rebels, not in rebellion at all. They are merely social beings behaving in an anti-social manner. They worship their own class, but they pretend to go one better and sneer at it. They are Forsyte *antis*, feeling snobbish about snobbery. Nevertheless, they want to attract attention and make money. That's why they are *anti*. It is the vicious circle of Forsytism. Money means more to them than it does to a Soames Forsyte, so they pretend to go one better, and despise it, but they will do anything to have it – things which Soames Forsyte would not have done.

If there is one thing more repulsive than the social being positive, it is the social being negative, the mere *anti*. In the great debacle of decency this gentleman is the most indecent. In a subtle way Bosinney and Irene are more dishonest and more indecent than Soames and Winifred, but they are *anti*, so they are glorified. It is pretty sickening.

The introduction to *The Island Pharisees* explains the whole show: 'Each man born into the world is born to go a journey, and for the most part he is born on the high road . . . As soon as he can toddle, he moves, by the queer instinct we call the love of life, along this road . . . his fathers went this way before him, they made this road for him to tread, and, when they bred him, passed into his fibre the love of doing things as they themselves had done them. So he walks on and on ... Suddenly, one day, without intending to, he notices a patch or opening in the hedge, leading to right or left, and he stands looking at the undiscovered. After that he stops at all the openings in the hedge; one day, with a beating heart, he tries one. And this is where the fun begins.' – Nine out of ten get back to the broad road again, and sidetrack no more. They snuggle down comfortably in the next inn, and think where they might have been. 'But the poor silly tenth is faring on. Nine times out of ten he goes down in a bog; the undiscovered has engulfed him.' But the tenth time he gets across, and a new road is opened to mankind.

It is a class-bound consciousness, or at least a hopeless social consciousness which sees life as a high road between two hedges. And the only way out is gaps in the hedge and excursions into naughtiness! These little *anti* excursions, from which the wayfarer slinks back to solid comfort nine times out of ten; an odd one goes down in a bog; and a very rare one finds a way across and opens out a new road.

In Mr Galsworthy's novels we see the nine, the ninety-nine, the nine hundred and ninety-nine slinking back to solid comfort; we see an odd Bosinney go under a bus, because he hadn't guts enough to do something else, the poor *anti!* but that rare figure sidetracking into the unknown we do *not* see. Because, as a matter of fact, the whole figure is faulty at that point. If life is a great highway, then it must forge ahead into the unknown. Sidetracking gets nowhere. That is mere *anti*. The tip of the road is always unfinished, in the wilderness. If it comes to a precipice and a cañon – well, then, there is need for some exploring. But we see Mr Galsworthy, after *The Country House*, very safe on the old highway, very secure in comfort, wealth, and renown. He at least has gone down in no bog, nor lost himself striking new paths. The hedges nowadays are ragged with gaps, anybody who likes strays out on the little trips of 'unconventions'. But the Forsyte road has not moved on at all. It has only become dishevelled and sordid with excursions doing the *anti* tricks and being 'unconventional', and leaving tin cans behind.

In the three early novels, *The Island Pharisees*, *The Man of Property*, *Fraternity*, it looked as if Mr Galsworthy might break through the blind end of the highway with the dynamite of satire, and help us out on to a new lap. But the sex ingredient of his dynamite was damp and muzzy, the explosion gradually fizzled off in sentimentality, and we are left in a worse state than before.

The later novels are purely commercial, and, if it had not been for the early novels, of no importance. They are popular, they sell well, and there's the end of them. They contain the explosive powder of the first books in minute quantities, fizzling as silly squibs. When you arrive at *To Let*, and the end, at least the *promised* end, of the Forsytes, what have you? Just money! Money, money, money and a certain snobbish silliness, and many more *anti* tricks and poses. Nothing else. The story is feeble, the characters have no blood and bones, the emotions are faked, faked, faked. It is one great fake. Not necessarily of Mr Galsworthy. The characters fake their own emotions. But that doesn't help us. And if you look closely at the characters, the meanness and low-level of vulgarity are very distasteful. You have all the Forsyte meanness, with none of the energy. Jolyon and Irene are meaner and more treacherous to their son than the older Forsytes were to theirs. The young ones are of a limited, mechanical, vulgar egoism far surpassing that of Swithin or James, their ancestors. There is in it all a vulgar sense of being rich, and therefore we do as we like: an utter incapacity for anything like *true* feeling, especially in the women, Fleur, Irene, Annette, June: a glib crassness, a youthful spontaneity which is just impertinence and lack of feeling; and all the time, a creeping, 'having' sort of vulgarity of money and self-will, money and self-will, so that we wonder sometimes if Mr Galsworthy is not treating his public in real bad faith, and being cynical and rancorous under his rainbow sentimentalism.

Fleur he destroys in one word: she is 'having'. It is perfectly true. We don't blame the young Jon for clearing out.

Irene he destroys in a phrase out of Fleur's mouth to June: 'Didn't she spoil your life too?' – and it is precisely what she did. Sneaking and mean, Irene prevented June from getting her lover. Sneaking and mean, she prevents Fleur. She is the bitch in the manger. She is the sneaking *anti*. Irene, the most beautiful woman on earth! And Mr Galsworthy, with the cynicism of a successful old sentimentalist, turns it off by making June say: 'Nobody can spoil a life, my dear. That's nonsense. Things happen, but we bob up.'

This is the final philosophy of it all. 'Things happen, but we bob up.' Very well, then, write the book in that key, the keynote of a frank old cynic. There's no point in sentimentalizing it and being a sneaking old cynic. Why pour out masses of feelings that pretend to be genuine and then turn it all off with: 'Things happen, but we bob up'?

It is quite true, things happen, and we bob up. If we are vulgar sentimentalists, we bob up just the same, so nothing has happened and nothing can happen. All is vulgarity. But it pays. There is money in it.

Vulgarity pays, and cheap cynicism smothered in sentimentalism pays better than anything else. Because nothing *can* happen to the degraded social being. So let's pretend it does, and then bob up!

It is time somebody began to spit out the jam of sentimentalism, at least, which smothers the 'bobbing-up' philosophy. It is time we turned a straight light on this horde of rats, these younger Forsyte sentimentalists whose name is legion. It is sentimentalism which is stifling us. Let the social beings keep on bobbing up while ever they can. But it is time an effort was made to turn a hosepipe on the sentimentalism they ooze over everything. The world is one sticky mess, in which the little Forsytes indeed may keep on bobbing still, but in which an honest feeling can't breathe.

But if the sticky mess gets much deeper, even the little Forsytes won't be able to bob up any more. They'll be smothered in their own slime along with everything else. Which is a comfort.

BENJAMIN FRANKLIN

Written 1917–18. *English Review*, December, 1928.
Studies in Classic American Literature, 1923

THE Perfectibility of Man! Ah heaven, what a dreary theme! The perfectibility of the Ford car! The perfectibility of which man? I am many men. Which of them are you going to perfect? I am not a mechanical contrivance.

Education! Which of the various me's do you propose to educate, and which do you propose to suppress?

Anyhow, I defy you. I defy you, oh society, to educate me or to suppress me, according to your dummy standards.

The ideal man! And which is he, if you please? Benjamin Franklin or Abraham Lincoln? The ideal man! Roosevelt or Porfirio Diaz?

There are other men in me, besides this patient ass who sits here in a tweed jacket. What am I doing, playing the patient ass in a tweed jacket? Who am I talking to? Who are you, at the other end of this patience?

Who are you? How many selves have you? And which of these selves do you want to be?

Is Yale College going to educate the self that is in the dark of you, or Harvard College?

The ideal self! Oh, but I have a strange and fugitive self shut out and howling like a wolf or a coyote under the ideal windows. See his red eyes in the dark? This is the self who is coming into his own.

The perfectibility of man, dear God! When every man as long as he remains alive is in himself a multitude of conflicting men. Which of these do you choose to perfect, at the expense of every other?

Old Daddy Franklin will tell you. He'll rig him up for you, the pattern American. Oh, Franklin was the first downright American. He knew what he was about, the sharp little man. He set up the first dummy American.

At the beginning of his career this cunning little Benjamin drew up for himself a creed that should 'satisfy the professors of every religion, but shock none'.

Now wasn't that a real American thing to do?

'*That there is one God who made all things.*'

(But Benjamin made Him.)

'*That He governs the world by His Providence.*'

(Benjamin knowing all about Providence.)

'*That He ought to be worshipped with adoration, prayer, and thanksgiving.*'

(Which costs nothing.)

'*But –*' But me no buts, Benjamin, saith the Lord.

'*But that the most acceptable service of God is doing good to men.*'

(God having no choice in the matter.)

'*That the soul is immortal.*'

(You'll see why, in the next clause.)

'*And that God will certainly reward virtue and punish vice, either here or hereafter.*'

Now if Mr Andrew Carnegie, or any other millionaire, had wished to invent a God to suit his ends, he could not have done better. Benjamin did it for him in the eighteenth century. God is the supreme servant of men who want to get on, to *produce*. Providence. The provider. The heavenly storekeeper. The everlasting Wanamaker.

And this is all the God the grandsons of the Pilgrim Fathers had left. Aloft on a pillar of dollars.

'*That the soul is immortal.*'

The trite way Benjamin says it!

But man has a soul, though you can't locate it either in his purse or his pocket-book or his heart or his stomach or his head. The *wholeness* of a man is his soul. Not merely that nice little comfortable bit which Benjamin marks out.

It's a queer thing is a man's soul. It is the whole of him. Which means it is the unknown him, as well as the known. It seems to me just funny, professors and Benjamins fixing the functions of the soul. Why, the soul of man is a vast forest, and all Benjamin intended was a neat back garden. And we've all got to fit into his kitchen garden scheme of things. Hail Columbia!

The soul of man is a dark forest. The Hercynian Wood that scared the Romans so, and out of which came the white-skinned hordes of the next civilization.

Who knows what will come out of the soul of man? The soul of man is a dark vast forest, with wild life in it. Think of Benjamin fencing it off!

Oh, but Benjamin fenced a little tract that he called the soul of man, and proceeded to get it into cultivation. Providence forsooth! And they think that bit of barbed wire is going to keep us in pound for ever? More fools they.

This is Benjamin's barbed wire fence. He made himself a list of virtues, which he trotted inside like a grey nag in a paddock.

1
TEMPERANCE

Eat not to fulness; drink not to elevation.

2
SILENCE

Speak not but what may benefit others or yourself; avoid trifling conversation.

3
ORDER

Let all your things have their places; let each part of your business have its time.

4
RESOLUTION

Resolve to perform what you ought; perform without fail what you resolve.

5
FRUGALITY

Make no expense but to do good to others or yourself – i.e., waste nothing.

6
INDUSTRY

Lose no time, be always employed in something useful; cut off all unnecessary action.

7
SINCERITY

Use no hurtful deceit; think innocently and justly, and, if you speak, speak accordingly.

8
JUSTICE

Wrong none by doing injuries, or omitting the benefits that are your duty.

9
MODERATION

Avoid extremes, forbear resenting injuries as much as you think they deserve.

10
CLEANLINESS

Tolerate no uncleanliness in body, clothes, or habitation.

11
TRANQUILLITY

Be not disturbed at trifles, or at accidents common or unavoidable.

12
CHASTITY

Rarely use venery but for health and offspring, never to dullness, weakness, or the injury of your own or another's peace or reputation.

13
HUMILITY

Imitate Jesus and Socrates.

A Quaker friend told Franklin that he, Benjamin, was generally considered proud, so Benjamin put in the Humility touch as an afterthought. The amusing part is the sort of humility it displays. 'Imitate Jesus and Socrates', and mind you don't outshine either of these two. One can just imagine Socrates and Alcibiades roaring in their cups over Philadelphian Benjamin, and Jesus looking at him a little puzzled, and murmuring: 'Aren't you wise in your own conceit, Ben?'

'Henceforth be masterless,' retorts Ben. 'Be ye each one his own master unto himself, and don't let even the Lord put His spoke in.' 'Each man his own master' is but a puffing up of masterlessness.

Well, the first of Americans practised this enticing list with assiduity, setting a national example. He had the virtues in columns, and gave himself good and bad marks according as he thought his behaviour deserved. Pity these conduct charts are lost to us. He only remarks that Order was his stumbling block. He could not learn to be neat and tidy.

Isn't it nice to have nothing worse to confess?

He was a little model, was Benjamin. Doctor Franklin. Snuff-coloured little man! Immortal soul and all!

The immortal soul part was a sort of cheap insurance policy.

Benjamin had no concern, really, with the immortal soul. He was too busy with social man.

1. He swept and lighted the streets of young Philadelphia.

2. He invented electrical appliances.

3. He was the centre of a moralizing club in Philadelphia, and he wrote the moral humorisms of Poor Richard.

4. He was a member of all the important councils of Philadelphia, and then of the American colonies.

5. He won the cause of American Independence at the French Court, and was the economic father of the United States.

Now what more can you want of a man? And yet he is *infra dig.*, even in Philadelphia.

I admire him. I admire his sturdy courage first of all, then his sagacity, then his glimpsing into the thunders of electricity, then his common-sense humour. All the qualities of a great man, and never more than a great citizen. Middle-sized, sturdy, snuff-coloured Doctor Franklin, one of the soundest citizens that ever trod or 'used venery'.

I do not like him.

And, by the way, I always thought books of Venery were about hunting deer.

There is a certain earnest *naïveté* about him. Like a child. And like a little old man. He has again become as a little child, always as wise as his grandfather, or wiser.

Perhaps, as I say, the most complete citizen that ever 'used venery'.

Printer, philosopher, scientist, author and patriot, impeccable husband and citizen, why isn't he an archetype?

Pioneers, Oh Pioneers! Benjamin was one of the greatest pioneers of the United States. Yet we just can't do with him.

What's wrong with him then? Or what's wrong with us?

I can remember, when I was a little boy, my father used to buy a scrubby yearly almanac with the sun and moon and stars on the cover. And it used to prophesy bloodshed and famine. But also crammed in corners it had little anecdotes and humorisms, with a moral tag. And I used to have my little priggish laugh at the woman who counted her chickens before they were hatched and so forth, and I was convinced that honesty was the best policy, also a little priggishly. The author of these bits was Poor Richard, and Poor Richard was Benjamin Franklin, writing in Philadelphia well over a hundred years before.

And probably I haven't got over those Poor Richard tags yet. I rankle still with them. They are thorns in young flesh.

Because, although I still believe that honesty is the best policy, I dislike policy altogether; though it is just as well not to count your chickens before they are hatched, it's still more hateful to count them with gloating when they *are* hatched. It has taken me many years and countless smarts to get out of that barbed wire moral enclosure that Poor Richard rigged up. Here am I now in tatters and scratched to ribbons, sitting in the middle of Benjamin's America looking at the barbed wire, and the fat sheep crawling under the fence to get fat outside, and the watchdogs yelling at the gate lest by chance anyone should get out by the proper exit. Oh America! Oh Benjamin! And I just utter a long loud curse against Benjamin and the American corral.

Moral America! Most moral Benjamin. Sound, satisfied Ben!

He had to go to the frontiers of his State to settle some disturbance among the Indians. On this occasion he writes:

'We found that they had made a great bonfire in the middle of the square; they were all drunk, men and women quarrelling and fighting. Their dark-coloured bodies, half-naked, seen only by the gloomy light of the bonfire, running after and beating one another with fire-brands, accompanied by their horrid yellings, formed a scene the most resembling our ideas of hell that could well be imagined. There was no appeasing the tumult, and we retired to our lodging. At midnight a number of them came thundering at our door, demanding more rum, of which we took no notice.

'The next day, sensible they had misbehaved in giving us that disturbance, they sent three of their counsellors to make their apology. The orator acknowledged the fault, but laid it upon the rum, and then endeavoured to excuse the rum by saying: "The Great Spirit, who made all things, made everything for some use: and whatever he designed anything for, that use it should always be put to. Now, when he had made the rum, he said: 'Let this be for the Indians to get drunk with.' And it must be so."

'And, indeed, if it be the design of Providence to extirpate these savages in order to make room for the cultivators of the earth, it seems not improbable that rum may be the appointed means. It has already annihilated all the tribes who formerly inhabited all the seacoast ...'

This, from the good doctor with such suave complacency, is a little disenchanting. Almost too good to be true.

But there you are! The barbed wire fence. 'Extirpate these savages in order to make room for the cultivators of the earth.' Oh, Benjamin Franklin! He even 'used venery' as a cultivator of seed.

Cultivate the earth, ye gods! The Indians did that, as much as they needed. And they left off there. Who built Chicago? Who cultivated the earth until it spawned Pittsburgh, Pa.?

The moral issue! Just look at it! Cultivation included. If it's a mere choice of Kultur or cultivation, I give it up.

Which brings us right back to our question, what's wrong with Benjamin, that we can't stand him? Or else, what's wrong with us, that we find fault with such a paragon?

Man is a moral animal. All right. I am a moral animal. And I'm going to remain such. I'm not going to be turned into a virtuous little automaton as Benjamin would have me. 'This is good, that is bad. Turn the little handle and let the good tap flow,' said Benjamin, and all America with him. 'But first of all extirpate those savages who are always turning on the bad tap.'

I am a moral animal. But I am not a moral machine. I don't work with a little set of handles or levers. The Temperance-silence-order-resolution-frugality-industry-sincerity-justice-moderation - cleanliness - tranquillity - chastity - humility keyboard is not going to get me going. I'm really not just an automatic piano with a moral Benjamin getting tunes out of me.

Here's my creed, against Benjamin's. This is what I believe:

'*That I am I.*'

'*That my soul is a dark forest.*'

'*That my known self will never be more than a little clearing in the forest.*'

'*That gods, strange gods, come forth from the forest into the clearing of my known self, and then go back.*'

'*That I must have the courage to let them come and go.*'

'*That I will never let mankind put anything over me, but that I will try always to recognize and submit to the gods in me and the gods in other men and women.*'

There is my creed. He who runs may read. He who prefers to crawl, or to go by gasoline, can call it rot.

Then for a 'list'. It is rather fun to play at Benjamin.

1
TEMPERANCE

Eat and carouse with Bacchus, or munch dry bread with Jesus, but don't sit down without one of the gods.

2
SILENCE

Be still when you have nothing to say; when genuine passion moves you, say what you've got to say, and say it hot.

3
ORDER

Know that you are responsible to the gods inside you and to the men in whom the gods are manifest. Recognize your superiors and your inferiors, according to the gods. This is the root of all order.

4
RESOLUTION

Resolve to abide by your own deepest promptings, and to sacrifice the smaller thing to the greater. Kill when you must, and be killed the same: the *must* coming from the gods inside you, or from the men in whom you recognize the Holy Ghost.

5
FRUGALITY

Demand nothing; accept what you see fit. Don't waste your pride or squander your emotion.

6
INDUSTRY
Lose no time with ideals; serve the Holy Ghost; never serve mankind.

7
SINCERITY
To be sincere is to remember that I am I, and that the other man is not me.

8
JUSTICE
The only justice is to follow the sincere intuition of the soul, angry or gentle. Anger is just, and pity is just, but judgement is never just.

9
MODERATION
Beware of absolutes. There are many gods.

10
CLEANLINESS
Don't be too clean. It impoverishes the blood.

11
TRANQUILLITY
The soul has many motions, many gods come and go. Try and find your deepest issue, in every confusion, and abide by that. Obey the man in whom you recognize the Holy Ghost; command when your honour comes to command.

12
CHASTITY
Never 'use' venery at all. Follow your passional impulse, if it be answered in the other being; but never have any motive in mind, neither offspring nor health nor even pleasure, nor even service. Only know that 'venery' is of the great gods. An offering-up of yourself to the very great gods, the dark ones, and nothing else.

13
HUMILITY
See all men and women according to the Holy Ghost that is within them. Never yield before the barren.

There's my list. I have been trying dimly to realize it for a long time, and only America and old Benjamin have at last goaded me into trying to formulate it.

And now I, at least, know why I can't stand Benjamin. He tries to take away my wholeness and my dark forest, my freedom. For how can any man be free, without an illimitable background? And Benjamin tries to shove me into a barbed wired paddock and make me grow potatoes or Chicagoes.

And how can I be free, without gods that come and go? But Benjamin won't let anything exist except my useful fellow-men, and I'm sick of them; as for his Godhead, his Providence, He is Head of nothing except a vast heavenly store that keeps every imaginable line of goods, from victrolas to cat-o'-nine tails.

And how can any man be free without a soul of his own, that he believes in and won't sell at any price? But Benjamin doesn't let me have a soul of my own. He says I am nothing but a servant of mankind – galley-slave I call it – and if I don't get my wages here below – that is, if Mr Pierpont Morgan or Mr Nosey Hebrew or the grand United States Government, the great US, US or SOMEOFUS, manages to scoop in my bit, along with their lump – why, never mind, I shall get my wages HEREAFTER.

Oh Benjamin! Oh Binjum! You do NOT suck me in any longer.

And why, oh why should the snuff-coloured little trap have wanted to take us all in? Why did he do it?

Out of sheer cussedness, in the first place. We do all like to get things inside a barbed-wire corral. Especially our fellow-men. We love to round them up inside the barbed-wire enclosure of FREEDOM, and make 'em work. '*Work! you free jewel! WORK!*' shouts the liberator, cracking his whip. Benjamin, I will not work. I do not choose to be a free democrat. I am absolutely a servant of my own Holy Ghost.

Sheer cussedness! But there was as well the salt of a subtler purpose. Benjamin was just in his eyeholes – to use an English vulgarism, meaning he was just delighted – when he was at Paris judiciously milking money out of the French monarchy for the overthrow of all monarchy. If you want to ride your horse to somewhere you must put a bit in his mouth. And Benjamin wanted to ride his horse so that it would upset the whole apple-cart of the old masters. He wanted the whole European apple-cart upset. So he had to put a strong bit in the mouth of his ass.

'Henceforth be masterless.'

That is, he had to break-in the human ass completely, so

that much more might be broken, in the long run. For the moment it was the British Government that had to have a hole knocked in it. The first real hole it ever had: the breach of the American rebellion.

Benjamin, in his sagacity, knew that the breaking of the old world was a long process. In the depths of his own underconsciousness he hated England, he hated Europe, he hated the whole corpus of the European being. He wanted to be American. But you can't change your nature and mode of consciousness like changing your shoes. It is a gradual shedding. Years must go by, and centuries must elapse before you have finished. Like a son escaping from the domination of his parents. The escape is not just one rupture. It is a long and half-secret process.

So with the American. He was a European when he first went over the Atlantic. He is in the main a recreant European still. From Benjamin Franklin to Woodrow Wilson may be a long stride, but it is a stride along the same road. There is no new road. The same old road, become dreary and futile. Theoretic and materialistic.

Why then did Benjamin set up this dummy of a perfect citizen as a pattern to America? Of course, he did it in perfect good faith, as far as he knew. He thought it simply was the true ideal. But what we *think* we do is not very important. We never really know what we are doing. Either we are materialistic instruments, like Benjamin, or we move in the gesture of creation, from our deepest self, usually unconscious. We are only the actors, we are never wholly the authors of our own deeds or works. IT is the author, the unknown inside us or outside us. The best we can do is to try to hold ourselves in unison with the deeps which are inside us. And the worst we can do is to try to have things our own way, when we run counter to IT, and in the long run get our knuckles rapped for our presumption.

So Benjamin contriving money out of the Court of France. He was contriving the first steps of the overthrow of all Europe, France included. You can never have a new thing without breaking an old. Europe happens to be the old thing.

America, unless the people in America assert themselves too much in opposition to the inner gods, should be the new thing. The new thing is the death of the old. But you can't cut the throat of an epoch. You've got to steal the life from it through several centuries.

And Benjamin worked for this both directly and indirectly. Directly, at the Court of France, making a small but very dangerous hole in the side of England, through which hole Europe has by now almost bled to death. And indirectly in Philadelphia, setting up this unlovely, snuff-coloured little ideal, or automaton, of a pattern American. The pattern American, this dry, moral, utilitarian little democrat, has done more to ruin the old Europe than any Russian nihilist. He has done it by slow attrition, like a son who has stayed at home and obeyed his parents, all the while silently hating their authority, and silently, in his soul, destroying not only their authority but their whole existence. For the American spiritually stayed at home in Europe. The spiritual home of America was, and still is, Europe. This is the galling bondage, in spite of several billions of heaped-up gold. Your heaps of gold are only so many muck-heaps, America, and will remain so till you become a reality to yourselves.

All this Americanizing and mechanizing has been for the purpose of overthrowing the past. And now look at America, tangled in her own barbed wire, and mastered by her own machines. Absolutely got down by her own barbed wire of shalt-nots, and shut up fast in her own 'productive' machines like millions of squirrels running in millions of cages. It is just a farce.

Now is your chance, Europe. Now let Hell loose and get your own back, and paddle your own canoe on a new sea, while clever America lies on her muck-heaps of gold, strangled in her own barbed wire of shalt-not ideals and shalt-not moralisms. While she goes out to work like millions of squirrels in millions of cages. Production!

Let Hell loose, and get your own back, Europe!

MOBY DICK

Written 1917–18. Rewritten 1922–3. *Studies in Classic American Literature*, 1923

MOBY DICK, or the White Whale.

A hunt. The last great hunt.

For what?

For Moby Dick, the huge white sperm whale: who is old, hoary, monstrous, and swims alone: who is unspeakably terrible in his wrath, having so often been attacked; and snow-white.

Of course he is a symbol.

Of what?

I doubt if even Melville knew exactly. That's the best of it.

He is warm-blooded and loveable. The South Sea Islanders, and Polynesians, and Malays, who worship shark, or crocodile, or weave endless frigate-bird distortions, why did they never worship the whale? So big!

Because the whale is not wicked. He doesn't bite. And their gods had to bite.

He's not a dragon. He is Leviathan. He never coils like the Chinese dragon of the sun. He's not a serpent of the waters. He is warm-blooded, a mammal. And hunted, hunted down.

It is a great book.

At first you are put off by the style. It reads like journalism. It seems spurious. You feel Melville is trying to put something over you. It won't do.

And Melville really is a bit sententious: aware of himself, self-conscious, putting something over even himself. But then it's not easy to get into the swing of a piece of deep mysticism when you just set out with a story.

Nobody can be more clownish, more clumsy and sententiously in bad taste, than Herman Melville, even in a great book like *Moby Dick*. He preaches and holds forth because he's not sure of himself. And he holds forth, often, so amateurishly.

The artist was so *much* greater than the man. The man is rather a tiresome New Englander of the ethical mystical-transcendentalist sort: Emerson, Longfellow, Hawthorne, etc. So unrelieved, the solemn ass even in humour. So hopelessly *au grand sérieux*, you feel like saying: Good God, what does it matter? If life is a tragedy, or a farce, or a disaster, or anything else, what do I care! Let life be what it likes. Give me a drink, that's what I want just now.

For my part, life is so many things I don't care what it is. It's not my affair to sum it up. Just now it's a cup of tea. This morning it was wormwood and gall. Hand me the sugar.

One wearies of the *grand sérieux*. There's something false about it. And that's Melville. Oh, dear, when the solemn ass brays! brays! brays!

But he was a deep, great artist, even if he was rather a sententious man. He was a real American in that he always felt his audience in front of him. But when he ceases to be American, when he forgets all audience, and gives us his sheer apprehension of the world, then he is wonderful, his book commands a stillness in the soul, an awe.

In his 'human' self, Melville is almost dead. That is, he hardly reacts to human contacts any more; or only ideally: or just for a moment. His human-emotional self is almost played out. He is abstract, self-analytical and abstracted. And he is more spell-bound by the strange slidings and collidings of Matter than by the things men do. In this he is like Dana. It is the material elements he really has to do with. His drama is with them. He was a futurist long before futurism found paint. The sheer naked slidings of the elements. And the human soul experiencing it all. So often, it is almost over the border: psychiatry. Almost spurious. Yet so great.

It is the same old thing as in all Americans. They keep their old-fashioned ideal frock-coat on, and an old-fashioned silk hat, while they do the most impossible things. There you are: you see Melville hugged in bed by a huge tattooed South Sea Islander, and solemnly offering burnt offering to this savage's little idol, and his ideal frock-coat just hides his shirt-tails and prevents us from seeing his bare posterior as he salaams, while his ethical silk hat sits correctly over his brow the while. That is so typically American: doing the most impossible things without taking off their spiritual get-up. Their ideals are like armour which has rusted in, and will never more come off. And meanwhile in Melville his bodily knowledge moves naked, a living quick among the stark elements. For with sheer physical vibrational sensitiveness, like a marvellous wireless-station, he registers the effects of the outer world. And he records also, almost beyond pain or pleasure, the extreme transitions of the isolated, far-driven soul, the soul which is now alone, without any real human contact.

The first days in New Bedford introduce the only human being who really enters into the book, namely, Ishmael, the 'I' of the book. And then the moment's heart's-brother, Queequeg, the tattooed, powerful South Sea harpooner, whom Melville loves as Dana loves 'Hope'. The advent of Ishmael's bedmate is amusing and unforgettable. But later the two swear 'marriage', in the language of the savages. For Queequeg has opened again the flood-gates of love and human connexion in Ishmael.

'As I sat there in that now lonely room, the fire burning low, in that mild stage when, after its first intensity has warmed the air, it then only glows to be looked at; the evening shades and phantoms gathering round the casements, and peering in upon us silent, solitary twain, I began to be sensible of strange feelings. I felt a melting in me. No more my splintered hand and maddened heart was turned against the wolfish world. This soothing savage had redeemed it. There he sat, his very indifference speaking a nature in which there lurked no civilized hypocrisies and bland deceits. Wild he was; a very sight of sights to see; yet I began to feel myself mysteriously drawn towards him.' – So they smoked together, and are clasped in each other's arms. The friendship is finally sealed when Ishmael offers sacrifice to Queequeg's little idol, Gogo.

'I was a good Christian, born and bred in the bosom of the infallible Presbyterian Church. How then could I unite with the idolater in worshipping his piece of wood? But what is worship? – to do the will of God – *that* is worship. And what is the will of God? – to do to my fellow-man what I would have my fellow-man do to me – *that* is the will of God.' – Which sounds like Benjamin Franklin, and is hopelessly bad theology. But it is real American logic. 'Now Queequeg is my fellow-man. And what do I wish that this Queequeg would do to me? Why, unite with me in my particular Presbyterian form of worship. Consequently, I must unite with him; ergo, I must turn idolater. So I kindled the shavings; helped prop up the innocent little idol; offered him burnt biscuit with Queequeg; salaamed before him twice or thrice; kissed his nose; and that done, we undressed and went to bed, at peace with our own consciences and all the world. But we did not go to sleep without some little chat. How it is I know not; but there is no place like bed for confidential disclosures between friends. Man and wife, they say, open the very bottom of their souls to each other; and some old couples often lie and chat over old times till nearly morning. Thus, then, lay I and Queequeg – a cosy, loving pair –'

You would think this relation with Queequeg meant something to Ishmael. But no. Queequeg is forgotten like yesterday's newspaper. Human things are only momentary excitements or amusements to the American Ishmael. Ishmael, the hunted. But much more Ishmael the hunter. What's a Queequeg? What's a wife? The white whale must be hunted down. Queequeg must be just 'KNOWN', then dropped into oblivion.

And what in the name of fortune is the white whale?

Elsewhere Ishmael says he loved Queequeg's eyes: 'large, deep eyes, fiery black and bold.' No doubt like Poe, he wanted to get the 'clue' to them. That was all.

The two men go over from New Bedford to Nantucket, and there sign on to the Quaker whaling ship, the *Pequod*. It is all strangely fantastic, phantasmagoric. The voyage of the soul. Yet curiously a real whaling voyage, too. We pass on into the midst of the sea with this strange ship and its incredible crew. The Argonauts were mild lambs in comparison. And Ulysses went *defeating* the Circes and overcoming the wicked hussies of the isles. But the *Pequod's* crew is a collection of maniacs fanatically hunting down a lonely, harmless white whale.

As a soul history, it makes one angry. As a sea yarn, it is marvellous: there is always something a bit over the mark, in sea yarns. Should be. Then again the masking up of actual seaman's experience with sonorous mysticism sometimes gets on one's nerves. And again, as a revelation of destiny the book is too deep even for sorrow. Profound beyond feeling.

You are some time before you are allowed to see the captain, Ahab: the mysterious Quaker. Oh, it is a God-fearing Quaker ship.

Ahab, the captain. The captain of the soul.

> I am the master of my fate,
> I am the captain of my soul.

Ahab!

'Oh, captain, my captain, our fearful trip is done.'

The gaunt Ahab, Quaker, mysterious person, only shows himself after some days at sea. There's a secret about him! What?

Oh, he's a portentous person. He stumps about on an ivory stump, made from sea-ivory. Moby Dick, the great white whale, tore off Ahab's leg at the knee, when Ahab was attacking him.

Quite right, too. Should have torn off both his legs, and a bit more besides.

But Ahab doesn't think so. Ahab is now a monomaniac. Moby Dick is his monomania. Moby Dick must DIE, or Ahab can't live any longer. Ahab is atheist by this.

All right.

This *Pequod*, ship of the American soul, has three mates.

1. Starbuck: Quaker, Nantucketer, a good responsible man of reason, forethought, intrepidity, what is called a dependable man. At the bottom, *afraid*.

2. Stubb: 'Fearless as fire, and as mechanical.' Insists on being reckless and jolly on every occasion. Must be afraid too, really.

3. Flask: Stubborn, obstinate, without imagination. To him 'the wondrous whale was but a species of magnified mouse or water-rat –'

There you have them: a maniac captain and his three mates, three splendid seamen, admirable whalemen, first-class men at their job.

America!

It is rather like Mr Wilson and his admirable 'efficient' crew, at the Peace Conference. Except that none of the Pequodders took their wives along.

A maniac captain of the soul, and three eminently practical mates.

Then such a crew. Renegades, castaways, cannibals: Ishmael, Quakers.

America!

Three giant harpooners, to spear the great white whale.

1. Queequeg, the South Sea Islander, all tattooed, big and powerful.

2. Tashtego, the Red Indian of the sea-coast, where the Indian meets the sea.

3. Daggoo, the huge black negro.

There you have them, three savage races, under the American flag, the maniac captain, with their great keen harpoons, ready to spear the white whale.

And only after many days at sea does Ahab's own boat-crew appear on deck. Strange, silent, secret, black-garbed. Malays, fire-worshipping Parsees. These are to man Ahab's boat, when it leaps in pursuit of that whale.

What do you think of the ship *Pequod,* the ship of the soul of an American?

Many races, many peoples, many nations, under the Stars and Stripes. Beaten with many stripes.

Seeing stars sometimes.

And in a mad ship, under a mad captain, in a mad, fanatic's hunt.

For what?

For Moby Dick, the great white whale.

But splendidly handled. Three splendid mates. The whole

thing practical, eminently practical in its working. American industry!

And all this practicality in the service of a mad, mad chase.

Melville manages to keep it a real whaling ship, on a real cruise, in spite of all fantastics. A wonderful, wonderful voyage. And a beauty that is so surpassing only because of the author's awful flounderings in mystical waters. He wanted to get metaphysically deep. And he got deeper than metaphysics. It is a surpassingly beautiful book, with an awful meaning, and bad jolts.

It is interesting to compare Melville with Dana, about the albatross – Melville a bit sententious. 'I remember the first albatross I ever saw. It was during a prolonged gale in waters hard upon the Antarctic seas. From my forenoon watch below I ascended to the overcrowded deck, and there, lashed upon the main hatches, I saw a regal feathered thing of unspotted whiteness, and with a hooked Roman bill sublime. At intervals it arched forth its vast, archangel wings – wondrous throbbings and flutterings shook it. Though bodily unharmed, it uttered cries, as some King's ghost in supernatural distress. Through its inexpressible strange eyes methought I peeped to secrets not below the heavens – the white thing was so white, its wings so wide, and in those for ever exiled waters, I had lost the miserable warping memories of traditions and of towns. I assert then, that in the wondrous bodily whiteness of the bird chiefly lurks the secret of the spell –'

Melville's albatross is a prisoner, caught by bait on a hook.

Well, I have seen an albatross, too: following us in waters hard upon the Antarctic, too, south of Australia. And in the Southern winter. And the ship, a P and O boat, nearly empty. And the lascar crew shivering.

The bird with its long, long wings following, then leaving us. No one knows till they have tried, how lost, how lonely those Southern waters are. And glimpses of the Australian coast.

It makes one feel that our day is only a day. That in the dark of the night ahead other days stir fecund, when we have lapsed from existence.

Who knows how utterly we shall lapse?

But Melville keeps up his disquisition about 'whiteness'. The great abstract fascinated him. The abstract where we end, and cease to be. White or black. Our white, abstract end!

Then again it is lovely to be at sea on the *Pequod*, with never a grain of earth to us.

'It was a cloudy, sultry afternoon; the seamen were lazily lounging about the decks, or vacantly gazing over into the lead-coloured waters. Queequeg and I were mildly employed weaving what is called a sword-mat, for an additional lashing to our boat. So still and subdued, and yet somehow preluding was all the scene, and such an incantation of reverie lurked in the air that each silent sailor seemed resolved into his own invisible self –'

In the midst of his preluding silence came the first cry: 'There she blows! there! there! there! She blows!' And then comes the first chase, a marvellous piece of true sea-writing, the sea, and sheer sea-beings on the chase, sea-creatures chased. There is scarcely a taint of earth – pure sea-motion.

'"Give way men," whispered Starbuck, drawing still further aft the sheet of his sail; "there is time to kill fish yet before the squall comes. There's white water again! – Close to! – Spring!" Soon after, two cries in quick succession on each side of us denoted that the other boats had got fast; but hardly were they overheard, when with a lightning-like hurtling whisper Starbuck said: "Stand up!" and Queequeg, harpoon in hand, sprang to his feet. – Though not one of the oarsmen was then facing the life and death peril so close to them ahead, yet their eyes on the intense countenance of the mate in the stern of the boat, they knew that the imminent instant had come; they heard, too, an enormous wallowing sound, as of fifty elephants stirring in their litter. Meanwhile the boat was still booming through the mist, the waves curbing and hissing around us like the erected crests of enraged serpents.

'"That's his hump. *There! There*, give it to him!" whispered Starbuck. – A short rushing sound leapt out of the boat; it was the darted iron of Queequeg. Then all in one welded motion came a push from astern, while forward the boat seemed striking on a ledge; the sail collapsed and exploded; a gush of scalding vapour shot up near by; something rolled and tumbled like an earthquake beneath us. The whole crew were half-suffocated as they were tossed helter-skelter into the white curling cream of the squall. Squall, whale, and harpoon had all blended together; and the whale, merely grazed by the iron, escaped –'

Melville is a master of violent, chaotic physical motion; he can keep up a whole wild chase without a flaw. He is as perfect at creating stillness. The ship is cruising on the Carrol Ground, south of St Helena. – 'It was while gliding through these latter waters that one serene and moonlight night, when all the waves rolled by like scrolls of silver; and by their soft, suffusing seethings, made what seemed a silvery silence, not a solitude; on such a silent night a silvery jet was seen far in advance of the white bubbles at the bow –'

Then there is the description of Brit. 'Steering northeastward from the Crozello we fell in with vast meadows of brit, the minute, yellow substance upon which the right whale largely feeds. For leagues and leagues it undulated round us, so that we seemed to be sailing through boundless fields of ripe and golden wheat. On the second day, numbers of right whales were seen, secure from the attack of a sperm whaler like the *Pequod.* With open jaws they sluggishly swam through the brit, which, adhering to the fringed fibres of that wondrous Venetian blind in their mouths, was in that manner separated from the water that escaped at the lip. As moving mowers who, side by side, slowly and seethingly advance their scythes through the long wet grass of the marshy meads, even so these monsters swam, making a strange, grassy, cutting sound; and leaving behind them endless swaths of blue on the yellow sea. But it was only the sound they made as they parted the brit which at all reminded one of mowers. Seen from the mast-heads, especially when they paused and were stationary for a while, their vast black forms looked more like masses of rock than anything else –'

This beautiful passage brings us to the apparition of the squid.

'Slowly wading through the meadows of brit, the *Pequod* still held her way northeastward towards the island of Java; a gentle air impelling her keel, so that in the surrounding serenity her three tall, tapering masts mildly waved to that languid breeze, as three mild palms on a plain. And still, at wide intervals, in the silvery night, that lonely, alluring jet would be seen –

'But one transparent-blue morning, when a stillness almost preternatural spread over the sea, however unattended with any stagnant calm; when the long burnished sunglade on the waters seemed a golden finger laid across them, enjoining secrecy; when all the slippered waves whispered together as they ran softly to; in this profound hush of the visible sphere a strange spectre was seen by Daggoo from the mainmast head.

'In the distance, a great white mass lazily rose, and rising higher and higher, and disentangling itself from the azure, at last gleamed before our prow like a snow-slide, new slid from the hills. Thus glistening for a moment, as slowly it subsided, and sank. Then once more arose, and silently gleamed. It seemed not a whale; and yet, is this Moby Dick? thought Daggoo –'

The boats were lowered and pulled to the scene.

'In the same spot where it sank, once more it slowly rose. Almost forgetting for the moment all thoughts of Moby Dick, we now gazed at the most wondrous phenomenon which the secret seas have hitherto revealed to mankind. A vast pulpy mass, furlongs in length and breadth, of a glancing cream-colour, lay floating on the water, innumerable long arms radiating from its centre, and curling and twisting like a nest of anacondas, as if blindly to clutch at any hapless object within reach. No perceptible face or front did it have; no conceivable token of either sensation or instinct; but undulated there on the billows, an unearthly, formless, chance-like apparition of life. And with a low sucking it slowly disappeared again.'

The following chapters, with their account of whale hunts, the killing, the stripping, the cutting up, are magnificent records of actual happening. Then comes the queer tale of the meeting of the *Jeroboam*, a whaler met at sea, all of whose men were under the domination of a religious maniac, one of the ship's hands. There are detailed descriptions of the actual taking of the sperm oil from a whale's head. Dilating on the smallness of the brain of a sperm whale, Melville significantly remarks – 'for I believe that much of a man's character will be found betokened in his backbone. I would rather feel your spine than your skull, whoever you are –' And of the whale, he adds:

'For, viewed in this light, the wonderful comparative smallness of his brain proper is more than compensated by the wonderful comparative magnitude of his spinal cord.'

In among the rush of terrible, awful hunts, come touches of pure beauty.

'As the three boats lay there on that gently rolling sea, gazing down into its eternal blue noon; and as not a single groan or cry of any sort, nay not so much as a ripple or a thought, came up from its depths; what landsman would have thought that beneath all that silence and placidity the utmost monster of the seas was writhing and wrenching in agony!'

Perhaps the most stupendous chapter is the one called *The Grand Armada*, at the beginning of Volume III. The *Pequod* was drawing through the Sunda Straits towards Java when she came upon a vast host of sperm whales. 'Broad on both bows, at a distance of two or three miles, and forming a great semicircle embracing one-half of the level horizon, a continuous chain of whale-jets were up-playing and sparkling in the noonday air.' Chasing this great herd, past the Straits of Sunda, themselves chased by Javan pirates, the whalers race on. Then the boats are lowered. At last that curious state of inert irresolution came over the whalers, when they were, as the seamen say, gallied. Instead of forging ahead in huge martial array they swam violently hither and thither, a surging sea of whales, no longer moving on. Starbuck's boat, made fast to a whale, is towed in amongst this howling Leviathan chaos. In mad career it cockles through the boiling surge of monsters, till it is brought into a clear lagoon in the very centre of the vast, mad, terrified herd. There a sleek pure calm reigns. There the females swam in peace, and the young whales came snuffing tamely at the boat, like dogs. And there the astonished seamen watched the love-making of these amazing monsters, mammals, now in rut far down in the sea – 'But far beneath this wondrous world upon the surface, another and still stranger world met our eyes, as we gazed over the side. For, suspended in these watery vaults, floated the forms of the nursing mothers of the whales, and those that by their enormous girth seemed shortly to become mothers. The lake, as I have hinted, was to a considerable depth exceedingly transparent; and as human infants while sucking will calmly and fixedly gaze away from the breast, as if leading two different lives at a time; and while yet drawing moral nourishment, be still spiritually feasting upon some unearthly reminiscence; even so did the young of these whales seem looking up towards us, but not at us, as if we were but a bit of gulf-weed in their newborn sight. Floating on their sides, the mothers also seemed quietly eyeing us. – Some of the subtlest secrets of the seas seemed divulged to us in this enchanted pond. We saw young Leviathan amours in the deep. And thus, though surrounded by circle upon circle of consternation and affrights, did these inscrutable creatures at the centre freely and fearlessly indulge in all peaceful concernments; yea, serenely revelled in dalliance and delight –'

There is something really overwhelming in these whale-hunts, almost superhuman or inhuman, bigger than life, more terrific than human activity. The same with the chapter on ambergris: it is so curious, so real, yet so unearthly. And again in the chapter called *The Cassock* – surely the oldest piece of phallicism in all the world's literature.

After this comes the amazing account of the Try-works, when the ship is turned into the sooty, oily factory in mid-ocean, and the oil is extracted from the blubber. In the night of the red furnace burning on deck, at sea, Melville has his startling experience of reversion. He is at the helm, but has turned to watch the fire: when suddenly he feels the ship rushing backward from him, in mystic reversion – 'Uppermost was the impression, that whatever swift, rushing thing I stood on was not so much bound to any haven ahead, as rushing from all havens astern. A stark bewildering feeling, as of death, came over me. Convulsively my hands grasped the tiller, but with the crazy conceit that the tiller was, somehow, in some enchanted way, inverted. My God! What is the matter with me, I thought!'

This dream-experience is a real soul-experience. He ends with an injunction to all men, not to gaze on the red fire when its redness makes all things look ghastly. It seems to him that his gazing on fire has evoked this horror of reversion, undoing.

Perhaps it had. He was water-born.

After some unhealthy work on the ship, Queequeg caught a fever and was like to die. 'How he wasted and wasted in those few, long-lingering days, till there seemed but little left of him but his frame and tattooing. But as all else in him thinned, and his cheek-bones grew sharper, his eyes, nevertheless, seemed growing fuller and fuller; they took on a strangeness of lustre; and mildly but deeply looked out at you there from his sickness, a wondrous testimony to that immortal health in him which could not die, or be weakened. And like circles on the water, which as they grow fainter, expand; so his eyes seemed rounding and rounding, like the circles of Eternity. An awe that cannot be named would steal over you as you sat by the side of this waning savage –'

But Queequeg did not die – and the *Pequod* emerges from the Eastern Straits, into the full Pacific. 'To my meditative Magian rover, this serene Pacific once beheld, must ever after be the sea of his adoption. It rolls the utmost waters of the world –'

In this Pacific the fights go on: 'It was far down the afternoon, and when all the spearings of the crimson fight were done, and floating in the lovely sunset sea and sky, sun and whale both died stilly together; then such a sweetness and such a plaintiveness, such inwreathing orisons curled up in that rosy air, that it almost seemed as if far over from the deep green convent valleys of the Manila isles, the Spanish land-breeze had gone to sea, freighted with these vesper hymns. Soothed again, but only soothed to deeper gloom, Ahab, who has steered off from the whale, sat intently watching his final wanings from the now tranquil boat. For that strange spectacle, observable in all sperm whales dying – the turning of the head sunwards, and so expiring – that strange spectacle, beheld of such a placid evening, somehow to Ahab conveyed wondrousness unknown before. "He turns and turns him to it; how slowly, but how steadfastly, his home-rendering and invoking brow, with his last dying motions. He too worships fire . . .'"

So Ahab soliloquizes: and so the warm-blooded whale turns for the last time to the sun, which begot him in the waters.

But as we see in the next chapter, it is the Thunder-fire which Ahab really worships: that living sundering fire of which he bears the brand, from head to foot: it is storm, the electric storm of the *Pequod*, when the corposants burn in high, tapering flames of supernatural pallor upon the masthead, and when the compass is reversed. After this all is fatality. Life itself seems mystically reversed. In these hunters of Moby Dick there is nothing but madness and possession. The captain, Ahab, moves hand in hand with the poor imbecile negro boy, Pip, who has been so cruelly demented, left swimming alone in the vast sea. It is the imbecile child of the sun hand in hand with the northern monomaniac, captain and master.

The voyage surges on. They meet one ship, then another. It is all ordinary day-routine, and yet all is a tension of pure madness and horror, the approaching horror of the last fight. 'Hither and thither, on high, glided the snow-white wings of small unspecked birds; these were the gentle thoughts of the feminine air; but to and fro in the deeps, far down in the bottomless blue, rushed mighty leviathans, sword-fish and sharks; and these were the strong, troubled, murderous thinkings of the masculine sea – ' On this day Ahab confesses his weariness, the weariness of his burden. 'But do I look very old, so very, very old, Starbuck? I feel deadly faint, and bowed, and humped, as though I were Adam staggering beneath the piled centuries since Paradise – ' It is the Gethsemane of Ahab, before the last fight: the Gethsemane of the human soul seeking the last self-conquest, the last attainment of extended consciousness – infinite consciousness.

At last they sight the whale. Ahab sees him from his hoisted perch at the masthead – 'From this height the whale was now seen some mile or so ahead, at every roll of the sea revealing his high, sparkling hump, and regularly jetting his silent spout into the air.'

The boats are lowered, to draw near the white whale. 'At length the breathless hunter came so nigh his seemingly unsuspectful prey that his entire dazzling hump was distinctly visible, sliding along the sea as if an isolated thing, and continually set in a revolving ring of finest, fleecy, greenish foam. He saw the vast involved wrinkles of the slightly projecting head beyond. Before it, far out on the soft Turkish rugged waters, went the glistening white shadow from his broad, milky forehead, a musical rippling playfully accompanying the shade; and behind, the blue waters interchangeably flowed over the moving valley of his steady wake; and on either side bright bubbles arose and danced by his side. But these were broken again by the light toes of hundreds of gay fowl softly feathering the sea, alternate with their fitful flight; and like to some flagstaff rising from the pointed hull of an argosy, the tall but shattered pole of a recent lance projected from the white whale's back; and at intervals one of the clouds of soft-toed fowls hovering, and to and fro shimmering like a canopy over the fish, silently perched and rocked on this pole, the long tail-feathers streaming like pennons.

'A gentle joyousness – a mighty mildness of repose in swiftness, invested the gliding whale –'

The fight with the whale is too wonderful, and too awful, to be quoted apart from the book. It lasted three days. The fearful sight, on the third day, of the torn body of the Parsee harpooner, lost on the previous day, now seen lashed on to the flanks of the white whale by the tangle of harpoon lines, has a mystic dream-horror. The awful and infuriated whale turns upon the ship, symbol of this civilized world of ours. He smites her with a fearful shock. And a few minutes later, from the last of the fighting whale-boats comes the cry: '"The ship! Great God, where is the ship?" Soon they, through the dim, bewildering mediums, saw her sidelong fading phantom, as in the gaseous Fata Morgana; only the uppermost masts out of the water; while fixed by infatuation, or fidelity, or fate, to their once lofty perches, the pagan harpooners still maintained their sinking lookouts on the sea. And now concentric circles seized the lone boat itself, and all its crew, and each floating oar, and every lance-pole, and spinning, animate and inanimate, all round and round in one voıtex, carried the smallest chip of the *Pequod* out of sight –'

The bird of heaven, the eagle, St John's bird, the Red Indian bird, the American, goes down with the ship, nailed by Tashtego's hammer, the hammer of the American Indian. The eagle of the spirit. Sunk!

'Now small fowls flew screaming over the yet yawning gulf; a sullen white surf beat against its steep sides; then all collapsed; and then the great shroud of the sea rolled on as it rolled five thousand years ago.'

So ends one of the strangest and most wonderful books in the world, closing up its mystery and its tortured symbolism. It is an epic of the sea such as no man has equalled; and it is a book of exoteric symbolism of profound significance, and of considerable tiresomeness.

But it is a great book, a very great book, the greatest book of the sea ever written. It moves awe in the soul.

The terrible fatality.

Fatality.

Doom.

Doom! Doom! Doom! Something seems to whisper it in the very dark trees of America. Doom!

Doom of what?

Doom of our white day. We are doomed, doomed. And the doom is in America. The doom of our white day.

Ah, well, if my day is doomed, and I am doomed with my day, it is something greater than I which dooms me, so I accept my doom as a sign of the greatness which is more than I am.

Melville knew. He knew his race was doomed. His white soul doomed. His great white epoch, doomed. Himself, doomed. The idealist, doomed. The spirit, doomed.

The reversion. 'Not so much bound to any haven ahead, as rushing from all havens astern.'

That great horror of ours! It is our civilization rushing from all havens astern.

The last ghastly hunt. The White Whale.

What then is Moby Dick? He is the deepest blood-being of the white race; he is our deepest blood-nature.

And he is hunted, hunted, hunted by the maniacal fanaticism of our white mental consciousness. We want to hunt him down. To subject him to our will. And in this maniacal conscious hunt of ourselves we get dark races and pale to help us, red, yellow, and black, east and west, Quaker and fire-worshipper, we get them all to help us in this ghastly maniacal hunt which is our doom and our suicide.

The last phallic being of the white man. Hunted into the death of upper consciousness and the ideal will. Our blood-self subjected to our will. Our blood-consciousness sapped by a parasitic mental or ideal consciousness.

Hot-blooded sea-born Moby Dick. Hunted by monomaniacs of the idea.

Oh God, oh God, what next, when the *Pequod* has sunk?

She sank in the war, and we are all flotsam.

Now what next?

Who knows? *Quién sabe? Quién sabe, señor?*

Neither Spanish nor Saxon America has any answer.

The *Pequod* went down. And the *Pequod* was the ship of the white American soul. She sank, taking with her Negro and Indian and Polynesian, Asiatic and Quaker and good, business-like Yankees and Ishmael: she sank all the lot of them.

Boom! as Vachel Lindsay would say.

To use the words of Jesus, IT IS FINISHED.

Consummatum est!

But *Moby Dick* was first published in 1851. If the Great White Whale sank the ship of the Great White Soul in 1851, what's been happening ever since?

Post mortem effects, presumably.

Because, in the first centuries, Jesus was Cetus, the Whale. And the Christians were the little fishes. Jesus, the Redeemer, was Cetus, Leviathan. And all the Christians all his little fishes.

WHITMAN

Written 1917–18. Rewritten 1922–3. *Studies in Classic American Literature*, 1923

Post mortem effects?

But what of Walt Whitman?

The 'good grey poet'.

Was he a ghost, with all his physicality?

The good grey poet.

Post mortem effects. Ghosts.

A certain ghoulish insistency. A certain horrible pottage of human parts. A certain stridency and portentousness. A luridness about his beatitudes.

Democracy! These States! Eidolons! Lovers, Endless Lovers!

One Identity!

One Identity!

I am he that aches with Amorous Love.

Do you believe me, when I say post mortem effects?

When the *Pequod* went down, she left many a rank and dirty steamboat still fussing in the seas. The *Pequod* sinks with all her souls, but their bodies rise again to man innumerable tramp steamers, and ocean-crossing liners. Corpses.

What we mean is that people may go on, keep on, and rush on, without souls. They have their ego, and their will; that is enough to keep them going.

So that you see, the sinking of the *Pequod* was only a metaphysical tragedy after all. The world goes on just the same. The ship of the *soul* is sunk. But the machine-manipulating body works just the same: digests, chews gum, admires Botticelli and aches with amorous love.

I am he that aches with Amorous Love.

What do you make of that? I am he that aches. First generalization. First uncomfortable universalization. With

AMOROUS! LOVE! Oh, God! Better a bellyache. A bellyache is at least specific. But the ACHE OF AMOROUS LOVE!

Think of having that under your skin. All that!

I AM HE THAT ACHES WITH AMOROUS LOVE.

Walter, leave off. You are not HE. You are just a limited Walter. And your ache doesn't include all Amorous Love, by any means. If you ache you only ache with a small bit of amorous love, and there's so much more stays outside the cover of your ache, that you might be a bit milder about it.

I AM HE THAT ACHES WITH AMOROUS LOVE.

CHUFF! CHUFF! CHUFF!

CHU-CHU-CHU-CHU-CHUFF!

Reminds one of a steam-engine. A locomotive. They're the only things that seem to me to ache with amorous love. All that steam inside them. Forty million foot-pounds pressure. The ache of AMOROUS LOVE. Steam-pressure. CHUFF!

An ordinary man aches with love for Belinda, or his Native Land, or the Ocean, or the Stars, or the Oversoul: if he feels that an ache is in the fashion.

It takes a steam-engine to ache with AMOROUS LOVE. All of it.

Walt was really too superhuman. The danger of the superman is that he is mechanical.

They talk of his 'splendid animality'. Well, he'd got it on the brain, if that's the place for animality.

I am he that aches with amorous love:
Does the earth gravitate, does not all matter, aching, attract all matter?
So the body of me to all I meet or know.

What can be more mechanical? The difference between life and matter is that life, living things, living creatures, have the instinct of turning right away from *some* matter, and of blissfully ignoring the bulk of most matter, and of turning towards only some certain bits of specially selected matter. As for living creatures all helplessly hurtling together into one great snowball, why, most very living creatures spend the greater part of their time getting out of the sight, smell, or sound of the rest of living creatures. Even bees only cluster on their own queen. And that is sickening enough. Fancy all white humanity clustering on one another like a lump of bees.

No, Walt, you give yourself away. Matter *does* gravitate, helplessly. But men are tricky-tricksy, and they shy all sorts of ways.

Matter gravitates because it *is* helpless and mechanical.

And if you gravitate the same, if the body of you gravitates to all you meet or know, why, something must have gone seriously wrong with you. You must have broken your main-spring.

You must have fallen also into mechanization.

Your Moby Dick must be really dead. That lonely phallic monster of the individual you. Dead mentalized.

I only know that my body doesn't by any means gravitate to all I meet or know. I find I can shake hands with a few people. But most I wouldn't touch with a long prop.

Your mainspring is broken, Walt Whitman. The main-spring of your own individuality. And so you run down with a great whirr, merging with everything.

You have killed your isolate Moby Dick. You have mentalized your deep sensual body, and that's the death of it.

I am everything and everything is me and so we're all One in One Identity, like the Mundane Egg, which has been addled quite a while.

> Whoever you are, to endless announcements –
> And of these one and all I weave the song of myself.

Do you? Well then, it just shows you haven't *got* any self. It's a mush, not a woven thing. A hotch-potch, not a tissue. Your self.

Oh, Walter, Walter, what have you done with it? What have you done with yourself? With your own individual self? For it sounds as if it had all leaked out of you, leaked into the universe.

Post-mortem effects. The individuality had leaked out of him.

No, no, don't lay this down to poetry. These are post-mortem effects. And Walt's great poems are really huge fat tomb-plants, great rank graveyard growths.

All that false exuberance. All those lists of things boiled in one pudding-cloth! No, No!

I don't want all those things inside me, thank you.

'I reject nothing,' says Walt.

If that is so, one must be a pipe open at both ends, so everything runs through.

Post mortem effects.

'I embrace ALL,' says Whitman. 'I weave all things into myself.'

Do you really! There can't be much left of *you* when you've done. When you've cooked the awful pudding of One Identity.

'And whoever walks a furlong without sympathy walks to his own funeral dressed in his own shroud.'

Take off your hat then, my funeral procession of one is passing.

This awful Whitman. This post-mortem poet. This poet with the private soul leaking out of him all the time. All his privacy leaking out in a sort of dribble, oozing into the universe.

Walt becomes in his own person the whole world, the whole universe, the whole eternity of time, as far as his rather sketchy knowledge of history will carry him, that is. Because to *be* a thing he had to know it. In order to assume the identity of a thing he had to know that thing. He was not able to assume one identity with Charlie Chaplin, for example, because Walt didn't know Charlie. What a pity! He'd have done poems, paeans and what not, Chants, Songs of Cinematernity.

Oh, Charlie, my Charlie, another film is done –

As soon as Walt *knew* a thing, he assumed a One Identity with it. If he knew that an Eskimo sat in a kyak, immediately there was Walt being little and yellow and greasy, sitting in a kyak.

Now will you tell me exactly what a kyak is?

Who is he that demands petty definition? Let him behold me *sitting in a kyak.*

I behold no such thing. I behold a rather fat old man full of a rather senile, self-conscious sensuosity.

DEMOCRACY. EN MASSE. ONE IDENTITY.

The universe is short, adds up to ONE.

ONE.

I.

Which is Walt.

His poems, *Democracy*, *En Masse*, *One Identity*, they are long sums in addition and multiplication, of which the answer is invariably MYSELF.

He reaches the state of ALLNESS.

And what then? It's all empty. Just an empty Allness. An addled egg.

Walt wasn't an Eskimo. A little, yellow, sly, cunning, greasy little Eskimo. And when Walt blandly assumed Allness, including Eskimoness, unto himself, he was just sucking the wind out of a blown egg-shell, no more. Eskimos are not minor little Walts. They are something that I am not, I know that. Outside the egg of my Allness chuckles the greasy little Eskimo. Outside the egg of Whitman's Allness too.

But Walt wouldn't have it. He was everything and everything was in him. He drove an automobile with a very fierce headlight, along the track of a fixed idea, through the darkness of this world. And he saw everything that way. Just as a motorist does in the night.

I, who happen to be asleep under the bushes in the dark, hoping a snake won't crawl into my neck; I, seeing Walt go by in his great fierce poetic machine, think to myself: What a funny world that fellow sees!

ONE DIRECTION! toots Walt in the car, whizzing along it.

Whereas there are myriads of ways in the dark, not to mention trackless wildernesses, as anyone will know who cares to come off the road – even the Open Road.

ONE DIRECTION! whoops America, and sets off in an automobile.

ALLNESS! shrieks Walt at a cross-road, going whizz over an unwary Red Indian.

ONE IDENTITY! chants democratic En masse, pelting behind in motor-cars, oblivious of the corpses under the wheels.

God save me, I feel like creeping down a rabbit-hole, to get away from all these automobiles rushing down the ONE IDENTITY track to the goal of ALLNESS.

A woman waits for me –

He might as well have said: 'The femaleness waits for my maleness.' Oh, beautiful generalization and abstraction! Oh, biological function.

'Athletic mothers of these States –' Muscles and wombs. They needn't have had faces at all.

As I see myself reflected in Nature,
As I see through a mist, One with inexpressible completeness, sanity, beauty,
See the bent head, and arms folded over the breast, the Female I see.

Everything was female to him: even himself. Nature just one great function.

This is the nucleus – after the child is born of woman, man is born of woman,
This is the bath of birth, the merge of small and large, and the outlet again –

'The Female I see –'

If I'd been one of his women, I'd have given him Female, with a flea in his ear.

Always wanting to merge himself into the womb of something or other.

'The Female I see –'

Anything, so long as he could merge himself.

Just a horror. A sort of white flux.

Post-mortem effects.

He found, as all men find, that you can't really merge in a woman, though you may go a long way. You can't manage the last bit. So you have to give it up, and try elsewhere if you *insist* on merging.

In *Calamus* he changes his tune. He doesn't shout and thump and exult any more. He begins to hesitate, reluctant, wistful.

The strange calamus has its pink-tinged root by the pond, and it sends up its leaves of comradeship, comrades from one root, without the intervention of woman, the female.

So he sings of the mystery of manly love, the love of comrades. Over and over he says the same thing: the new world will be built on the love of comrades, the new great dynamic of life will be manly love. Out of this manly love will come the inspiration for the future.

Will it though? Will it?

Comradeship! Comrades! This is to be the new Democracy of Comrades. This is the new cohering principle in the world: Comradeship.

Is it? Are you sure?

It is the cohering principle of true soldiery, we are told in *Drum Taps*. It is the cohering principle in the new unison for creative activity. And it is extreme and alone, touching the confines of death. Something terrible to bear, terrible to be responsible for. Even Walt Whitman felt it. The soul's last and most poignant responsibility, the responsibility of comradeship, of manly love.

Yet you are beautiful to me, you faint-tinged roots, you make me think of death.
Death is beautiful from you (what indeed is finally beautiful except death and love?)
I think it is not for life I am chanting here my chant of lovers, I think it must be for death,
For how calm, how solemn it grows to ascend to the atmosphere of lovers,
Death or life, I am then indifferent, my soul declines to prefer
(I am not sure but the high soul of lovers welcomes death most)
Indeed, O death, I think now these leaves mean precisely the same as you mean –

This is strange, from the exultant Walt.

Death!

Death is now his chant! Death!

Merging! And Death! Which is the final merge.

The great merge into the womb. Woman.

And after that, the merge of comrades: man-for-man love.

And almost immediately with this, death, the final merge of death.

There you have the progression of merging. For the great mergers, woman at last becomes inadequate. For those who love to extremes. Woman is inadequate for the last merging. So the next step is the merging of man-for-man love. And this is on the brink of death. It slides over into death.

David and Jonathan. And the death of Jonathan.

It always slides into death.

The love of comrades.

Merging.

So that if the new Democracy is to be based on the love of comrades, it will be based on death too. It will slip so soon into death.

The last merging. The last Democracy. The last love. The love of comrades.

Fatality. And fatality.

Whitman would not have been the great poet he is if he had not taken the last steps and looked over into death. Death, the last merging, that was the goal of his manhood.

To the mergers, there remains the brief love of comrades, and then Death.

Whereto answering, the sea
Delaying not, hurrying not
Whispered me through the night, very plainly before daybreak,
Lisp'd to me the low and delicious word death,
And again death, death, death, death.
Hissing melodions, neither like the bird nor like my arous'd child's heart,
But edging near as privately for me rustling at my feet,
Creeping thence steadily up to my ears and laving me softly all over,
Death, death, death, death, death –

Whitman is a very great poet, of the end of life. A very great post mortem poet, of the transitions of the soul as it loses its integrity. The poet of the soul's last shout and shriek, on the confines of death. *Aprés moi le déluge.*

But we have all got to die, and disintegrate.

We have got to die in life, too, and disintegrate while we live.

But even then the goal is not death.

Something else will come.

Out of the cradle endlessly rocking.

We've got to die first, anyhow. And disintegrate while we still live.

Only we know this much: Death is not the *goal*. And Love, and merging, are now only part of the death-process. Comradeship – part of the death-process. Democracy – part of the death-process. The new Democracy – the brink of death. One Identity – death itself.

We have died, and we are still disintegrating.

But IT IS FINISHED.

Consummatum est.

Whitman, the great poet, has meant so much to me. Whitman, the one man breaking a way ahead. Whitman, the one pioneer. And only Whitman. No English pioneers, no French. No European pioneer-poets. In Europe the would-be pioneers are mere innovators. The same in America. Ahead of Whitman, nothing. Ahead of all poets, pioneering into the wilderness of unopened life, Whitman. Beyond him, none. His wide, strange camp at the end of the great high-road. And lots of new little poets camping on Whitman's camping ground now. But none going really beyond. Because Whitman's camp is at the end of the road, and on the edge of a great precipice. Over the precipice, blue distances, and the blue hollow of the future. But there is no way down. It is a dead end.

Pisgah. Pisgah sights. And Death. Whitman like a strange, modern, American Moses. Fearfully mistaken. And yet the great leader.

The essential function of art is moral. Not aesthetic, not decorative, not pastime and recreation. But moral. The essential function of art is moral.

But a passionate, implicit morality, not didactic. A morality which changes the blood, rather than the mind. Changes the blood first. The mind follows later, in the wake.

Now Whitman was a great moralist. He was a great leader. He was a great changer of the blood in the veins of men.

Surely it is especially true of American art, that it is all essentially moral. Hawthorne, Poe, Longfellow, Emerson, Melville: it is the moral issue which engages them. They all feel uneasy about the old morality. Sensuously, passionally, they all attack the old morality. But they know nothing better, mentally. Therefore they give tight mental allegiance to a morality which all their passion goes to destroy. Hence the duplicity which is the fatal flaw in them: most fatal in the most perfect American work of art, *The Scarlet Letter*. Tight mental allegiance given to a morality which the passional self repudiates.

Whitman was the first to break the mental allegiance. He was the first to smash the old moral conception that the soul of man is something 'superior' and 'above' the flesh. Even Emerson still maintained this tiresome 'superiority' of the soul. Even Melville could not get over it. Whitman was the first heroic seer to seize the soul by the scruff of her neck and plant her down among the potsherds.

'There!' he said to the soul. 'Stay there!'

Stay there. Stay in the flesh. Stay in the limbs and lips and in the belly. Stay in the breast and womb. Stay there, Oh Soul, where you belong.

Stay in the dark limbs of Negroes. Stay in the body of the prostitute. Stay in the sick flesh of the syphilitic. Stay in the marsh where the calamus grows. Stay there, Soul, where you belong.

The Open Road. The great home of the Soul is the open road. Not heaven, not paradise. Nor 'above'. Not even 'within'. The soul is neither 'above' nor 'within'. It is a wayfarer down the open road.

Not by meditating. Not by fasting. Not by exploring heaven after heaven, inwardly, in the manner of the great mystics. Not by exaltation. Not by ecstasy. Not by any of those ways does the soul come into her own.

Only by taking the open road.

Not through charity. Not through sacrifice. Not even through love. Not through good works. Not through these does the soul accomplish herself.

Only through the journey down the open road.

The journey itself, down the open road. Exposed to full contact. On two slow feet. Meeting whatever comes down the open road. In company with those that drift in the same measure along the same way. Towards no goal. Always the open road.

Having no known direction even. Only the soul remaining true to herself in her going.

Meeting all the other wayfarers along the road. And how? How meet them, and how pass? With sympathy, says Whitman. Sympathy. He does not say love. He says sympathy. Feeling with. Feel with them as they feel with themselves. Catching the vibration of their soul and flesh as we pass.

It is a new great doctrine. A doctrine of life. A new great morality. A morality of actual living, not of salvation. Europe has never got beyond the morality of salvation. America to this day is deathly sick with saviourism. But Whitman, the greatest and the first and the only American teacher, was no Saviour. His morality was no morality of salvation. His was a morality of the soul living her life, not saving herself. Accepting the contact with other souls along the open way, as they lived their lives. Never trying to save them. As leave try to arrest them and throw them in gaol. The soul living her life along the incarnate mystery of the open road.

This was Whitman. And the true rhythm of the American continent speaking out in him. He is the first white aboriginal.

'In my Father's house are many mansions.'

'No,' said Whitman. 'Keep out of mansions. A mansion may be heaven on earth, but you might as well be dead. Strictly avoid mansions. The soul is herself when she is going on foot down the open road.'

It is the American heroic message. The soul is not to pile up defences round herself. She is not to withdraw and seek her heavens inwardly, in mystical ecstasies. She is not to cry to some God beyond, for salvation. She is to go down the open road, as the road opens, into the unknown, keeping company with those whose soul draws them near to her, accomplishing nothing save the journey, and the works incident to the journey, in the long life-travel into the unknown, the soul in her subtle sympathies accomplishing herself by the way.

This is Whitman's essential message. The heroic message of the American future. It is the inspiration of thousands of Americans to-day, the best souls of to-day, men and women.

And it is a message that only in America can be fully understood, finally accepted.

Then Whitman's mistake. The mistake of his interpretation of his watchword: Sympathy. The mystery of SYMPATHY. He still confounded it with Jesus' LOVE, and with Paul's CHARITY. Whitman, like all the rest of us, was at the end of the great emotional highway of Love. And because he couldn't help himself, he carried on his Open Road as a prolongation of the emotional highway of Love, beyond Calvary. The highway of love ends at the foot of the Cross. There is no beyond. It was a hopeless attempt to prolong the highway of love.

He didn't follow his Sympathy. Try as he might, he kept on automatically interpreting it as Love, as Charity. Merging!

This merging, *en masse*, One Identity, Myself monomania was a carry-over from the old Love idea. It was carrying the idea of Love to its logical physical conclusion. Like Flaubert and the leper. The decree of unqualified Charity, as the soul's one means of salvation, still in force.

Now Whitman wanted his soul to save itself; *he* didn't want to save it. Therefore he did not need the great Christian receipt for saving the soul. He needed to supersede the Christian Charity, the Christian Love, within himself, in order to give his Soul her last freedom. The highroad of Love is no Open Road. It is a narrow, tight way, where the soul walks hemmed in between compulsions.

Whitman wanted to take his Soul down the open road. And he failed in so far as he failed to get out of the old rut of Salvation. He forced his Soul to the edge of a cliff, and he looked down into death. And there he camped, powerless. He had carried out his Sympathy as an extension of Love and Charity. And it had brought him almost to madness and soul-death. It gave him his forced, unhealthy, post-mortem quality.

His message was really the opposite of Henley's rant:

I am the master of my fate,
I am the captain of my soul.

Whitman's essential message was the Open Road. The leaving of the soul free unto herself, the leaving of his fate to her and to the loom of the open road. Which is the bravest doctrine man has ever proposed to himself.

Alas, he didn't quite carry it out. He couldn't quite break the old maddening bond of the love-compulsion; he couldn't quite get out of the rut of the charity habit – for Love and Charity have degenerated now into habit: a bad habit.

Whitman said Sympathy. If only he had stuck to it! Because Sympathy means feeling with, not feeling for. He kept on having a passionate feeling *for* the negro slave, or the prostitute, or the syphilitic – which is merging. A sinking of Walt Whitman's soul in the souls of these others.

He wasn't keeping to his open road. He was forcing his soul down an old rut. He wasn't leaving her free. He was forcing her into other people's circumstances.

Supposing he had felt true sympathy with the negro slave? He would have felt *with* the negro slave. Sympathy – compassion – which is partaking of the passion which was in the soul of the negro slave.

What was the feeling in the negro's soul?

'Ah, I am a slave! Ah, it is bad to be a slave! I must be free myself. My soul will die unless she frees herself. My soul says I must free myself.'

Whitman came along, and saw the slave, and said to himself: 'That negro slave is a man like myself. We share the same identity. And he is bleeding with wounds. Oh, oh, is it not myself who am also bleeding with wounds?'

This was not *sympathy*. It was merging and self-sacrifice. 'Bear ye one another's burdens': 'Love thy neighbour as thyself': 'Whatsoever ye do unto him, ye do unto me.'

If Whitman had truly *sympathized*, he would have said: 'That negro slave suffers from slavery. He wants to free himself. His soul wants to free him. He has wounds, but they are the price of freedom. The soul has a long journey from slavery to freedom. If I can help him I will: I will not take over his wounds and his slavery to myself. But I will help him fight the power that enslaves him when he wants to be free, if he wants my help, since I see in his face that he needs to be free. But even when he is free, his soul has many journeys down the open road, before it is a free soul.'

And of the prostitute Whitman would have said:

'Look at that prostitute! Her nature has turned evil under her mental lust for prostitution. She has lost her soul. She knows it herself. She likes to make men lose their souls. If she tried to make me lose my soul, I would kill her. I wish she may die.'

But of another prostitute he would have said:

'Look! She is fascinated by the Priapic mysteries. Look, she will soon be worn to death by the Priapic usage. It is the way of her soul. She wishes it so.'

Of the syphilitic he would say:

'Look! She wants to infect all men with syphilis. We ought to kill her.'

And of still another syphilitic:

'Look! She has a horror of her syphilis. If she looks my way I will help her to get cured.'

This is sympathy. The soul judging for herself, and preserving her own integrity.

But when, in Flaubert, the man takes the leper to his naked body: when Bubu de Montparnasse takes the girl because he knows she's got syphilis; when Whitman embraces an evil prostitute: that is not sympathy. The evil prostitute has no desire to be embraced with love; so if you sympathize with her, you won't try to embrace her with love. The leper loathes his leprosy, so if you sympathize with him, you'll loathe it too. The evil woman who wishes to infect all men with her syphilis hates you if you haven't got syphilis. If you sympathize, you'll feel her hatred, and you'll hate too, you'll hate her. Her feeling is hate, and you'll share it. Only your soul will choose the direction of its own hatred.

The soul is a very perfect judge of her own motions, if your mind doesn't dictate to her. Because the mind says Charity! Charity! you don't have to force your soul into kissing lepers or embracing syphilitics. Your lips are the lips of your soul, your body is the body of your soul; your own single, individual soul. That is Whitman's message. And your soul hates syphilis and leprosy. Because it *is* a soul, it hates these things, which are against the soul. And therefore to force the body of your soul into contact with uncleanness is a great violation of your soul. The soul wishes to keep clean and whole. The soul's deepest will is to preserve its own integrity, against the mind and the whole mass of disintegrating forces.

Soul sympathizes with soul. And that which tries to kill my soul, my soul hates. My soul and my body are one. Soul and body wish to keep clean and whole. Only the mind is capable of great perversion. Only the mind tries to drive my soul and body into uncleanness and unwholesomeness.

What my soul loves, I love.

What my soul hates, I hate.

When my soul is stirred with compassion, I am compassionate.

What my soul turns away from, I turn away from.

That is the *true* interpretation of Whitman's creed: the true revelation of his Sympathy.

And my soul takes the open road. She meets the souls that are passing, she goes along with the souls that are going her way. And for one and all, she has sympathy. The sympathy of love, the sympathy of hate, the sympathy of simple proximity; all the subtle sympathizings of the incalculable soul, from the bitterest hate to passionate love.

It is not I who guide my soul to heaven. It is I who am guided by my own soul along the open road, where all men tread. Therefore, I must accept her deep motions of love, or hate, or compassion, or dislike, or indifference. And I must go where she takes me, for my feet and my lips and my body are my soul. It is I who must submit to her.

This is Whitman's message of American democracy.

The democracy, where soul meets soul, in the open road. Democracy. American democracy where all journey down the open road, and where a soul is known at once in its going. Not by its clothes or appearance. Whitman did away with that. Not by its family name. Not even by its reputation. Whitman and Melville both discounted that. Not by a progression of piety, or by works of Charity. Not by works at all.

Not by anything, but just itself. The soul passing unenhanced, passing on foot and being no more than itself. And recognized, and passed by or greeted according to the soul's dictate. If it be a great soul, it will be worshipped in the road.

The love of man and woman: a recognition of souls, and a communion of worship. The love of comrades: a recognition of souls, and a communion of worship. Democracy: a recognition of souls, all down the open road, and a great soul seen in its greatness, as it travels on foot among the rest, down the common way of the living. A glad recognition of souls, and a gladder worship of great and greater souls, because they are the only riches.

Love, and Merging, brought Whitman to the Edge of Death! Death! Death!

But the exultance of his message still remains. Purified of MERGING, purified of MYSELF, the exultant message of American Democracy, of souls in the Open Road, full of glad recognition, full of fierce readiness, full of the joy of worship, when one soul sees a greater soul.

The only riches, the great souls.

GIOVANNI VERGA

Written spring 1922. *Phoenix*, 1936

It seems curious that modern Italian literature has made so little impression on the European consciousness. A hundred years ago, when Manzoni's *I Promessi Sposi* came out, it met with European applause. Along with Sir Walter Scott and Byron, Manzoni stood for 'Romance' to all Europe. Yet where is Manzoni now, even compared to Scott and Byron? Actually, I mean. Nominally, *I Promessi Sposi* is a classic, in fact, it is usually considered *the* classic Italian novel. It is set in all 'literature courses'. But who reads it? Even in Italy, who reads it? And yet, to my thinking, it is one of the best and most interesting novels ever written: surely a greater book than *Ivanhoe* or *Paul et Virginie* or *Werther*. Why then does nobody read it? Why is it found boring? When I gave a good English translation to the late Katherine Mansfield, she said, to my astonishment: I couldn't read it. Too long and boring.

It is the same with Giovanni Verga. After Manzoni, he is Italy's accepted greatest novelist. Yet nobody takes any notice of him. He is, as far as anybody knows his name, just the man who wrote the libretto to *Cavalleria Rusticana*. Whereas, as a matter of fact, Verga's story *Cavalleria Rusticana* is as much superior to Mascagni's rather cheap music as wine is superior to sugar-water. Verga is one of the greatest masters of the short story. In the volume *Novelle Rusticane* and in the volume entitled *Cavalleria Rusticana* are some of the best short stories ever written. They are sometimes as short and as poignant as Chekhov. I prefer them to Chekhov. Yet nobody reads them. They are 'too depressing'. They don't depress me half as much as Chekhov does. I don't understand the popular taste.

Verga wrote a number of novels, of different sorts: very different. He was born about 1850, and died, I believe, at the beginning of 1921. So he is a modern. At the same time, he is a classic. And at the same time, again, he is old-fashioned.

The earlier novels are rather of the French type of the seventies – Octave Feuillet, with a touch of Gyp. There is the depressing story of the Sicilian young man who made a Neapolitan marriage, and on the last page gives his wife a much-belated slap across the face. There is the gruesome book, *Tigre Reale*, of the Russian countess – or princess, whatever it is – who comes to Florence and gets fallen in love with by the young Sicilian, with all the subsequent horrid affair: the weird woman dying of consumption, the man weirdly infatuated, in the suicidal South-Italian fashion. It is a bit in the manner of Matilda Serao. And though unpleasant, it is impressive.

Verga himself was a Sicilian, from one of the lonely agricultural villages in the south of the island. He was a gentleman – but not a rich one, presumably: with some means. As a young man, he went to Naples, then he worked at journalism in Milan and Florence. And finally he retired to Catania, to an exclusive, aristocratic old age. He was a shortish, broad man with a big red moustache. He never married.

His fame rests on his two long Sicilian novels, *I Malavoglia* and *Mastro-don Gesualdo*, also on the books of short pieces, *Cavalleria Rusticana*, *Novelle Rusticane*, and *Vagabondaggio*. These are all placed in Sicily, as is the short novel, *Storia di una Capinera*. Of this last little book, one of the leading literary young Italians in Rome said to me the other day: Ah, yes, Verga! *Some* of his things! But a thing like *Storia di una Capinera*, now, is ridiculous.

But why? It is rather sentimental, maybe. But it is no more sentimental than *Tess*. And the sentimentality seems to me to belong to the Sicilian characters in the book, it is true to type, quite as much so as the sentimentality of a book like Dickens' *Christmas Carol*, or George Eliot's *Silas Marner*, both of which works are 'ridiculous', if you like, without thereby being wiped out of existence.

The trouble with Verga, as with all Italians, is that he never seems quite to know where he is. When one reads Manzoni, one wonders if he is not more 'Gothic' or Germanic, than Italian. And Verga, in the same way, seems to have a borrowed outlook on life: but this time, borrowed from the French. With d'Annunzio the same, it is hard to believe he is really being himself. He gives one the impression of 'acting up'. Pirandello goes on with the game to-day. The Italians are always that way: always acting up to somebody else's vision of life. Men like Hardy, Meredith, Dickens, they are just as sentimental and false as the Italians, in their own way. It only happens to be our own brand of falseness and sentimentality.

And yet, perhaps, one can't help feeling that Hardy, Meredith, Dickens, and Maupassant and even people like the Goncourts and Paul Bourget, false in part though they be, are still looking on life with their own eyes. Whereas the Italians give one the impression that they are always borrowing somebody else's eyes to see with, and then letting loose a lot of emotion into a borrowed vision.

This is the trouble with Verga. But on the other hand, everything he does has a weird quality of Verga in it, quite distinct and like nothing else. And yet, perhaps the gross vision of the man is not quite his own. All his movements are his own. But his main motive is borrowed.

This is the unsatisfactory part about all Italian literature, as far as I know it.

The main motive, the gross vision of all the nineteenth-century literature, is what we may call the emotional-democratic vision or motive. It seems to me that since 1860 or even 1830, the Italians have always borrowed their ideals of democracy from the northern nations, and poured great emotion into them without ever being really grafted by them. Some of the most wonderful martyrs for democracy have been Neapolitan men of birth and breeding. But none the less, it seems a mistake: an attempt to live by somebody else's lights.

Verga's first Sicilian novel, *I Malavoglia*, is of this sort. It was considered his greatest work. It is a great book. But it is *parti pris*. It is one-sided. And therefore it dates. There is too much, too much of the tragic fate of the poor, in it. There is a sort of wallowing in tragedy: the tragedy of the humble. It belongs to a date when the 'humble' were almost the most fashionable thing. And the Malavoglia family are most humbly humble. Sicilians of the sea-coast, fishers, small traders – their humble tragedy is so piled on, it becomes almost disastrous. The book was published in America under the title of *The House by the Medlar Tree*, and can still be obtained. It is a great book, a great picture of poor life in Sicily, on the coast just north of Catania. But it is rather overdone on the pitiful side. Like the woebegone pictures by Bastien Lepage. Nevertheless, it is essentially a true picture, and different from anything else in literature. In most books of the period – even in *Madame Bovary*, to say nothing of Balzac's earlier *Lys dans la Vallée* – one has to take off about twenty per cent of the tragedy. One does it in Dickens, one does it in Hawthorne, one does it all the time, with all the great writers. Then why not with Verga? Just knock off about twenty per cent of the tragedy in *I Malavoglia*, and see what a great book remains. Most books that live, live in spite of the author's laying it on thick. Think of *Wuthering Heights*. It is quite as impossible to an Italian as even *I Malavoglia* is to us. But it is a great book.

The trouble with realism – and Verga was a realist – is that the writer, when he is a truly exceptional man like Flaubert or like Verga, tries to read his own sense of tragedy into people much smaller than himself. I think it is a final criticism against *Madame Bovary* that people such as Emma Bovary and her husband Charles simply are too insignificant to carry the full weight of Gustave Flaubert's sense of tragedy. Emma and Charles Bovary are a couple of little people. Gustave Flaubert is not a little person. But, because he is a realist and does not believe in 'heroes', Flaubert insists on pouring his own deep and bitter tragic consciousness into the little skins of the country doctor and his uneasy wife. The result is a discrepancy. *Madame Bovary* is a great book and a very wonderful picture of life. But we cannot help resenting the fact that the great tragic soul of Gustave Flaubert is, so to speak, given only the rather commonplace bodies of Emma and Charles Bovary. There's a misfit. And to get over the misfit you have to let in all sorts of seams of pity. Seams of pity, which won't be hidden.

The great tragic soul of Shakespeare borrows the bodies of kings and princes – not out of snobbism, but out of natural affinity. You can't put a great soul into a commonplace person. Commonplace persons have commonplace souls. Not all the noble sympathy of Flaubert or Verga for Bovarys and Malavoglias can prevent the said Bovarys and Malavoglias from being commonplace persons. They were deliberately chosen because they *were* commonplace, and not heroic. The authors insisted on the treasure of the humble. But they had to lend the humble by far the best part of their own treasure, before the said humble could show any treasure at all.

So, if *I Malavoglia* dates, so does *Madame Bovary*. They belong to the emotional-democratic, treasure-of-the-humble period of the nineteenth century. The period is just now rather out of fashion. We still feel the impact of the treasure-of-the-humble too much. When the emotion will have quite gone out of us, we can accept *Madame Bovary* and *I Malavoglia* in the same free spirit with the same detachment as that in which we accept Dickens or Richardson.

Mastro-don Gesualdo, however, is not nearly so much treasure-of-the-humble as *I Malavoglia*. Here, Verga is not dealing with the disaster of poverty, and calling it tragedy. On the contrary, he is a little bored by poverty. He must have a hero who wins out, and makes his pile, and then succumbs under the pile.

Mastro-don Gesualdo started life as a barefoot peasant brat, not a don at all. He becomes very rich. But all he gets out of it is a great tumour of bitterness inside, which kills him.

Verga must have known, in actual life, the prototype of Gesualdo. We see him in the marvellous realistic story in *Cavalleria Rusticana*, of a fat little peasant, who has become enormously rich, grinding his labourers, and now is diseased and must die. This little fellow is quite unheroic. He has the indomitable greedy will, but nothing else of Gesualdo's rather attractive character.

Gesualdo is attractive, and, in a sense, heroic. But still he is not allowed to emerge in the old heroic sense, with swagger and nobility and head-and-shoulders taller than anything else. He is allowed to have exceptional qualities, and above all, exceptional force. But these things do not make a hero of a man. A hero must be a hero by grace of God, and must have an inkling of the same. Even the old Paladin heroes had a great idea of themselves as exemplars. And Hamlet had the same. 'O cursed spite that ever I was born to set it right.' Hamlet didn't succeed in setting anything right, but he felt that way. And so all heroes must feel.

But Gesualdo, and Jude, and Emma Bovary are not allowed to feel any of these feelings. As far as *destiny* goes, they felt no more than anybody else. And this is because they belong to the realistic world.

Gesualdo is just an ordinary man with extraordinary energy. That, of course, is the intention. But he is a Sicilian. And here lies the difficulty. Because the realistic-democratic age has dodged the dilemma of having no heroes by having every man his own hero. This is reached by what we call subjective intensity, and in this subjectively-intense every-man-his-own-hero business the Russians have carried us to the greatest lengths. The merest scrub of a pick-pocket is so phenomenally aware of his own soul, that we are made to bow down before the imaginary coruscations that go on inside him. That is almost the whole of Russian literature: the phenomenal coruscations of the souls of quite commonplace people.

Of course your soul will coruscate, if you think it does. That's why the Russians are so popular. No matter how much of a shabby animal you may be, you can learn from Dostoievsky and Chekhov, etc., how to have the most tender, unique, coruscating soul on earth. And so you may be most vastly important to yourself. Which is the private aim of all men. The hero had it openly. The commonplace person has it inside himself, though outwardly he says: Of course I'm no better than anybody else! His very asserting it shows he doesn't think it for a second. Every character in Dostoievsky or Chekhov thinks himself *inwardly* a nonesuch, absolutely unique.

And here you get the blank opposite, in the Sicilians. The

Sicilians simply don't have any subjective idea of themselves, or any souls. Except, of course, that funny little *alter ego* of a soul which can be prayed out of purgatory into paradise, and is just as objective as possible.

The Sicilian, in our sense of the word, doesn't have any soul. He just hasn't got our sort of subjective consciousness, the soulful idea of himself. Souls, to him, are little naked people uncomfortably hopping on hot bricks, and being allowed at last to go up to a garden where there is music and flowers and sanctimonious society, Paradise. Jesus is a man who was crucified by a lot of foreigners and villains, and who can help you against the villainous lot nowadays: as well as against witches and the rest.

The self-tortured Jesus, the self-tortured Hamlet, simply does not exist. Why should a man torture himself? Gesualdo would ask in amazement. Aren't there scoundrels enough in the world to torture him?

Of course, I am speaking of the Sicilians of Verga's day, fifty and sixty years ago, before the great emigration to America, and the great return, with dollars and bits of self-aware souls: at least politically self-aware.

So that in *Mastro-don Gesualdo* you have the very antithesis of what you get in *The Brothers Karamazov*. Anything more un-Russian than Verga it would be hard to imagine: save Homer. Yet Verga has the same sort of pity as the Russians. And, with the Russians, he is a realist. He won't have heroes, nor appeals to gods above nor below.

The Sicilians of to-day are supposed to be the nearest thing to the classic Greeks that is left to us: that is, they are the nearest descendants on earth. In Greece to-day there are no Greeks. The nearest thing is the Sicilian, the eastern and south-eastern Sicilian.

And if you come to think of it, Gesualdo Motta might really be a Greek in modern setting, except that he is not intellectual. But this many Greeks were not. And he has the energy, the quickness, the vividness of the Greek, the same vivid passion for wealth, the same ambition, the same lack of scruples, the same queer openness, without ever really openly committing himself. He is not a bit furtive, like an Italian. He is astute instead, far too astute and Greek to let himself be led by the nose. Yet he has a certain frankness, far more than an Italian. And far less fear than an Italian. His boldness and his queer sort of daring are Sicilian rather than Italian, so is his independent manliness.

He is Greek above all in not having any soul or any lofty ideals. The Greeks were far more bent on making an audacious splendid impression than on fulfilling some noble purpose. They loved the splendid look of a thing, the splendid ring of words. Even tragedy was to them a grand gesture, rather than something to mope over. Peak and pine they would not, and unless some Fury pursued them to punish them for their sins, they cared not a straw for sins: their own or anyone else's.

As for being burdened with souls, they were not such fools.

But alas, ours is the day of souls, when soul pays, and when having a soul is as important to the young as a solitaire to a valetudinarian. If you don't have feelings about your soul, what sort of person can you be?

And Gesualdo didn't have feelings about his soul. He was remorselessly and relentlessly objective, like all people that belong to the sun. In the sun men are objective, in the mist and snow, subjective. Subjectivity is largely a question of the thickness of your overcoat.

When you get to Ceylon, you realize that, to the swarthy Cingalese, even Buddhism is a purely objective affair. And we have managed to spiritualize it to such a subjective pitch.

Then you have the setting to the hero. The south-Sicilian setting to *Mastro-don Gesualdo* is perhaps nearer to the true medieval than anything else in modern literature, even barring the Sardinian medievalism of Grazia Deledda. You have the Sicily of the Bourbons, the Sicily of the kingdom of Naples. The island is incredibly poor and incredibly backward. There are practically no roads for wheeled vehicles, and consequently no wheeled vehicles, neither carts nor carriages, outside the towns. Everything is packed on asses or mules, man travels on horseback or on foot, or, if sick, in a mule litter. The land is held by the great landowners, the peasants are almost serfs. It is as wild, as poor, and in the ducal houses of Palermo even as splendid and ostentatious as Russia.

Yet how different from Russia! Instead of the wild openness of the north, you have the shut-in, guarded watchfulness of the old Mediterranean. For centuries, the people of the Mediterranean have lived on their guard, intensely on their guard, on the watch, wary, always wary, and holding aloof. So it is even to-day, in the villages: aloof, holding aloof, each individual inwardly holding aloof from the others; and this in spite of the returned 'Americans'.

How utterly different it is from Russia, where the people are always – in the books – expanding to one another, and pouring out tea and their souls to one another all night long. In Sicily, by nightfall, nearly every man is barricaded inside his own house. Save in the hot summer, when the night is more or less turned into day.

It all seems, to some people, dark and squalid and brutal and boring. There is no soul, no enlightenment at all. There is not one single enlightened person. If there had been, he would have departed long ago. He could not have stayed.

And for people who seek enlightenment, oh, how boring! But if you have any physical feeling for life, apart from nervous feelings such as the Russians have, nerves, nerves – if you have any appreciation for the southern way of life, then what a strange, deep fascination there is in *Mastro-don Gesualdo*! Perhaps the deepest nostalgia I have ever felt has been for Sicily, reading Verga. Not for England or anywhere else – for Sicily, the beautiful, that which goes deepest into the blood. It is so clear, so beautiful, so like the physical beauty of the Greek.

Yet the lives of the people all seem so squalid, so pottering, so despicable: like a crawling of beetles. And then, the moment you get outside the grey and squalid walls of the village, how wonderful in the sun, with the land lying apart. And isolated, the people too have some of the old Greek singleness, carelessness, dauntlessness. It is only when they bunch together as citizens that they are squalid. In the countryside, they are portentous and subtle, like the wanderers in the Odyssey. And their relations are all curious and immediate, objective. They are so little aware of themselves, and so much aware of their own effects.

It all depends what you are looking for. Gesualdo's life-long love-affair with Diodata is, according to our ideas, quite impossible. He puts no value on sentiment at all: or almost none: again a real Greek. Yet there is a strange forlorn beauty in it, impersonal, a bit like Rachel or Rebecca. It is of the old, old world, when man is aware of his own belongings, acutely, but only very dimly aware of his own feelings. And feelings you are not aware of, you don't have.

Gesualdo seems so potent, so full of potency. Yet nothing emerges, and he never says anything. It is the very reverse of the Russian, who talks and talks, out of impotence.

And you have a wretched, realistic kind of tragedy for the end. And you feel, perhaps the book was all about nothing, and Gesualdo wasn't worth the labour of Verga.

But that is because we are spiritual snobs, and think, because a man can fume with 'To be or not to be', therefore he is a person to be taken account of. Poor Gesualdo had never heard of it: To be or not to be, and he wouldn't have taken any notice if he had. He lived blindly, with the impetuosity of blood and muscles, sagacity and will, and he never woke up to himself. Whether he would have been any the better for waking up to himself, who knows!

PREFACE TO THE AMERICAN EDITION OF NEW POEMS

Date of writing uncertain. *New Poems*, New York, 1920. *Phoenix*, 1936

It seems when we hear a skylark singing as if sound were running into the future, running so fast and utterly without consideration, straight on into futurity. And when we hear a nightingale, we hear the pause and the rich, piercing rhythm of recollection, the perfected past. The lark may sound sad, but with the lovely lapsing sadness that is almost a swoon of hope. The nightingale's triumph is a paean, but a death-paean.

So it is with poetry. Poetry is, as a rule, either the voice of the far future, exquisite and ethereal, or it is the voice of the past, rich, magnificent. When the Greeks heard the *Iliad* and the *Odyssey* they heard their own past calling in their hearts, as men far inland sometimes hear the sea and fall weak with powerful, wonderful regret, nostalgia; or else their own future rippled its time-beats through their blood, as they followed the painful, glamorous progress of the Ithacan. This was Homer to the Greeks: their Past, splendid with battles won and death achieved, and their Future, the magic wandering of Ulysses through the unknown.

With us it is the same. Our birds sing on the horizons. They sing out of the blue, beyond us, or out of the quenched night. They sing at dawn and sunset. Only the poor, shrill, tame canaries whistle while we talk. The wild birds begin before we are awake, or as we drop into dimness, out of waking. Our poets sit by the gateways, some by the east, some by the west. As we arrive and as we go out our hearts surge with response. But whilst we are in the midst of life, we do not hear them.

The poetry of the beginning and the poetry of the end must have that exquisite finality, perfection which belongs to all that is far off. It is in the realm of all that is perfect. It is of the nature of all that is complete and consummate. This completeness, this consummateness, the finality and the perfection are conveyed in exquisite form: the perfect symmetry, the rhythm which returns upon itself like a dance where the hands link and loosen and link for the supreme moment of the end. Perfected bygone moments, perfected moments in the glimmering futurity, these are the treasured gem-like lyrics of Shelley and Keats.

But there is another kind of poetry: the poetry of that which is at hand: the immediate present. In the immediate present there is no perfection, no consummation, nothing finished. The strands are all flying, quivering, intermingling into the web, the waters are shaking the moon. There is no round, consummate moon on the face of running water, nor on the face of the unfinished tide. There are no gems of the living plasm. The living plasm vibrates unspeakably, it inhales the future, it exhales the past, it is the quick of both, and yet it is neither. There is no plasmic finality, nothing crystal, permanent. If we try to fix the living tissue, as the biologists fix it with formation, we have only a hardened bit of the past, bygone life under our observation.

Life, the ever-present, knows no finality, no finished crystallization. The perfect rose is only a running flame, emerging and flowing off, and never in any sense at rest, static, finished. Herein lies its transcendent liveliness. The whole tide of all life and all time suddenly heaves, and appears before us as an apparition, a revelation. We look at the very white quick of nascent creation. A water-lily heaves herself from the flood, looks around, gleams, and is gone. We have seen the incarnation, the quick of the ever-whirling flood. We have seen the invisible. We have seen, we have touched, we have partaken of the very substance of creative change, creative mutation. If you tell me about the lotus, tell me of nothing changeless or eternal. Tell me of the mystery of the inexhaustible, forever-unfolding creative spark. Tell me of the incarnate disclosure of the flux, mutation in blossom, laughter and decay perfectly open in their transit, nude in their movement before us.

Let me feel the mud and the heavens in my lotus. Let me feel the heavy, silting, sucking mud, the spinning of sky winds. Let me feel them both in purest contact, the nakedness of sucking weight, nakedly passing radiance. Give me nothing fixed, set, static. Don't give me the infinite or the eternal: nothing of infinity, nothing of eternity. Give me the still, white seething, the incandescence and the coldness of the incarnate moment: the moment, the quick of all change and haste and opposition: the moment, the immediate present, the Now. The immediate moment is not a drop of water running downstream. It is the source and issue, the bubbling up of the stream. Here, in this very instant moment, up bubbles the stream of time, out of the wells of futurity, flowing on to the oceans of the past. The source, the issue, the creative quick.

There is poetry of this immediate present, instant poetry, as well as poetry of the infinite past and the infinite future. The seething poetry of the incarnate Now is supreme, beyond even the everlasting gems of the before and after. In its quivering momentaneity it surpasses the crystalline, pearl-hard jewels, the poems of the eternities. Do not ask for the qualities of the unfading timeless gems. Ask for the whiteness which is the seethe of mud, ask for that incipient putrescence which is the skies falling, ask for the never-pausing, never-ceasing life itself. There must be mutation, swifter than iridescence, haste, not rest, come-and-go, not fixity, inconclusiveness, immediacy, the quality of life itself, without denouement or close. There must be the rapid momentaneous association of things which meet and pass on the for ever incalculable journey of creation: everything left in its own rapid, fluid relationship with the rest of things.

This is the unrestful, ungraspable poetry of the sheer present, poetry whose very permanency lies in its wind-like transit. Whitman's is the best poetry of this kind. Without beginning and without end, without any base and pediment, it sweeps past for ever, like a wind that is for ever in passage and unchainable. Whitman truly looked before and after. But he did not sigh for what is not. The clue to all his utterance lies in the sheer appreciation of the instant moment, life surging itself into utterance at its very well-head. Eternity is only an abstraction from the actual present. Infinity is only a great reservoir of recollection, or a reservoir of aspiration: man-made. The quivering nimble hour of the present, this is the quick of Time. This is the immanence. The quick of the universe is the *pulsating carnal self* mysterious and palpable. So it is always.

Because Whitman put this into his poetry, we fear him and respect him so profoundly. We should not fear him if he sang only of the 'old unhappy far-off things', or of the 'wings of the morning'. It is because his heart beats with the urgent, insurgent Now, which is even upon us all, that we dread him. He is so near the quick.

From the foregoing it is obvious that the poetry of the instant present cannot have the same body or the same motion as the poetry of the before and after. It can never submit to the same conditions. It is never finished. There is no rhythm which returns upon itself, no serpent of eternity with its tail in its own mouth. There is no static perfection, none of that finality which we find so satisfying because we are so frightened.

Much has been written about free verse. But all that can be said, first and last, is that free verse is, or should be direct utterance from the instant, whole man. It is the soul and the mind and body surging at once, nothing left out. They speak all together. There is some confusion, some discord. But the confusion and the discord only belong to the reality, as noise belongs to the plunge of water. It is no use inventing fancy laws for free verse, no use drawing a melodic line which all the feet must toe. Free verse toes no melodic line, no matter what drill-sergeant. Whitman pruned away his clichés – perhaps his clichés of rhythm as well as of phrase. And this is about all we can do, deliberately, with free verse. We can get rid of the stereotyped movements and the old hackneyed associations of sound or sense. We can break down those artificial conduits and canals through which we do so love to force our utterance. We can break the stiff neck of habit. We can be in ourselves spontaneous and flexible as flame, we can see that utterance rushes out without artificial form or artificial smoothness. But we cannot positively prescribe any motion, any rhythm. All the laws we invent or discover – it amounts to pretty much the same – will fail to apply to free verse. They will only apply to some form of restricted, limited un-free verse.

All we can say is that free verse does *not* have the same nature as restricted verse. It is not of the nature of reminiscence. It is not the past which we treasure in its perfection between our hands. Neither is it the crystal of the perfect future, into which we gaze. Its tide is neither the full, yearning flow of aspiration, nor the sweet, poignant ebb of remembrance and regret. The past and the future are the two great bournes of human emotion, the two great homes of the human days, the two eternities. They are both conclusive, final. Their beauty is the beauty of the goal, finished, perfected. Finished beauty and measured symmetry belong to the stable, unchanging eternities.

But in free verse we look for the insurgent naked throb of the instant moment. To break the lovely form of metrical verse, and to dish up the fragments as a new substance, called *vers libre*, this is what most of the free-versifiers accomplish. They do not know that free verse has its own *nature*, that it is neither star nor pearl, but instantaneous like plasm. It has no goal in either eternity. It has no finish. It has no satisfying stability, satisfying to those who like the immutable. None of this. It is the instant; the quick; the very jetting source of all will-be and has-been. The utterance is like a spasm, naked contact with all influences at once. It does not want to get anywhere. It just takes place.

For such utterance any externally applied law would be mere shackles and death. The law must come new each time from within. The bird is on the wing in the winds, flexible to every breath, a living spark in the storm, its very flickering depending upon its supreme mutability and power of change. Whence such a bird came: whither it goes: from what solid earth it rose up, and upon what solid earth it will close its wings and settle, this is not the question. This is a question of before and after. Now, *now*, the bird is on the wing in the winds.

Such is the rare new poetry. One realm we have never conquered: the pure present. One great mystery of time is *terra incognita* to us: the instant. The most superb mystery we have hardly recognized: the immediate, instant self. The quick of all time is the instant. The quick of all the universe, of all creation, is the incarnate, carnal self. Poetry gave us the clue: free verse: Whitman. Now we know.

The ideal – what is the ideal? A figment. An abstraction. A static abstraction, abstracted from life. It is a fragment of the before or the after. It is a crystallized aspiration, or a crystallized remembrance: crystallized, set, finished. It is a thing set apart, in the great storehouse of eternity, the storehouse of finished things.

We do not speak of things crystallized and set apart. We speak of the instant, the immediate self, the very plasm of the self. We speak also of free verse.

All this should have come as a preface to *Look! We Have Come Through!* But is it not better to publish a preface long after the book it belongs to has appeared? For then the reader will have had his fair chance with the book, alone.

ACCUMULATED MAIL

Written 1925. *The Borzoi*, December, 1925.
Phoenix, 1936

IF there is one thing I don't look forward to it's my mail.

Look out! Look out! Look out!
Look out! The postman comes,
His double knocking makes us start,
It rouses echoes in the heart,
It wakens expectation, and hope and agitation, etc., etc.

So we used to sing, in school.

Now, the postman is no knocker. He pitches the mail-bag into a box on a tree, and kicks his horse forward.

And when one has been away, and a heap of letters and printed stuff slithers out under one's eyes, there is neither hope nor expectation in the heart, but only repulsion, as if it were something nauseous one had to eat.

Business letters – all rather dreary. Bank letters, with the nasty green used-up cheques, and a dwindling small balance. Family letters: *We are so disappointed you are not coming to England. We wanted you to see the baby, he is so bonny: the new house, it is awfully nice: the show of the daffodils and crocuses down the garden.* Friends' letters: *The winter has been very trying.* And then the unknown correspondents. They are the worst ... *If you saw my little blue-eyed darling, you could not refuse her anything – not even an autograph* ... The high-school students somewhere in Massachusetts or in Maryland are in the habit of choosing by name some unknown man, whom they accept as a sort of guide. A group has chosen me – will I send them a letter of encouragement or of help in the battle of life? Well, I would willingly, but what on earth am I to say to them? *My dear young people: I daren't advise you to do as I do, for it's no fun, writing books. And I won't advise you, for your own sakes, to do as I say. For in details I'm sure I'm wrong. My dear young people, perhaps I need your encouragement more than you need mine* ... Well, that's no message.

Then there's the letter signed 'A Mother' – from Lenton, Nottingham: telling me she has been reading *Sons and Lovers*, and is there not misery enough in Nottingham (my home town) without my indicating where vice can be found, and (to cut short) how it can be practised? She saw a young woman reading *Sons and Lovers*, but was successful in preventing her from finishing the book. And the book was so well written, it was a pity the author could not have kept it clean. 'As it is, although so interesting, it cannot be mentioned in polite society.' Signed 'A Mother'. (Let us hope the young woman who was saved from finishing *Sons and Lovers* may also be saved from becoming in her turn, A Mother!)

Then the letter from some gentleman in New York beginning: *I am afraid you may consider this letter an impertinence.* If he was afraid, then what colossal impertinence to carry on to two sheets, and then post his impudence to me. The substance was: *I should like to know, in the controversy between you and Norman Douglas* (I didn't know myself that there was a controversy), *how it was the Magnus manuscript came into your hands, and you came to publish it, when clearly it was left to Douglas? In this case, why should you be making a lot of money out of another man's work? – Of course. I know it is your* Introduction *which sells the book. Magnus's manuscript is trash, and not worth reading. Still for the satisfaction of myself and many of my readers, I wish you could make it clear how you come to be profiting by a work that is not your own.*

Apparently this gentleman's sense of his own impertinence only drove him deeper. He has obviously read neither Magnus's work nor my *Introduction* – else he would plainly have seen that this MS was detained by Magnus's creditors, at his death, and handed by them to me, in the poor hope of recovering some of the money lost with that little adventurer. Moreover, if I wrote the only part of the book that is worth reading (*I* don't say so) – the only part for which people buy the book (they're not *my* words) – then it is my work they buy! This out of my genteel correspondent's own mouth – because *I* do *not* consider Magnus's work trash. Finally, if I get half proceeds for a book of which practically half was written by me and the other half sells on my account, who in heaven's name is going to be impertinent to me? Nobody, without a kick in the pants. As for Douglas, if he could have paid the dead man's debts, he might have 'executed' the dead man's literary works to his heart's content. Why doesn't he do something with the rest of the remains? Was this poor Foreign Legion MS the only egg in the nest? Anyhow, let us hope that those particular debts for which this MS was detained, will now be paid. And R.I.P. Anyhow, I shan't be a rich man on the half profits.

But this is not all my precious mail ... From a London editor and a friend (soi-disant): *Perhaps you would understand other people better if you did not think that you were always right.* How one learns things about oneself! Or is it really about the other person? I always find that my critics, pretending to criticize me, are analysing themselves. My own private opinion is that I have been, as far as people go, almost every time wrong! Anyhow, my desire to 'understand other people better' is turning to dread of finding out any more about them. This 'friend' goes on to say, will I ask my literary agent to let him have some articles of mine at a considerably cheaper figure than the agent puts on them?

It is not done yet. There is Mr Muir's article about me in the *Nation*. Never did I feel so baffled, confronting myself in my worst moments, as I feel when I read this 'elucidation' of myself. I hope it isn't my fault that Mr Muir plays such havoc between two stools. I think I read that he is a young man, and younger critic. It seems a pity he hasn't 'A Mother' to take the books from him before he can do himself any more harm. Truly, I don't want him to read them. 'There remain his gifts, splendid in their imperfection' – this is Mr Muir about me – 'thrown recklessly into a dozen books, fulfilling themselves in none. His chief title to greatness is that he has brought a new mode of seeing into literature, a new beauty which is also one of the oldest things in the world. It is the beauty of the ancient instinctive life which civilized man has almost forgotten. Mr Lawrence has picked up a thread of life left behind by mankind: and at some time it will be woven in with the others, making human life more complete, as all art tends to . . . Life has come to him fresh from the minting at a time when it seemed to everyone soiled and banal. He has many faults, and many of these are wilful. He has not fulfilled the promise shown in *Sons and Lovers* and *The Rainbow*. He has not submitted himself to any discipline. The will (in Mr Lawrence's characters) is not merely weak and inarticulate, it is in abeyance; it does not come into action. To this tremendous extent the tragedy in Mr Lawrence's novels fails in significance. We remember the scenes in his novels; we forget the names of his men and women. We should not know any of them if we met them in the street, as we should know Anna Karenina, or Crevel, or Soames Forsyte . . .' (Who is Crevel?)

Now listen, you, Mr Muir, and my dear readers. You read me for your own sakes, not for mine. You do me no favour by reading me. I am not indebted to you in the least if you spend two dollars on a book. You do it entirely for your own delectation. Spend the dollars on chewing-gum, it keeps the mouth busy and doesn't fly to the brain. I shall live just as blithely, unbought and unsold. When you buy chewing-gum, do you feel you acquire divine rights over the mind and soul of Mr Wrigley? If you do, it's like your impudence. Therefore get it out of your head that you are throned aloft like the gods, called upon to utter divine judgement. Your lofty seats, after all, are more like tall baby-chairs than thrones of the gods of judgement . . . But here goes, for an answer.

1. I have lunched with Mr Banality, and I'm sure I should know him if I met him in the street . . . Is that my fault, or his? – Alas, that I should recognize people in the street, by their noses, bonnets, or beauty. I don't care about their noses, bonnets, or beauty. Does nothing exist beyond that which is recognizable in the street? – How does my cat recognize me in the dark? – Ugh, thank God, there are more and other sorts of vision than the kodak sort which Mr Muir esteems above all others.

2. 'The will is not merely weak and inarticulate, it is in abeyance.' – Ah, my dear Mr Muir, the will of the modern young gentleman may not be in your opinion weak and

inarticulate, but certainly it is as mechanical as a Ford car engine. To this extent is the tragedy of modern young men insignificant. Oh, you little gods in the machine, stop the engine for a bit, do!

3. 'He has not submitted himself to any discipline.' – Try, Mr Muir *et al.*, putting your little iron will into abeyance for one hour daily, and see if it doesn't need a harder discipline than this doing of your 'daily dozen' and all your other mechanical repetitions. Believe me, to-day, the little god in a Ford machine cannot get at the thing worth having, not even with the most praiseworthy little engine of a will.

4. 'He has not fulfilled the promise of *Sons and Lovers* and *The Rainbow*.' – Just after *The Rainbow* was published, the most eminent figure in English letters told me to my nose that this work was a failure. Now, after ten years, Mr Muir finds it 'promising'. Go ahead, O Youth. But whatever promise you read into *The Rainbow*, remember it's like the little boy who 'promised' his mother to be good if she'd 'promise' to take him to the pantomime. I promise nothing, inside or out of *The Rainbow*.

5. 'Life has come to him fresh from the minting at a time when it seemed to everyone stale and banal.' – Come! Come! Mr Muir! With all that 'spirit' of yours, and all that 'intellect', and with all that 'will', and all that 'discipline', do you dare to confess that (I suppose you lump yourself in among everyone) life seemed to you stale and banal? – If so, something must be badly wrong with you and your psychic equipment, and Mr Lawrence wouldn't be in your shoes for all the money and the 'cleverness' in the world.

6. 'Mr Lawrence has picked up a thread of life left behind by mankind.' – Darn your socks with it, Mr Muir!

7. 'It is the beauty of the ancient instinctive life which civilized man has almost forgotten.' – He may have forgotten it, but he can put a label on it and price it at a figure and let it go cheap, in one and a half minutes. Ah, my dear Mr Muir, when do you consider ancient life ended, and 'civilized' life began? And which is stale and banal? Wherein does staleness lie, Mr Muir? As for 'ancient life', it may be ancient to you,

but it is still alive and kicking in some people. And 'ancient life' is far more deeply conscious than you can even imagine. And its discipline goes into regions where you have no existence.

8. 'His chief title to greatness is that he has brought a new mode of seeing into literature, a new beauty,' etc., etc. – Easy, of course, as re-trimming an old hat. Michael Arlen does it better! Looks more modish, the old hat. – But shouldn't it be a new mode of 'feeling' or 'knowing' rather than of 'seeing'? Since none of my characters would be recognizable in the street?

9. 'There remain his gifts, splendid in their imperfection.' – Ugh, Mr Muir, think how horrible for us all, if I were perfect! or even if I had 'perfect' gifts! – Isn't splendour enough for you, Mr Muir? Or do you find the peacock more 'perfect' when he is moulting and has lost his tail, and therefore isn't so exaggerated, but is more 'down to normal'? – For 'perfection' is only one of the attributes of 'the normal' and 'the average' in modern thought.

Well, I don't want to be just or to be kind. There is a further justice and a greater kindness than this niggling tolerance business, and suffering fools gladly. Fools bore me – but I don't mean Mr Muir. He is a phoenix, compared to most. I wonder what it is that the rainbow – I mean the natural phenomenon – stands for in my own consciousness! I don't know all it means to me. – Is this lack of intellectual capacity on my part? Or is it because the rainbow is somehow not quite 'normal', and therefore not quite fit for intellectual appreciation? Of course, white light passing through prisms of falling raindrops makes a rainbow. Let us therefore sell it by the yard.

For me, give me a little splendour, and I'll leave perfection to the small fry.

But oh, my other anonymous little critic, what shall I say to thee? *Mr Lawrence's horses are all mares or stallions.*

Honi soit qui mal y pense, my dear, though I'm sure the critic is a gentleman (I daren't say a *man*) and not a lady.

Little critics' horses (sic) are all geldings.

Another little critic: 'Mr Lawrence's introspective intelligence is too feeble to balance this melodramatic fancy in activities which cater for a free play of mind.'

Retort simple: Mr Lawrence's intelligence would prevent his writing such a sentence down, and sending it to print. – What can those activities be which 'cater for a free play of mind' (whatever that may mean) and at the same time have 'introspective intelligence' (what quite is this?) balancing 'melodramatic fancy' (what is this either?) within them?

Same critic, finishing the same sentence: '... and so, since criticism begins at home, his (Mr Lawrence's) latter-day garment of philosopher and preacher is shot through with the vulgarity of aggressive self-ignorance.'

Retort simple: If criticism begins at home, then the professional, and still more so the amateur critic (I suspect this gentleman to be the latter), is never by any chance at home. He is always out sponging on some author. As for a 'latter-day garment of philosopher and preacher' (I never before knew a philosopher and a preacher transmogrified into a garment) being 'shot through with the vulgarity of aggressive self-ignorance', was it grapeshot, or duck-shot, or just shot-silk effect?

Alas, this young critic is 'shot through with ignorance' even more extensive than that of self. Or perhaps it is only his garment of critic and smart little fellow which is so shot through, *percé* or *miroité*, according to fancy – 'melodramatic fancy' balanced by 'introspective intelligence', 'in activities which cater for a free play of mind'.

'We cater to the Radical Trade,' says Jimmie Higgins' advertisement.

Another friend and critic: 'Lawrence is an artist, but his intellect is not up to his art.'

You might as well say: Mr Lawrence rides a horse but he doesn't wear his stirrups round his neck. And the accusation is just. Because he hopes to heaven he is riding a horse that is alive of itself, not a wooden hobbyhorse suitable for the nursery. – And he does his best to keep his feet in the stirrups, and to leave his intellect under his hat, when he is riding his naughty steed. No, my dears! I guess, as an instrument, my intellect is as good as yours. But instead of sitting in my own wheelbarrow (the intellect is a sort of wheelbarrow about the place) and whipping it ecstatically over the head, I just wheel out what dump I've got, and forget the old barrow again, till next time.

And now, thank God, I can throw all my mail, letters, used cheques, pamphlets, periodicals, clippings from the 'press', Ave Marias, paternosters, and bunk, into the fire. – When I get a particularly smelly bit of sentiment, I always burn it slowly, invoking the Lord thus: 'Lord! *Herrgott! nimm du diesen Opferrauch!* Take Thou this smoke of sacrifice. – This sacrifice of blood is no longer acceptable, for blood has turned to water; all is vapour! Therefore, O Lord, this choice titbit of the spirit, this kidney-fat of sentiment, accept it, O Lord, from Thy servant ... This firstling of the sentimental herd, this young ram without spot or blemish, from the aesthetic flock, this adamantine young he-goat, from the troops of human 'stunts' – see, Lord, I cut their throats and burn the cardboard fat of them. Lord of the Spirit, Lord of the Universal Mind, Lord of the cosmic will, snuff up the smoke of this burnt-paper offering, for it makes my eyes smart –'

I wish they'd make His eyes smart as well! this Lord of sentimentalism, aestheticism, and stunts. One day I'll make a sacrifice to Him too: to my own Lord, who broods at the centre of all the worlds, over His fathomless Desire.

MAKING PICTURES

Written April, 1929. *Creative Art*, July, 1929.
The Studio, July, 1929. *Vanity Fair*,
August, 1929. *Assorted Articles*, 1930

ONE has to eat one's own words. I remember I used to assert, perhaps I even wrote it: Everything that can possibly be painted has been painted, every brush-stroke that can possibly be laid on canvas has been laid on. The visual arts are at a dead end. Then suddenly, at the age of forty, I begin painting myself and am fascinated.

Still, going through the Paris picture shops this year of grace, and seeing the Dufys and Chiricos, etc., and the Japanese Foujita with his wish-wash nudes with pearl-button eyes, the same weariness comes over one. They are all so would-be, they make such efforts. They at least have nothing to paint. In the midst of them a graceful Friesz flower-piece, or a blotting-paper Laurencin, seems a masterpiece. At least here is a bit of *natural* expression in paint. Trivial enough, when compared to the big painters, but still, as far as they go, real.

What about myself, then! What am I doing, bursting into paint? I am a writer, I ought to stick to ink. I have found my medium of expression; why, at the age of forty, should I suddenly want to try another?

Things happen, and we have no choice. If Maria Huxley hadn't come rolling up to our house near Florence with four rather large canvases, one of which she had busted, and presented them to me because they had been abandoned in her house, I might never have started in on a real picture in my life. But those nice stretched canvases were too tempting. We had been painting doors and window-frames in the house, so there was a little stock of oil, turps, and colour in powder, such as one buys from an Italian drogheria. There were several brushes for house-painting. There was a canvas on which the unknown owner had made a start – mud-grey, with the beginnings of a red-haired man. It was a grimy and ugly beginning, and the young man who had made it had wisely gone no further. He certainly had had no inner compulsion: nothing in him, as far as paint was concerned, or if there was anything in him, it had stayed in, and only a bit of themud-grey 'group' had come out.

So for the sheer fun of covering a surface and obliterating that mud-grey, I sat on the floor with the canvas propped against a chair – and with my house-paint brushes and colours in little casseroles. I disappeared into that canvas. It is to me the most exciting moment – when you have a blank canvas and a big brush full of wet colour, and you plunge. It is just like diving into a pond – then you start frantically to swim. So far as I am concerned, it is like swimming in a baffling current and being rather frightened and very thrilled, gasping and striking out for all you're worth. The knowing eye watches sharp as a needle; but the picture comes clean out of instinct, intuition and sheer physical action. Once the instinct and intuition gets into the brush-tip, the picture *happens*, if it is to be a picture at all.

At least, so my first picture happened – the one I have called 'A Holy Family'. In a couple of hours there it all was, man, woman, child, blue shirt, red shawl, pale room – all in the rough, but, as far as I am concerned, a picture. The struggling comes later. But the picture itself comes in the first rush, or not at all. It is only when the picture has come into being that one can struggle and make it *grow* to completion.

Ours is an excessively conscious age. We *know* so much, we feel so little. I have lived enough among painters and around studios to have had all the theories – and how contradictory they are – rammed down my throat. A man has to have a gizzard like an ostrich to digest all the brass-tacks and wire nails of modern art theories. Perhaps all the theories, the utterly indigestible theories, like nails in an ostrich's gizzard, do indeed help to grind small and make digestible all the emotional and aesthetic pabulum that lies in an artist's soul. But they can serve no other purpose. Not even corrective. The modern theories of art make real pictures impossible. You only get these expositions, critical ventures in paint, and fantastic negations. And the bit of fantasy that may lie in the negation – as in a Dufy or a Chirico – is just the bit that has escaped theory and perhaps saves the picture. Theorize, theorize all you like – but when you start to paint, shut your theoretic eyes and go for it with instinct and intuition.

Myself, I have always loved pictures, the pictorial art. I never went to an art school, I have had only one real lesson in painting in all my life. But of course I was thoroughly drilled in 'drawing', the solid-geometry sort, and the plaster-cast sort, and the pin-wire sort. I think the solid-geometry sort, with all the elementary laws of perspective, was valuable. But the pin-wire sort and the plaster-cast light-and-shade sort was harmful. Plaster-casts and pin-wire outlines were always so repulsive to me, I quite early decided I 'couldn't draw'. I couldn't draw, so I could never do anything on my own. When I did paint jugs of flowers or bread and potatoes, or cottages in a lane, copying from Nature, the result wasn't very thrilling. Nature was more or less of a plaster-cast to me – those plaster-cast heads of Minerva or figures of Dying Gladiators which so unnerved me as a youth. The 'object', be it what it might, was always slightly repulsive to me once I sat down in front of it, to paint it. So, of course, I decided I couldn't really paint. Perhaps I can't. But I verily believe I can make pictures, which is to me all that matters in this respect. The art of painting consists in making pictures – and so many artists accomplish canvases without coming within miles of painting a picture.

I learnt to paint from copying other pictures – usually reproductions, sometimes even photographs. When I was a boy, how I concentrated over it! Copying some perfectly worthless scene reproduction in some magazine. I worked with almost dry water-colour, stroke by stroke, covering half a square-inch at a time, each square-inch perfect and completed, proceeding in a kind of mosaic advance, with no idea at all of laying on a broad wash. Hours and hours of intense concentration, inch by inch progress, in a method entirely wrong – and yet those copies of mine managed, when they were finished, to have a certain something that delighted me: a certain glow of life, which was beauty to me. A picture lives with the life you put into it. If you put no *life* into it – no thrill, no concentration of delight or exaltation of visual discovery – then the picture is dead, like so many canvases, no matter how much thorough and scientific work is put into it. Even if you only copy a purely banal reproduction of an old bridge, some sort of keen, delighted awareness of the old bridge or of its atmosphere, or the image it has kindled inside you, can go over on to the paper and give a certain touch of life to a banal conception.

It needs a certain purity of spirit to be an artist, of any sort. The motto which should be written over every School of Art is: 'Blessed are the pure in spirit, for theirs is the kingdom of heaven'. But by 'pure in spirit' we mean pure in spirit. An artist may be a profligate and, from the social point of view, a scoundrel. But if he can paint a nude woman, or a couple of apples, so that they are a living image, then he was pure in spirit, and, for the time being, his was the kingdom of heaven. This is the beginning of all art, visual or literary or musical: be pure in spirit. It isn't the same as goodness. It is much more difficult and nearer the divine. The divine isn't only good, it is all things.

One may see the divine in natural objects; I saw it to-day, in the frail, lovely little camellia flowers on long stems, here on the bushy and splendid flower-stalls of the Ramblas in Barcelona. They were different from the usual fat camellias, more like gardenias, poised delicately, and I saw them like a vision. So now, I could paint them. But if I had bought a handful, and started in to paint them 'from nature', then I should have lost them. By staring at them I should have lost them. I have learnt by experience. It is personal experience only. Some men can only get at a vision by staring themselves blind, as it were: like Cézanne; but staring kills my vision. That's why I could never 'draw' at school. One was supposed to draw what one stared at.

The only thing one can look into, stare into, and see only vision, is the vision itself: the visionary image. That is why I am glad I never had any training but the self-imposed training of copying other men's pictures. As I grew more ambitious, I copied Leader's landscapes, and Frank Brangwyn's cartoon-like pictures, then Peter de Wint and Girtin water-colours. I can never be sufficiently grateful for the series of English water-colour painters, published by the *Studio* in eight parts, when I was a youth. I had only six of the eight parts, but they were invaluable to me. I copied them with the greatest joy, and found some of them extremely difficult. Surely I put as much labour into copying from those water-colour reproductions as most modern art students put into all their years of study. And I had enormous profit from it. I not only acquired a considerable technical skill in handling water-colour – let any man try copying the English water-colour artists, from Paul Sandby and Peter de Wint and Girtin, up to Frank Brangwyn and the impressionists like Brabazon, and he will see how much skill he requires – but also I developed my visionary awareness. And I believe one can only develop one's visionary awareness by close contact with the vision itself: that is, by knowing pictures, real vision pictures, and by dwelling on them, and really dwelling in them. It is a great delight, to dwell in a picture. But it needs a purity of spirit, a sloughing of vulgar sensation and vulgar interest, and above all, vulgar contact that few people know how to perform. Oh, if art schools only taught that! If, instead of saying: This drawing is wrong, incorrect, badly drawn, etc., they would say: Isn't this in bad taste? isn't it insensitive? isn't that an insentient curve with none of the delicate awareness of life in it? – But art is treated all wrong. It is treated as if it were a science, which it is not. Art is a form of religion, minus the Ten Commandment business, which is sociological. Art is a form of supremely delicate awareness and atonement – meaning at-one-ness, the state of being at one with the object. But is the great atonement in delight? – for I can never look on art save as a form of delight.

All my life I have from time to time gone back to paint, because it gave me a form of delight that words can never give. Perhaps the joy in words goes deeper and is for that reason more unconscious. The *conscious* delight is certainly stronger in paint. I have gone back to paint for real pleasure – and by paint I mean copying, copying either in oils or waters. I think the greatest pleasure I ever got came from copying Fra Angelico's 'Flight into Egypt' and Lorenzetti's big picture of the Thebaid, in each case working from photographs and putting in my own colour; or perhaps even more a Carpaccio picture in Venice. Then I *really* learned what life, what powerful life has been put into every curve, every motion of a great picture. Purity of spirit, sensitive awareness, intense eagerness to portray an inward vision, how it all comes. The English water-colours are frail in comparison – and the French and the Flemings are shallow. The great Rembrandt I never tried to copy, though I loved him intensely, even more than I do now; and Rubens I never tried, though I always liked him so much, only he seemed so spread out. But I have copied Peter de Hooch and Vandyck, and others that I forget. Yet none of them gave me the deep thrill of the Italians, Carpaccio, or the lovely 'Death of Procris' in the National Gallery, or that 'Wedding' with the scarlet legs, in the Uffizi, or a Giotto from Padua. I must have made many copies in my day, and got endless joy out of them.

Then suddenly, by having a blank canvas, I discovered I could make a picture myself. That is the point, to make a picture on a blank canvas. And I was forty before I had the real courage to try. Then it became an orgy, making pictures.

I have learnt now not to work from objects, not to have models, not to have a technique. Sometimes, for a water-colour, I have worked direct from a model. But it always spoils the *picture*. I can only use a model when the picture is already made; then I can look at the model to get some detail which the vision failed me with, or to modify something which I *feel* is unsatisfactory and I don't know why. Then a model may give a suggestion. But at the beginning, a model only spoils the picture. The picture must all come out of the artist's inside, awareness of forms and figures. We can call it memory, but it is more than memory. It is the image as it lives in the consciousness, alive like a vision, but unknown. I believe many people have, in their consciousness, living images that would give them the greatest joy to bring out. But they don't know how to go about it. And teaching only hinders them.

To me, a picture has delight in it, or it isn't a picture. The saddest pictures of Piero della Francesca or Sodoma or Goya have still that indescribable delight that goes with the real picture. Modern critics talk a lot about ugliness, but I never saw a real picture that seemed to me ugly. The theme may be ugly, there may be a terrifying, distressing, almost repulsive quality, as in El Greco. Yet it is all, in some strange way, swept up in the delight of a picture. No artist, even the gloomiest, ever painted a picture without the curious delight in image-making.

INTRODUCTION TO THESE PAINTINGS

Written 1929. *The Paintings of D. H. Lawrence*, Mandrake Press, 1929. *Phoenix*, 1936

THE reason the English produce so few painters is not that they are, as a nation, devoid of a genuine feeling for visual art: though to look at their productions, and to look at the mess which has been made of actual English landscape, one might really conclude that they were, and leave it at that. But it is not the fault of the God that made them. They are made with aesthetic sensibilities the same as anybody else. The fault lies in the English attitude to life.

The English, and the Americans following them, are paralysed by fear. That is what thwarts and distorts the Anglo-Saxon existence, this paralysis of fear. It thwarts life, it distorts vision, and it strangles impulse: this overmastering fear. And fear of what, in heaven's name? What is the Anglo-Saxon stock so petrified with fear about? We have to answer that before we can understand the English failure in the visual arts: for, on the whole, it is a failure.

It is an old fear, which seemed to dig in to the English soul at the time of the Renaissance. Nothing could be more lovely and fearless than Chaucer. But already Shakespeare is morbid with fear, fear of consequences. That is the strange phenomenon of the English Renaissance: this mystic terror of the consequences, the consequences of action. Italy, too, had her reaction, at the end of the sixteenth century, and showed a similar fear. But not so profound, so overmastering. Aretino was anything but timorous he was bold as any Renaissance novelist, and went one better.

What appeared to take full grip on the northern consciousness at the end of the sixteenth century was a terror, almost a horror of sexual life. The Elizabethans, grand as we think them, started it. The real 'mortal coil' in Hamlet is all sexual; the young man's horror of his mother's incest, sex carrying with it a wild and nameless terror which, it seems to me, it had never carried before. Oedipus and Hamlet are very different in this respect. In Oedipus there is no recoil in horror from sex itself: Greek drama never shows us that. The horror, when it is present in Greek tragedy, is against *destiny*, man caught in the toils of destiny. But with the Renaissance itself, particularly in England, the horror is sexual. Orestes is dogged by destiny and driven mad by the Eumenides. But Hamlet is over-powered by horrible revulsion from his physical connexion with his mother, which makes him recoil in similar revulsion from Ophelia and almost from his father, even as a ghost. He is horrified at the merest suggestion of physical connexion, as if it were an unspeakable taint.

This, no doubt, is all in the course of the growth of the 'spiritual-mental' consciousness, at the expense of the instinctive-intuitive consciousness. Man came to have his own body in horror, especially in its sexual implications: and so he began to suppress with all his might his instinctive-intuitive consciousness, which is so radical, so physical, so sexual. Cavalier poetry, love poetry, is already devoid of body. Donne, after the exacerbated revulsion-attraction excitement of his earlier poetry, becomes a divine. 'Drink to me only with thine eyes', sings the cavalier: an expression incredible in Chaucer's poetry. 'I could not love thee, dear, so much, loved I not honour more', sings the Cavalier lover. In Chaucer the 'dear' and the 'honour' would have been more or less identical.

But with the Elizabethans the grand rupture had started in the human consciousness, the mental consciousness recoiling in violence away from the physical, instinctive-intuitive. To the Restoration dramatists sex is, on the whole, a dirty business, but they more or less glory in the dirt. Fielding tries in vain to defend the Old Adam. Richardson with his calico purity and his underclothing excitements sweeps all before him. Swift goes mad with sex and excrement revulsion. Sterne flings a bit of the same excrement humorously around. And physical consciousness gives a last song in Burns, then is dead. Wordsworth, Keats, Shelley, the Brontës, all are post-mortem poets.

The essential instinctive-intuitive body is dead, and worshipped in death – all very unhealthy. Till Swinburne and Oscar Wilde try to start a revival from the mental field. Swinburne's 'white thighs' are purely mental.

Now, in England – and following, in America – the physical self was not just fig-leafed over or suppressed in public, as was the case in Italy and on most of the Continent. In England it excited a strange horror and terror. And this extra morbidity came, I believe, from the great shock of syphilis and the realization of the consequences of the disease. Wherever syphilis, or 'pox', came from, it was fairly new in England, at the end of the fifteenth century. But by the end of the sixteenth, its ravages were obvious, and the shock of them had just penetrated the thoughtful and the imaginative consciousness. The royal families of England and Scotland were syphilitic; Edward VI and Elizabeth born with the inherited consequences of the disease. Edward VI died of it, while still a boy. Mary died childless and in utter depression. Elizabeth had no eyebrows, her teeth went rotten; she must have felt herself, somewhere, utterly unfit for marriage, poor thing. That was the grisly horror that lay behind the glory of Queen Bess. And so the Tudors died out: and another syphilitic-born unfortunate came to the throne, in the person of James I. Mary Queen of Scots had no more luck than the Tudors, apparently. Apparently Darnley was reeking with the pox, though probably at first she did not know it. But when the Archbishop of St Andrews was christening her baby James, afterwards James I of England, the old clergyman was so dripping with pox that she was terrified lest he should give it to the infant. And she need not have troubled, for the wretched infant had brought it into the world with him, from that fool Darnley. So James I of England slobbered and shambled, and was the wisest fool in Christendom, and the Stuarts likewise died out, the stock enfeebled by the disease.

With the royal families of England and Scotland in this condition, we can judge what the noble houses, the nobility of both nations, given to free living and promiscuous pleasure, must have been like. England traded with the East and with America; England, unknowingly, had opened her doors to the disease. The English aristocracy travelled and had curious taste in loves. And pox entered the blood of the nation, particularly of the upper classes, who had more chance of infection. And after it had entered the blood, it entered the consciousness, and hit the vital imagination.

It is possible that the effects of syphilis and the conscious realization of its consequences gave a great blow to the Spanish psyche, precisely at this period. And it is possible that Italian society, which was on the whole so untravelled, had no connexion with America, and was so privately self-contained, suffered less from the disease. Someone ought to make a thorough study of the effects of 'pox' on the minds and the emotions and imaginations of the various nations of Europe, at about the time of our Elizabethans.

The apparent effect on the Elizabethans and the Restoration wits is curious. They appear to take the whole thing as a joke. The common oath, 'Pox on you!' was almost funny. But how common the oath was! How the word 'pox' was in every mind and in every mouth. It is one of the words that haunt Elizabethan speech. Taken very manly, with a great deal of Falstaffian bluff, treated as a huge joke! Pox! Why, he's got the pox! Ha-ha! What's he been after?

There is just the same attitude among the common run of men today with regard to the minor sexual diseases. Syphilis is no longer regarded as a joke, according to my experience. The very word itself frightens men. You could joke with the word 'pox'. You can't joke with the word 'syphilis'. The change of word has killed the joke. But men still joke about *clap!* which is a minor sexual disease. They pretend to think it manly, even, to have the disease, or to have had it. 'What! never had a shot of clap!' cries one gentleman to another. 'Why, where have you been all your life?' If we changed the word and insisted on 'gonorrhoea', or whatever it is, in place of 'clap', the joke would die. Anyhow I have had young men come to me green and quaking, afraid they've caught a 'shot of clap'.

Now, in spite of all the Elizabethan jokes about pox, pox

was no joke to them. A joke may be a very brave way of meeting a calamity, or it may be a very cowardly way. Myself, I consider the Elizabethan pox joke a purely cowardly attitude. They didn't think it funny, for by God it *wasn't* funny. Even poor Elizabeth's lack of eyebrows and her rotten teeth were not funny. And they knew it. They may not have known it was the direct result of pox: though probably they did. This fact remains, that no man can contract syphilis, or any deadly sexual disease, without feeling the most shattering and profound terror go through him, through the very roots of his being. And no man can look without a sort of horror on the effects of a sexual disease in another person. We are so constituted that we are all at once horrified and terrified. The fear and dread has been so great that the pox joke was invented as an evasion, and following that, the great hush! hush! was imposed. Man was *too* frightened: that's the top and bottom of it.

But now, with remedies discovered, we need no longer be *too* frightened. We can begin, after all these years, to face the matter. After the most fearful damage has been done.

For the overmastering fear is poison to the human psyche. And this overmastering fear, like some horrible secret tumour, has been poisoning our consciousness ever since the Elizabethans, who first woke up with dread to the entry of the original syphilitic poison into the blood.

I know nothing about medicine and very little about disease, and my facts are such as I have picked up in casual reading. Nevertheless I am convinced that the secret awareness of syphilis, and the utter secret terror and horror of it, has had an enormous and incalculable effect on the English consciousness and on the American. Even when the fear has never been formulated, there it has lain, potent and overmastering. I am convinced that *some* of Shakespeare's horror and despair, in his tragedies, arose from the shock of his consciousness of syphilis. I don't suggest for one moment Shakespeare ever contracted syphilis. I have never had syphilis myself. Yet I know and confess how profound is my fear of the disease, and more than fear, my horror. In fact, I don't think I am so very much afraid of it. I am more horrified, inwardly and deeply, at the idea of its existence.

All this sounds very far from the art of painting. But it is not so far as it sounds. The appearance of syphilis in our midst gave a fearful blow to our sexual life. The real natural innocence of Chaucer was impossible after that. The very sexual act of procreation might bring as one of its consequences a foul disease, and the unborn might be tainted from the moment of conception. Fearful thought! It is truly a fearful thought, and all the centuries of getting used to it won't help us. It remains a fearful thought, and to free ourselves from this fearful dread we should use all our wits and all our efforts, not stick our heads in the sand of some idiotic joke, or still more idiotic don't-mention-it. The fearful thought of the consequences of syphilis, or of any sexual disease, upon the unborn gives a shock to the impetus of fatherhood in any man, even the cleanest. Our consciousness is a strange thing, and the knowledge of a certain fact may wound it mortally, even if the fact does not touch us directly. And so I am certain that *some* of Shakespeare's father-murder complex, *some* of Hamlet's horror of his mother, of his uncle, of all old men came from the feeling that fathers may transmit syphilis, or syphilis-consequences, to children. I don't know even whether Shakespeare was actually aware of the consequences to a child born of a syphilitic father or mother. He may not have been, though most probably he was. But he certainly was aware of the effects of syphilis itself, especially on men. And this awareness struck at his deep sex imagination, at his instinct for fatherhood, and brought in an element of terror and abhorrence there where men should feel anything but terror and abhorrence, into the procreative act.

The terror-horror element which had entered the imagination with regard to the sexual and procreative act was at least partly responsible for the rise of Puritanism, the beheading of the king-father Charles, and the establishment of the New England colonies. If America really sent us syphilis, she got back the full recoil of the horror of it, in her puritanism.

But deeper even than this, the terror-horror element led to

the crippling of the consciousness of man. Very elementary in man is his sexual and procreative being, and on his sexual and procreative being depend many of his deepest instincts and the flow of his intuition. A deep instinct of his kinship joins men together, and the kinship of flesh-and-blood keeps the warm flow of intuitional awareness streaming between human beings. Our true awareness of one another is intuitional, not mental. Attraction between people is really instinctive and intuitional, not an affair of judgement. And in mutual attraction lies perhaps the deepest pleasure in life, mutual attraction which may make us 'like' our travelling companion for the two or three hours we are together, then no more; or mutual attraction that may deepen to powerful love, and last a life-time.

The terror-horror element struck a blow at our feeling of physical communion. In fact, it almost killed it. We have become ideal beings, creatures that exist in idea, to one another, rather than flesh-and-blood kin. And with the collapse of the feeling of physical, flesh-and-blood kinship, and the substitution of our ideal, social or political oneness, came the failing of our intuitive awareness, and the great unease, the *nervousness* of mankind. We are *afraid* of the instincts. We are *afraid* of the intuition within us. We suppress the instincts, and we cut off our intuitional awareness from one another and the world. The reason being some great shock to the procreative self. Now we know one another only as ideal or social or political entities, fleshless, bloodless, and cold, like Bernard Shaw's creatures. Intuitively we are dead to one another, we have all gone cold.

But by intuition alone can man *really* be aware of man, or of the living, substantial world. By intuition alone can man live and know either woman or world, and by intuition alone can he bring forth again images of magic awareness which we call art. In the past men brought forth images of magic awareness, and now it is the convention to admire these images. The convention says, for example, we must admire Botticelli or Giorgione, so Baedeker stars the pictures, and we admire them. But it is all a fake. Even those that get a thrill, even when they call it ecstasy, from these old pictures are only undergoing cerebral excitation. Their deeper responses, down in the intuitive and instinctive body, are not touched. They cannot be, because they are dead. A dead intuitive body stands there and gazes at the corpse of beauty: and usually it is completely and honestly bored. Sometimes it feels a mental coruscation which it calls an ecstasy or an aesthetic response.

Modern people, but particularly English and Americans, *cannot* feel anything with the whole imagination. They can see the living body of imagery as little as a blind man can see colour. The imaginative vision, which includes physical, intuitional perception, they *have not got*. Poor things, it is dead in them. And they stand in front of a Botticelli Venus, which they know as conventionally 'beautiful', much as a blind man might stand in front of a bunch of roses and pinks and monkey-musk, saying: 'Oh, do tell me which is red; let me feel red! Now let me feel white! Oh, let me feel it! What is this I am feeling? Monkey-musk? Is it white? Oh, do you say it is yellow blotched with orange-brown? Oh, but I can't feel it! What *can* it be? Is white velvety, or just silky?'

So the poor blind man! Yet he may have an acute perception of alive beauty. Merely by touch and scent, his intuitions being alive, the blind man may have a genuine and soul-satisfying experience of imagery. But not pictorial images. These are forever beyond him.

So those poor English and Americans in front of the Botticelli Venus. They stare so hard; they do so *want* to see. And their eyesight is perfect. But all they can see is a sort of nude woman on a sort of shell on a sort of pretty greenish water. As a rule they rather dislike the 'unnaturalness' or 'affectation' of it. If they are high-brows they may get a little self-conscious thrill of aesthetic excitement. But real imaginative awareness, which is so largely physical, is denied them. *Ils n'ont pas de quoi*, as the Frenchman said of the angels, when asked if they made love in heaven.

Ah, the dear high-brows who gaze in a sort of ecstasy and get a correct mental thrill! Their poor high-brow bodies stand there as dead as dust-bins, and can no more feel the sway of complete imagery upon them than they can feel any other real sway. *Ils n'ont pas de quoi.* The instincts and the intuitions are so nearly dead in them, and they fear even the feeble remains. Their fear of the instincts and intuitions is even greater than that of the English Tommy who calls: 'Eh, Jack! Come an' look at this girl standin' wi' no clothes on, an' two blokes spittin' at 'er.' That is his vision of Botticelli's Venus. It is, for him, complete, for he is void of the image-seeing imagination. But at least he doesn't have to work up a cerebral excitation, as the high-brow does, who is really just as void.

All alike, cultured and uncultured, they are still dominated by that unnamed, yet overmastering dread and hate of the instincts deep in the body, dread of the strange intuitional awareness of the body, dread of anything but ideas, which *can't* contain bacteria. And the dread all works back to a dread of the procreative body, and is partly traceable to the shock of the awareness of syphilis.

The dread of the instincts included the dread of intuitional awareness. 'Beauty is a snare' – 'Beauty is but skin-deep' – 'Handsome is as handsome does' – 'Looks don't count' – 'Don't judge by appearances' – if we only realized it, there are thousands of these vile proverbs which have been dinned into us for over two hundred years. They are all of them false. Beauty is not a snare, nor is it skin-deep, since it always involves a certain loveliness of modelling, and handsome doers are often ugly and objectionable people, and if you ignore the look of the thing you plaster England with slums and produce at last a state of spiritual depression that is suicidal, and if you don't judge by appearances, that is, if you can't trust the impression which things make on you, you are a fool. But all these base-born proverbs born in the cash-box, hit direct against the intuitional consciousness. Naturally, man gets a great deal of his life's satisfaction from beauty, from a certain sensuous pleasure in the look of the thing. The old Englishman built his hut of a cottage with a childish joy in its appearance, purely intuitional and direct. The modern Englishman has a few borrowed ideas, simply doesn't know *what* to feel, and makes a silly mess of it: though perhaps he is improving, hopefully, in this field of architecture and house-building. The intuitional faculty, which alone relates us in direct awareness to physical things and substantial presences, is atrophied and dead, and we don't know *what* to feel. We know we ought to feel something, but what? – Oh, tell us what! And this is true of all nations, the French and Italians as much as the English. Look at new French suburbs! Go through the crockery and furniture departments in the *Dames de France* or any big shop. The blood in the body stands still, before such *crétin* ugliness. One has to decide that the modern bourgeois is a *crétin*.

This movement against the instincts and the intuition took a moral tone in all countries. It started in hatred. Let us never forget that modern morality has its roots in hatred, a deep, evil hate of the instinctive, intuitional, procreative body. This hatred is made more virulent by fear, and an extra poison is added to the fear by unconscious horror of syphilis. And so we come to modern bourgeois consciousness, which turns upon the secret poles of fear and hate. That is the real pivot of all bourgeois consciousness in all countries: fear and hate of the instinctive, intuitional, procreative body in man or woman. But of course this fear and hate had to take on a righteous appearance, so it became moral, said that the instincts, intuitions and all the activities of the procreative body were evil, and promised a *reward* for their suppression. That is the great clue to bourgeois psychology: the reward business. It is screamingly obvious in Maria Edgeworth's tales, which must have done unspeakable damage to ordinary people. Be good, and you'll have money. Be wicked, and you'll be penniless at last, and the good ones will have to offer you a little charity. This is sound working morality in the world. And it makes one realize that, even to Milton, the true hero of *Paradise Lost* must be Satan. But by this baited morality the masses were caught and enslaved to industrialism before ever they knew it; the good got hold of the goods, and our modern 'civilization' of money, machines, and wage-slaves was inaugurated. The very pivot of it, let us never forget, being fear and hate, the most intimate fear and hate, fear and hate of one's own instinctive, intuitive body, and fear and hate of every other man's and every other woman's warm, procreative body and imagination.

Now it is obvious what result this will have on the plastic arts, which depend entirely on the representation of substantial bodies, and on the intuitional perception of the *reality* of substantial bodies. The reality of substantial bodies can only be perceived by the imagination, and the imagination is a kindled state of consciousness in which intuitive awareness predominates. The plastic arts are all imagery, and imagery is the body of our imaginative life, and our imaginative life is a great joy and fulfilment to us, for the imagination is a more powerful and more comprehensive flow of consciousness than our ordinary flow. In the flow of true imagination we know in full, mentally and physically at once, in a greater, enkindled awareness. At the maximum of our imagination we are religious. And if we deny our imagination, and have no imaginative life, we are poor worms who have never lived.

In the seventeenth and eighteenth centuries we have the deliberate denial of intuitive awareness, and we see the results on the arts. Vision became more optical, less intuitive and painting began to flourish. But what painting! Watteau, Ingres, Poussin, Chardin have some real imaginative glow still. They are still somewhat free. The puritan and the intellectual has not yet struck them down with his fear and hate obsession. But look at England! Hogarth, Reynolds, Gainsborough, they are all already bourgeois. The coat is really more important than the man. It is amazing how important clothes suddenly become, how they *cover* the subject. An old Reynolds colonel in a red uniform is much more a uniform than an individual, and as for Gainsborough, all one can say is: What a lovely dress and hat! What really expensive Italian silk! This painting of garments continued in vogue, till pictures like Sargent's seem to be nothing but yards and yards of satin from the most expensive shops, having some pretty head popped on the top. The imagination is quite dead. The optical vision, a sort of flashy coloured photography of the eye, is rampant.

In Titian, in Velasquez, in Rembrandt the people are there

inside their clothes all right, and the clothes are imbued with the life of the individual, the gleam of the warm procreative body comes through all the time, even if it be an old, half-blind woman or a weird, ironic little Spanish princess. But modern people are nothing inside their garments, and a head sticks out at the top and hands stick out of the sleeves, and it is a bore. Or, as in Lawrence or Raeburn, you have something very pretty but almost a mere cliché, with very little instinctive or intuitional perception to it.

After this, and apart from landscape and water-colour, there is strictly no English painting that exists. As far as I am concerned, the pre-Raphaelites don't exist; Watts doesn't, Sargent doesn't, and none of the moderns.

There is the exception of Blake. Blake is the only painter of imaginative pictures, apart from landscape, that England has produced. And unfortunately there is so little Blake, and even in that little the symbolism is often artificially imposed. Nevertheless, Blake paints with real intuitional awareness and solid instinctive feeling. He dares handle the human body, even if he sometimes makes it a mere ideograph. And no other Englishman has ever dared handle it with alive imagination. Painters of composition-pictures in England, of whom perhaps the best is Watts, never quite get beyond the level of cliché, sentimentalism, and *funk*. Even Watts is a failure, though he made some sort of try: even Etty's nudes in York fail imaginatively, though they have some feeling for flesh. And the rest, the Leightons, even the moderns don't really do anything. They never get beyond studio models and clichés of the nude. The image never gets across to us, to seize intuitively. It remains merely optical.

Landscape, however, is different. Here the English exist and hold their own. But, for me, personally, landscape is always waiting for something to occupy it. Landscape seems to be *meant* as a background to an intenser vision of life, so to my feeling painted landscape is background with the real subject left out.

Nevertheless, it can be very lovely, especially in water-colour, which is a more bodiless medium, and doesn't aspire to very substantial existence, and is so small that it doesn't try to make a very deep seizure on the consciousness. Water-colour will always be more of a statement than an experience.

And landscape, on the whole, is the same. It doesn't call up the more powerful responses of the human imagination, the sensual passional responses. Hence it is the favourite modern form of expression in painting. There is no deep conflict. The instinctive and intuitional consciousness is called into play, but lightly, superficially. It is not confronted with any living, procreative body.

Hence the English have delighted in landscape, and have succeeded in it well. It is a form of escape for them, from the actual human body they so hate and fear, and it is an outlet for their perishing aesthetic desires. For more than a century we have produced delicious water-colours, and Wilson, Crome, Constable, Turner are all great landscape-painters. Some of Turner's landscape compositions are, to my feelings, among the finest that exist. They still satisfy me more even than Van Gogh's or Cézanne's landscapes, which make a more violent assault on the emotions, and repel a little for that reason. Somehow I don't want landscape to make a violent assault on my feelings. Landscape is background with the figures left out or reduced to minimum, so let it stay back. Van Gogh's surging earth and Cézanne's explosive or rattling planes worry me. Not being profoundly interested in landscape, I prefer it to be rather quiet and unexplosive.

But, of course, the English delight in landscape is a delight in escape. It is always the same. The northern races are so innerly afraid of their own bodily existence, which they believe fantastically to be an evil thing – you could never find them feel anything but uneasy shame, or an equally shameful gloating, over the fact that a man was having intercourse with his wife, in his house next door – that all they cry for is an escape. And, especially, art must provide that escape.

It is easy in literature. Shelley is pure escape: the body is sublimated into sublime gas. Keats is more difficult – the body can still be *felt* dissolving in waves of successive death – but the death-business is very satisfactory. The novelists have even a better time. You can get some of the lasciviousness of Hetty Sorrell's 'sin', and you can enjoy condemning her to penal servitude for life. You can thrill to Mr Rochester's *passion*, and you can enjoy having his eyes burnt out. So it is, all the way: the novel of 'passion'!

But in paint it is more difficult. You cannot paint Hetty Sorrell's sin or Mr Rochester's passion without being really shocking. And you *daren't* be shocking. It was this fact that unsaddled Watts and Millais. Both might have been painters if they hadn't been Victorians. As it is, each of them is a washout.

Which is the poor, feeble history of art in England, since we can lay no claim to the great Holbein. And art on the continent, in the last century? It is more interesting, and has a fuller story. An artist *can* only create what he really religiously *feels* is truth, religious truth really *felt*, in the blood and the bones. The English could never think anything connected with the body *religious* – unless it were the eyes. So they painted the social appearance of human beings, and hoped to give them wonderful eyes. But they *could* think landscape religious, since it had no sensual reality. So they felt religious about it and painted it as well as it could be painted, maybe, from their point of view.

And in France? In France it was more or less the same, but with a difference. The French, being more rational, decided that the body had its place, but that it should be rationalized. The Frenchman of today has the most reasonable and rationalized body possible. His conception of sex is basically hygienic. A certain amount of copulation is good for you. *Ça fait du bien au corps!* sums up the physical side of a Frenchman's ideas of love, marriage, food, sport and all the rest. Well, it is more sane, anyhow, than the Anglo-Saxon terrors. The Frenchman is afraid of syphilis and afraid of the procreative body, but not quite so deeply. He has known for a long time that you can take precautions. And he is not profoundly imaginative.

Therefore he has been able to paint. But his tendency, just like that of all the modern world, has been to get away from the body, while still paying attention to its hygiene, and still not violently quarrelling with it. Puvis de Chavannes is really as sloppy as all the other spiritual sentimentalizers. Renoir is jolly: *ça fait du bien au corps!* is his attitude to the flesh. If a woman didn't have buttocks and breasts, she wouldn't be paintable, he said, and he was right. *Ça fait du bien au corps!* What do you paint with, Maître? – With my penis, and be damned! Renoir didn't try to get away from the body. But he had to dodge it in some of its aspects, rob it of its natural terrors, its natural demonishness. He is delightful, but a trifle banal. *Ça fait du bien au corps!* Yet how infinitely much better he is than any English equivalent.

Courbet, Daumier, Degas, they all painted the human body. But Daumier satirized it, Courbet saw it as a toiling thing, Degas saw it as a wonderful instrument. They all of them deny it its finest qualities, its deepest instincts, its purest intuitions. They prefer, as it were, to industrialize it. They deny it the best imaginative existence.

And the real grand glamour of modern French art, the real outburst of delight came when the body was at last dissolved of its substance, and made part and parcel of the sunlight-and-shadow scheme. Let us say what we will, but the real grand thrill of modern French art was the discovery of light, the discovery of light, and all the subsequent discoveries, of the impressionists, and of the post-impressionists, even Cézanne. No matter how Cézanne may have reacted from the impressionists, it was they, with their deliriously joyful discovery of light and 'free' colour, who really opened his eyes. Probably the most joyous moment in the whole history of painting was the moment when the incipient impressionists discovered light, and with it, colour. Ah, then they made the grand, grand escape into freedom, into infinity, into light and delight. They escaped from the tyranny of solidity and the menace of mass-form. They escaped, they escaped from the dark procreative body which so haunts a man, they escaped into the open air, *plein air* and *plein soleil*: light and almost ecstasy.

Like every other human escape, it meant being hauled back later with the tail between the legs. Back comes the truant, back to the old doom of matter, of corporate existence, of the body sullen and stubborn and obstinately refusing to be transmuted into pure light, pure colour, or pure anything. It is not concerned with purity. Life isn't. Chemistry and mathematics and ideal religion are, but these are only small bits of life, which is itself bodily, and hence neither pure nor impure.

After the grand escape into impressionism and pure light, pure colour, pure bodilessness – for what is the body but a shimmer of lights and colours! – poor art came home truant and sulky, with its tail between its legs. And it is this return which now interests us. We know the escape was illusion, illusion, illusion. The cat had to come back. So now we despise the 'light' blighters too much. We haven't a good word for them. Which is nonsense, for they too are wonderful, even if their escape was into *le grand néant*, the great nowhere.

But the cat came back. And it is the home-coming tom that now has our sympathy: Renoir, to a certain extent, but mostly Cézanne, the sublime little grimalkin, who is followed by Matisse and Gauguin and Derain and Vlaminck and Braque and all the host of other defiant and howling cats that have come back, perforce, to form and substance and *thereness*, instead of delicious nowhereness.

Without wishing to labour the point, one cannot help being amused at the dodge by which the impressionists made the grand escape from the body. They metamorphosed it into a pure assembly of shifting lights and shadows, all coloured. A web of woven, luminous colour was a man, or a woman – and so they painted her, or him: a web of woven shadows and gleams. Delicious! and quite true as far as it goes. A purely optical truth: which paint is supposed to be. And they painted delicious pictures: a little too delicious. They bore us, at the moment. They bore people like the very modern critics intensely. But very modern critics need not be so intensely bored. There is something very lovely about the good impressionist pictures. And ten years hence critics will be bored by the present run of post-impressionists, though not so passionately bored, for these post-impressionists don't move us as the impressionists moved our fathers. We have to persuade ourselves, and we have to persuade one another to be impressed by the post-impressionists, on the whole. On the whole, they rather depress us. Which is perhaps good for us.

But modern art criticism is in a curious hole. Art has suddenly gone into rebellion, against all the canons of accepted religion, accepted good form, accepted everything. When the cat came back from the delicious impressionist excursion, it came back rather tattered, but bristling and with its claws out. The glorious escape was all an illusion. There was substance in the world, a thousand times be damned to it! There *was* the body, the great lumpy body. There it was. You had it shoved down your throat. What really existed was lumps, lumps. Then paint 'em. Or else paint the thin 'spirit' with gaps in it and looking merely dishevelled and 'found out'. Paint had found the spirit out.

This is the sulky and rebellious mood of the post-impressionists. They still hate the body – hate it. But, in a rage, they admit its existence, and paint it as huge lumps, tubes, cubes, planes, volumes, spheres, cones, cylinders, all the 'pure' or mathematical forms of substance. As for landscape, it comes in for some of the same rage. It has also suddenly gone lumpy. Instead of being nice and ethereal and non-sensual, it was discovered by Van Gogh to be heavily, overwhelmingly substantial and sensual. Van Gogh took up landscape in heavy spadefuls. And Cézanne had to admit it. Landscapes, too, after being, since Claude Lorraine, a thing of pure luminosity and floating shadow, suddenly exploded, and came tumbling back on to canvases of artists in lumps. With Cézanne, landscape 'crystallized', to use one of the favourite terms of the critics, and it has gone on crystallizing into cubes, cones, pyramids, and so forth ever since.

The impressionists brought the world at length, after centuries of effort, into the delicious oneness of light. At last, at last! Hail, holy Light! the great natural One, the universal, the universalizer! We are not divided, all one body we – one in Light, lovely light! No sooner had this paean gone up than the post-impressionists, like Judas, gave the show away. They exploded the illusion, which fell back to the canvas of art in a chaos of lumps.

This new chaos, of course, needed new apologists who therefore rose up in hordes to apologize, almost, for the new chaos. They felt a little guilty about it, so they took on new notes of effrontery, defiant as any Primitive Methodists, which, indeed, they are: the Primitive Methodists of art criticism. These evangelical gentlemen at once ran up their chapels, in a Romanesque or Byzantine shape, as was natural for a primitive and a methodist, and started to cry forth their doctrines in the decadent wilderness. They discovered once more that the aesthetic experience was an ecstasy, an ecstasy granted only to the chosen few, the elect, among whom said critics were, of course, the arch-elect. This was outdoing Ruskin. It was almost Calvin come to art. But let scoffers scoff, the aesthetic ecstasy was vouchsafed only to the few, the elect, and even then only when they had freed their minds of false doctrines. They had renounced the mammon of 'subject' in pictures, they went whoring no more after the Babylon of painted 'interest', nor did they hanker after the flesh-pots of artistic 'representation'. Oh, purify yourselves, ye who would know the aesthetic ecstasy, and be lifted up to the 'white peaks of artistic inspiration'. Purify yourselves of all base hankering for a tale that is told, and of all low lust for likenesses. Purify yourselves, and know the one supreme way, the way of Significant Form. I am the revelation and the way! I am Significant Form, and my unutterable name is Reality. Lo, I am Form and I am Pure, behold, I am Pure Form. I am the revelation of Spiritual Life, moving behind the veil. I come forth and make myself known, and I am Pure Form, behold, I am Significant Form.

So the prophets of the new era in art cry aloud to the multitude, in exactly the jargon of the revivalists, for revivalists they are. They will revive the Primitive Methodbrethren, the Byzantines, the Ravennese, the early Italian and French primitives (which ones, in particular, we aren't told); these were Right, these were Pure, these were Spiritual, these were Real! And the builders of early Romanesque churches,

O my brethren! these were holy men, before the world went a-whoring after Gothic. Oh, return, my brethren, to the Primitive Method. Lift up your eyes to Significant Form, and be saved.

Now myself, brought up a Nonconformist as I was, I just was never able to understand the language of salvation. I never knew what they were talking about, when they raved about being saved, and safe in the arms of Jesus, and Abraham's bosom, and seeing the great light, and entering into glory: I just was puzzled, for what did it *mean*? It seemed to work out as getting rather drunk on your own self-importance, and afterwards coming dismally sober again and being rather unpleasant. That was all I could see in actual experience of the entering-into-glory business. The term itself, like something which ought to mean something but somehow doesn't, stuck on my mind like an irritating burr, till I decided that it was just an artificial stimulant to the individual self-conceit. How could I enter into glory, when glory is just an abstraction of a human state, and not a separate reality at all? If glory means anything at all, it means the thrill a man gets when a great many people look up to him with mixed awe, reverence, delight. To-day, it means Rudolph Valentino. So that the cant about entering into glory is just used fuzzily to enhance the individual sense of self-importance – one of the rather cheap cocaine-phrases.

And I'm afraid 'aesthetic ecstasy' sounds to me very much the same, especially when accompanied by exhortations. It so sounds like another great uplift into self-importance, another apotheosis of personal conceit; especially when accompanied by a lot of jargon about the pure world of reality existing behind the veil of this vulgar world of accepted appearances, and of the entry of the elect through the doorway of visual art. Too evangelical altogether, too much chapel and Primitive Methodist, too obvious a trick for advertising one's own self-glorification. The ego, as an American says, shuts itself up and paints the inside of the walls sky-blue, and thinks it is in heaven.

And then the great symbols of this salvation. When the

evangelical says: Behold the lamb of God: – what on earth does he want one to behold? Are we invited to look at a lamb, with woolly, muttony appearance, frisking and making its little pills? Awfully nice, but what *has* it got to do with God or my soul? Or the cross? What *do* they expect us to see in the cross? A sort of gallows? Or the mark we use to cancel a mistake? – cross it out! That the cross by itself was supposed to *mean* something always mystified me. The same with the Blood of the Lamb. – Washed in the Blood of the Lamb! always seemed to me an extremely unpleasant suggestion. And when Jerome says: He who has once washed in the blood of Jesus need never wash again! – I feel like taking a hot bath at once, to wash off even the suggestion.

And I find myself equally mystified by the cant phrases like Significant Form and Pure Form. They are as mysterious to me as the Cross and the Blood of the Lamb. They are just the magic jargon of invocation, nothing else. If you want to invoke an aesthetic ecstasy, stand in front of a Matisse and whisper fervently under your breath: 'Significant Form! Significant Form!' – and it will come. It sounds to me like a form of masturbation, an attempt to make the body react to some cerebral formula.

No, I am afraid modern criticism has done altogether too much for modern art. If painting survives this outburst of ecstatic evangelism, which it will, it is because people do come to their senses, even after the silliest vogue.

And so we can return to modern French painting, without having to quake before the bogy, or the Holy Ghost of Significant Form: a bogy which doesn't exist if we don't mind leaving aside our self-importance when we look at a picture.

The actual fact is that in Cézanne modern French art made its first step back to real substance, to objective substance, if we may call it so. Van Gogh's earth was still subjective earth, himself projected into the earth. But Cézanne's apples are a real attempt to let the apple exist in its own separate entity, without transfusing it with personal emotion. Cézanne's great effort was, as it were, to shove the apple away from him, and let it live of itself. It seems a small thing to do: yet it is the first real sign that man has made for several thousands of years that he is willing to admit that matter *actually* exists. Strange as it may seem, for thousands of years, in short, ever since the mythological 'Fall', man has been preoccupied with the constant preoccupation of the denial of the existence of matter, and the proof that matter is only a form of spirit. And then, the moment it is done, and we realize finally that matter is only a form of energy, whatever that may be, in the same instant matter rises up and hits us over the head and makes us realize that it exists absolutely, since it is compact energy itself.

Cézanne felt it in paint, when he felt for the apple. Suddenly he felt the tyranny of mind, the white, worn-out arrogance of the spirit, the mental consciousness, the enclosed ego in its sky-blue heaven self-painted. He felt the sky-blue prison. And a great conflict started inside him. He was dominated by his old mental consciousness, but he wanted terribly to escape the domination. He wanted to *express* what he suddenly, convulsedly knew! the existence of matter. He terribly wanted to paint the real existence of the body, to make it artistically palpable. But he couldn't. He hadn't got there yet. And it was the torture of his life. He wanted to be himself in his own procreative body – and he couldn't. He was, like all the rest of us, so intensely and exclusively a mental creature, or a spiritual creature, or an egoist, that he could no longer identify himself with his intuitive body. He wanted to, terribly. At first he determined to do it by sheer bravado and braggadocio. But no good; it couldn't be done that way. He had, as one critic says, to become humble. But it wasn't a question of becoming humble. It was a question of abandoning his cerebral conceit and his 'willed ambition' and coming down to brass tacks. Poor Cézanne, there he is in his self-portraits, even the early showy ones, peeping out like a mouse and saying: I *am* a man of flesh, am I not? For he was not quite, as none of us are. The man of flesh has been slowly destroyed through centuries, to give place to the man of spirit, the mental man, the ego, the self-conscious I. And in his artistic soul Cézanne knew it, and wanted to rise in the flesh. He couldn't do it, and it embittered him. Yet, with his apple, he did shove the stone from the door of the tomb.

He wanted to be a man of flesh, a real man: to get out of the sky-blue prison into real air. He wanted to live, really live in the body, to know the world through his instincts and his intuitions, and to be himself in his procreative blood, not in his mere mind and spirit. He wanted it, he wanted it terribly. And whenever he tried, his mental consciousness, like a cheap fiend, interfered. If he wanted to paint a woman, his mental consciousness simply overpowered him and wouldn't let him paint the woman of flesh, the first Eve who lived before any of the fig-leaf nonsense. He couldn't do it. If he wanted to paint people intuitively and instinctively, he couldn't do it. His mental concepts shoved in front, and these he *wouldn't* paint – mere representations of what the *mind* accepts, not what the intuitions gather – and they, his mental concepts, wouldn't let him paint from intuition; they shoved in between all the time, so he painted his conflict and his failure, and the result is almost ridiculous.

Woman he was not allowed to know by intuition; his mental self, his ego, that bloodless fiend, forbade him. Man, other men, he was likewise not allowed to know – except by a few, few touches. The earth likewise he was not allowed to know: his landscapes are mostly acts of rebellion against the mental concept of landscape. After a fight tooth-and-nail for forty years, he did succeed in knowing an apple, fully; and, not quite as fully, a jug or two. That was all he achieved.

It seems little, and he died embittered. But it is the first step that counts, and Cézanne's apple is a great deal, more than Plato's Idea. Cézanne's apple rolled the stone from the mouth of the tomb, and if poor Cézanne couldn't unwind himself from his cerements and mental winding-sheet, but had to lie still in the tomb, till he died, still he gave us a chance.

The history of our era is the nauseating and repulsive history of the crucifixion of the procreative body for the glorification of the spirit, the mental consciousness. Plato was an arch-priest of this crucifixion. Art, that handmaid, humbly and honestly served the vile deed, through three thousand years at least. The Renaissance put the spear through the side of the already crucified body, and syphilis put poison into the wound made by the imaginative spear. It took still three hundred years for the body to finish: but in the eighteenth century it became a corpse, a corpse with an abnormally active mind: and to-day it stinketh.

We, dear reader, you and I, we were born corpses, and we are corpses. I doubt if there is even one of us who has ever known so much as an apple, a whole apple. All we know is shadows, even of apples. Shadows of everything, of the whole world, shadows even of ourselves. We are inside the tomb, and the tomb is wide and shadowy like hell, even if sky-blue by optimistic paint, so we think it is all the world. But our world is a wide tomb full of ghosts, replicas. We are all spectres, we have not been able to touch even so much as an apple. Spectres we are to one another. Spectre you are to me, spectre I am to you. Shadow you are even to yourself. And by shadow I mean idea, concept, the abstracted reality, the ego. We are not solid. We don't live in the flesh. Our instincts and intuitions are dead, we live wound round with the winding-sheet of abstraction. And the touch of anything solid hurts us. For our instincts and intuitions, which are our feelers of touch and knowing through touch, they are dead, amputated. We walk and talk and eat and copulate and laugh and evacuate wrapped in our winding-sheets, all the time wrapped in our winding-sheets.

So that Cézanne's apple hurts. It made people shout with pain. And it was not till his followers had turned him again into an abstraction that he was ever accepted. Then the critics stepped forth and abstracted his good apple into Significant Form, and henceforth Cézanne was saved. Saved for democracy. Put safely in the tomb again, and the stone rolled back. The resurrection was postponed once more.

As the resurrection will be postponed *ad infinitum* by the good bourgeois corpses in their cultured winding-sheets. They will run up a chapel to the risen body, even if it is only an apple, and kill it on the spot. They are wide awake, are the corpses, on the alert. And a poor mouse of a Cézanne is alone in the years. Who else shows a spark of awakening life, in our marvellous civilized cemetery? All is dead, and dead breath teaching with phosphorescent effulgence about aesthetic ecstasy and Significant Form. If only the dead would bury their dead. But the dead are not dead for nothing. Who buries his own sort? The dead are cunning and alert to pounce on any spark of life and bury *it*, even as they have already buried Cézanne's apple and put up to it a white tombstone of Significant Form.

For who of Cézanne's followers does anything but follow at the triumphant funeral of Cézanne's achievements? They follow him in order to bury him, and they succeed. Cézanne is deeply buried under all the Matisses and Vlamincks of his following, while the critics read the funeral homily.

It is quite easy to accept Matisse and Vlaminck and Friesz and all the rest. They are just Cézanne abstracted again. They are all just tricksters, even if clever ones. They are all mental, mental egoists, egoists, egoists. And therefore they are all acceptable now to the enlightened corpses of connoisseurs. You needn't be afraid of Matisse and Vlaminck and the rest. They will never give your corpse-anatomy a jar. They are just shadows, minds mountebanking and playing charades on canvas. They may be quite amusing charades, and I am all for the mountebank. But of course it is all games inside the cemetery, played by corpses and *hommes d'esprit*, even *femmes d'esprit*, like Mademoiselle Laurencin. As for *l'esprit*, said Cézanne, I don't give a fart for it. Perhaps not! But the connoisseurs will give large sums of money. Trust the dead to pay for their amusement, when the amusement is deadly!

The most interesting figure in modern art, and the only really interesting figure, is Cézanne: and that, not so much because of his achievement as because of his struggle. Cézanne was born in Aix in Provence in 1839: small, timorous, yet sometimes bantam defiant, sensitive, full of grand ambition, yet ruled still deeper by a naïve, Mediterranean sense of truth or reality, imagination, call it what you will. He is not a big figure. Yet his struggle is truly heroic. He was a bourgeois, and one must never forget it. He had a moderate bourgeois income. But a bourgeois in Provence is much more real and human than a bourgeois in Normandy. He is much nearer the actual people, and the actual people are much less subdued by awe of his respectable bourgeois money.

Cézanne was naïve to a degree, but not a fool. He was rather insignificant, and grandeur impressed him terribly. Yet still stronger in him was the little flame of life where he *felt* things to be true. He didn't betray himself in order to get success, because he couldn't: to his nature it was impossible: he was too pure to be able to betray his own small real flame for immediate rewards. Perhaps that is the best one can say of a man, and it puts Cézanne, small and insignificant as he is, among the heroes. He would *not* abandon his own vital imagination.

He was terribly impressed by physical splendour and flamboyancy, as people usually are in the lands of the sun. He admired terribly the splendid virtuosity of Paul Veronese and Tintoretto, and even of later and less good baroque painters. He wanted to be like that – terribly he wanted it. And he tried very, very hard, with bitter effort. And he always failed. It is a cant phrase with the critics to say 'he couldn't draw'. Mr Fry says: 'With all his rare endowments, he happened to lack the comparatively common gift of illustration, the gift that any draughtsman for the illustrated papers learns in a school of commercial art.'

Now this sentence gives away at once the hollowness of modern criticism. In the first place, can one learn a 'gift' in a school of commercial art, or anywhere else? A gift surely is given, we tacitly assume, by God or Nature or whatever higher power we hold responsible for the things we have no choice in.

Was, then, Cézanne devoid of this gift? Was he simply incapable of drawing a cat so that it would look like a cat? Nonsense! Cézanne's work is full of accurate drawing. His more trivial pictures, suggesting copies from other masters, are perfectly well drawn – that is, conventionally: so are some of the landscapes, so even is that portrait of M. Geffroy and his books, which is, or was, so famous. Why all these cant phrases about not being able to draw? Of course Cézanne could draw, as well as anybody else. And he had learned everything that was necessary in the art-schools.

He *could* draw. And yet, in his terrifically earnest compositions in the late Renaissance or baroque manner, he drew so badly. Why? Not because he couldn't. And not because he was sacrificing 'significant form' to 'insignificant form', or mere slick representation, which is apparently what artists themselves mean when they talk about drawing. Cézanne knew all about drawing: and he surely knew as much as his critics do about significant form. Yet he succeeded neither in drawing so that things looked right, nor combining his shapes so that he achieved real form. He just failed.

He failed, where one of his little slick successors would have succeeded with one eye shut. And why? Why did Cézanne fail in his early pictures? Answer that, and you'll know a little better what art is. He didn't fail because he understood nothing about drawing or significant form or aesthetic ecstasy. He knew about them all, and didn't give a spit for them.

Cézanne failed in his earlier pictures because he was trying with his mental consciousness to do something which his living Provençal body didn't want to do, or couldn't do. He terribly wanted to do something grand and voluptuous and sensuously satisfying, in the Tintoretto manner. Mr Fry calls that his 'willed ambition', which is a good phrase, and says he had to learn humility, which is a bad phrase.

The 'willed ambition' was more than a mere willed ambition – it was a genuine desire. But it was a desire that thought it would be satisfied by ready-made baroque expressions, whereas it needed to achieve a whole new marriage of mind and matter. If we believed in reincarnation, then we should have to believe that after a certain number of new incarnations into the body of an artist, the soul of Cézanne *would* produce grand and voluptuous and sensually rich pictures – but not at all in the baroque manner. Because the pictures he actually did produce with undeniable success are the first steps in that direction, sensual and rich, with not the slightest hint of baroque, but new, the man's new grasp of substantial reality.

There was, then, a certain discrepancy between Cézanne's *notion* of what he wanted to produce, and his other, intuitive knowledge of what he *could* produce. For whereas the mind works in possibilities, the intuitions work in actualities, and what you *intuitively* desire, that is possible to you. Whereas what you mentally or 'consciously' desire is nine times out of ten impossible: hitch your wagon to a star, and you'll just stay where you are.

So the conflict, as usual, was not between the artist and his medium, but between the artist's *mind* and the artist's *intuition* and *instinct*. And what Cézanne had to learn was not humility – cant word! – but honesty, honesty with himself. It was not a question of any gift or significant form or aesthetic ecstasy: it was a question of Cézanne being himself, just Cézanne. And when Cézanne is himself he is not Tintoretto, nor Veronese, nor anything baroque at all. Yet he is something *physical*, and even sensual: qualities which he had identified with the masters of virtuosity.

In passing, if we think of Henri Matisse, a real virtuoso, and imagine him possessed with a 'willed ambition' to paint grand and flamboyant baroque pictures, then we know at once that he would not have to 'humble' himself at all, but that he would start in and paint with great success grand and flamboyant modern-baroque pictures. He would succeed because he has the gift of virtuosity. And the gift of virtuosity simply means that you don't have to humble yourself, or even be honest with yourself, because you are a clever mental creature who is capable at will of making the intuitions and instincts subserve some mental concept: in short, you can prostitute your body to your mind, your instincts and intuitions you can prostitute to your 'willed ambition', in a sort of masturbation process, and you can produce the impotent glories of virtuosity. But Veronese and Tintoretto are real painters; they are not mere *virtuosi*, as some of the later men are.

The point is very important. Any creative act occupies the

whole consciousness of a man. This is true of the great discoveries of science as well as of art. The truly great discoveries of science and real works of art are made by the whole consciousness of man working together in unison and oneness: instinct, intuition, mind, intellect all fused into one complete consciousness, and grasping what we may call a complete truth, or a complete vision, a complete revelation in sound. A discovery, artistic or otherwise, may be more or less intuitional, more or less mental: but intuition will have entered into it, and mind will have entered too. The whole consciousness is concerned in every case. – And a painting requires the activity of the whole imagination, for it is made of imagery, and the imagination is that form of complete consciousness in which predominates the intuitive awareness of forms, images, the *physical* awareness.

And the same applies to the genuine appreciation of a work of art, or the *grasp* of a scientific law, as to the production of the same. The whole consciousness is occupied, not merely the mind alone, or merely the body. The mind and the spirit alone can never really grasp a work of art, though they may, in a masturbating fashion, provoke the body into an ecstasized response. The ecstasy will die out into ash and more ash. And the reason we have so many trivial scientists promulgating fantastic 'facts' is that so many modern scientists likewise work with the mind alone, and *force* the intuitions and instincts into a prostituted acquiescence. The very statement that water is H_2O is a mental *tour de force*. With our bodies we know that water is *not* H_2O, our intuitions and instincts both know it is not so. But they are bullied by the impudent mind. Whereas if we said that water, under certain circumstances, produces two volumes of hydrogen to one of oxygen, then the intuitions and instincts would agree entirely. But that water is *composed* of two volumes of hydrogen to one of oxygen we cannot physically believe. It needs something else. Something is missing. Of course, alert science does not ask us to believe the commonplace assertion of: *water* is H_2O, but school children have to believe it.

A parallel case is all this modern stuff about astronomy,

stars, their distances and speeds and so on, talking of billions and trillions of miles and years and so forth: it is just occult. The mind is revelling in words, the intuitions and instincts are just left out, or prostituted into a sort of ecstasy. In fact, the sort of ecstasy that lies in absurd figures such as 2,000,000,000,000,000,000,000,000,000 miles or years or tons, figures which abound in modern *scientific* books on astronomy, is just the sort of aesthetic ecstasy that the over-mental critics of art assert they experience to-day from Matisse's pictures. It is all poppycock. The body is either stunned to a corpse, or prostituted to ridiculous thrills, or stands coldly apart.

When I read how far off the suns are, and what they are made of, and so on, and so on, I believe all I am *able* to believe, with the true imagination. But when my intuition and instinct can grasp no more, then I call my mind to a halt. I am not going to accept mere mental asseverations. The mind can assert anything, and pretend it has proved it. My beliefs I test on my body, on my intuitional consciousness, and when I get a response there, then I accept. The same is true of great scientific 'laws', like the law of evolution. After years of acceptance of the 'laws' of evolution – rather desultory or 'humble' acceptance – now I realize that my vital imagination makes great reservations. I find I can't, with the best will in the world, believe that the species have 'evolved' from one common life-form. I just can't feel it, I have to violate my intuitive and instinctive awareness of something else, to make myself believe it. But since I know that my intuitions and instincts may still be held back by prejudice, I seek in the world for someone to make me intuitively and instinctively feel the truth of the 'law' – and I don't find anybody. I find scientists, just like artists, asserting things they are *mentally* sure of, in fact cocksure, but about which they are much too egoistic and ranting to be *intuitively, instinctively* sure. When I find a man, or a woman, intuitively and instinctively sure of anything, I am all respect. But for scientific or artistic braggarts how can one have respect? The intrusion of the egoistic element is a sure proof of intuitive uncertainty. No man who is sure by instinct and intuition *brags*, though he may fight tooth and nail for his beliefs.

Which brings us back to Cézanne, why he couldn't draw, and why he couldn't paint baroque masterpieces. It is just because he was real, and could only believe in his own expression when it expressed a moment of wholeness or completeness of consciousness in himself. He could not prostitute one part of himself to the other. He *could* not masturbate, in paint or words. And that is saying a very great deal, to-day; the great day of the masturbating consciousness, when the mind prostitutes the sensitive responsive body, and just forces the reactions. The masturbating consciousness produces all kinds of novelties, which thrill for the moment, then go very dead. I cannot produce a single genuinely new utterance.

What we have to thank Cézanne for is not his humility, but for his proud high spirit that refused to accept the glib utterances of his facile mental self. He wasn't poor-spirited enough to be facile – nor humble enough to be satisfied with visual and emotional clichés. Thrilling as the baroque masters were to him in themselves, he realized that as soon as he reproduced them he produced nothing but cliché. The mind is full of all sorts of memory, visual, tactile, emotional memory, memories, groups of memories, systems of memories. A cliché is just a worn-out memory that has no more emotional or intuitional root, and has become a habit. Whereas a novelty is just a new grouping of clichés, a new arrangement of accustomed memories. That is why a novelty is so easily accepted: it gives the little shock or thrill of surprise, but it does not *disturb* the emotional and intuitive self. It forces you to see nothing new. It is only a novel compound of clichés. The work of most of Cézanne's successors is just novel, just a new arrangement of clichés, soon growing stale. And the clichés are Cézanne's clichés, just as in Cézanne's own earlier pictures the clichés were all, or mostly, baroque clichés.

Cézanne's early history as a painter is a history of his fight with his own cliché. His consciousness wanted a new realization. And his ready-made mind offered him all the time a ready-made expression. And Cézanne, far too inwardly proud and haughty to accept the ready-made clichés that came from his mental consciousness, stocked with memories, and which appeared mocking at him on his canvas, spent most of his time smashing his own forms to bits. To a true artist, and to the living imagination, the cliché is the deadly enemy. Cézanne had a bitter fight with it. He hammered it to pieces a thousand times. And still it reappeared.

Now again we can see why Cézanne's drawing was so bad. It was bad because it represented a smashed, mauled cliché, terribly knocked about. If Cézanne had been willing to accept his own baroque cliché, his drawing would have been perfectly conventionally 'all right', and not a critic would have had a word to say about it. But when his drawing was conventionally all right, to Cézanne himself it was mockingly all wrong, it was cliché. So he flew at it and knocked all the shape and stuffing out of it, and when it was so mauled that it was all wrong, and he was exhausted with it, he let it go; bitterly, because it still was not what he wanted. And here comes in the comic element in Cézanne's pictures. His rage with the cliché made him distort the cliché sometimes into parody, as we see in pictures like *The Pasha* and *La Femme*. 'You *will* be cliché, will you?' he gnashes. 'Then *be* it!' And he shoves it in a frenzy of exasperation over into parody. And the sheer exasperation makes the parody still funny; but the laugh is a little on the wrong side of the face.

This smashing of the cliché lasted a long way into Cézanne's life; indeed, it went with him to the end. The way he worked over and over his forms was his nervous manner of laying the ghost of his cliché, burying it. Then when it disappeared perhaps from his forms themselves, it lingered in his composition, and he had to fight with the *edges* of his forms and contours, to bury the ghost there. Only his colour he knew was not cliché. He left it to his disciples to make it so.

In his very best pictures, the best of the still-life compositions, which seem to me Cézanne's greatest achievement, the fight with the cliché is still going on. But it was in the still-life pictures he learned his final method of *avoiding* the cliché; just leaving gaps through which it fell into nothingness. So he makes his landscape succeed.

In his art, all his life long, Cézanne was tangled in a twofold activity. He wanted to express something, and before he could do it he had to fight the hydra-headed cliché, whose last head he could never lop off. The fight with the cliché is the most obvious thing in his pictures. The dust of battle rises thick and the splinters fly wildly. And it is this dust of battle and flying of splinters which his imitators still so fervently imitate. If you give a Chinese dressmaker a dress to copy, and the dress happens to have a darned rent in it, the dressmaker carefully tears a rent in the new dress, and darns it in exact replica. And this seems to be the chief occupation of Cézanne's disciples, in every land. They absorb themselves reproducing imitation mistakes. He let off various explosions in order to blow up the stronghold of the cliché, and his followers make grand firework imitations of the explosions, without the faintest inkling of the true attack. They do, indeed, make an onslaught on representation, true-to-life representation: because the explosion in Cézanne's pictures blew them up. But I am convinced that what Cézanne himself wanted *was* representation. He *wanted* true-to-life representation. Only he wanted it *more* true to life. And once you have got photography, it is a very, very difficult thing to get representation *more* true-to-life: which it has to be.

Cézanne was a realist, and he wanted to be true to life. But he would not be content with the optical cliché. With the impressionists, purely optical vision perfected itself and fell *at once* into clichés, with a startling rapidity. Cézanne saw this. Artists like Courbet and Daumier were not purely optical, but the other element in these two painters, the intellectual element, was cliché. To the optical vision they added the concept of force-pressure, almost like an hydraulic brake, and this force-pressure concept is mechanical, a cliché, though still popular. And Daumier added mental satire, and Courbet added a touch of a sort of socialism: both cliché and unimaginative.

Cézanne wanted something that was neither optical nor mechanical nor intellectual. And to introduce into our world of vision something which is neither optical nor mechanical nor intellectual-psychological requires a real revolution. It was a revolution Cézanne began, but which nobody, apparently, has been able to carry on.

He wanted to touch the world of substance once more with the intuitive touch, to be aware of it with the intuitive awareness, and to express it in intuitive terms. That is, he wished to displace our present mode of mental-visual consciousness, the consciousness of mental concepts, and substitute a mode of consciousness that was predominantly intuitive, the awareness of touch. In the past the primitives painted intuitively, but *in the direction* of our present mental-visual, conceptual form of consciousness. They were working away from their own intuition. Mankind has never been able to trust the intuitive consciousness, and the decision to accept the trust marks a very great revolution in the course of human development.

Without knowing it, Cézanne, the timid little conventional man sheltering behind his wife and sister and the Jesuit father, was a pure revolutionary. When he said to his models: 'Be an apple! Be an apple!' he was uttering the foreword to the fall not only of Jesuits and the Christian idealists together, but to the collapse of our whole way of consciousness, and the substitution of another way. If the human being is going to be primarily an apple, as for Cézanne it was, then you are going to have a new world of men: a world which has very little to say, men that can sit still and just be physically there, and be truly non-moral. That was what Cézanne meant with his: 'Be an apple!' He knew perfectly well that the moment the model began to intrude her personality and her 'mind', it would be cliché and moral, and he would have to paint cliché. The only part of her that was not banal, known *ad nauseam*, living cliché, the only part of her that was not living cliché was her appleyness. Her body, even her very sex, was known, nauseously: *connu! connu!* the endless chance of known cause-and-effect, the infinite web of the hated cliché which nets us all down in utter boredom. He knew it all, he hated it all, he refused it all, this timid and 'humble' little man. He knew, as an artist, that the only bit of a woman which nowadays escapes being ready-made and ready-known cliché is the appley part of her. Oh, be an apple, and leave out all your thoughts, all your feelings, all your mind and all your personality, which we know all about and find boring beyond endurance. Leave it all out – and be an apple! It is the appleyness of the portrait of Cézanne's wife that makes it so permanently interesting: the appleyness, which carries with it also the feeling of knowing the other side as well, the side you don't see, the hidden side of the moon. For the intuitive apperception of the apple is so *tangibly* aware of the apple that it is aware of it *all round*, not only just of the front. The eye sees only fronts, and the mind, on the whole, is satisfied with fronts. But intuition needs all-roundedness, and instinct needs insideness. The true imagination is for ever curving round to the other side, to the back of presented appearance.

So to my feeling the portraits of Madame Cézanne, particularly the portrait in the red dress, are more interesting than the portrait of M. Geffroy, or the portraits of the housekeeper or the gardener. In the same way the *Card-Players* with two figures please me more than those with four.

But we have to remember, in his figure-paintings, that while he was painting the appleyness he was also deliberately painting *out* the so-called humanness, the personality, the 'likeness', the physical cliché. He had deliberately to paint it out, deliberately to make the hands and face rudimentary, and so on, because if he had painted them in fully they would have been cliché. He *never* got over the cliché denominator, the intrusion and interference of the ready-made concept, when it came to people, to men and women. Especially to women he could only give a cliché response – and that maddened him. Try as he might, women remained a known, ready-made cliché object to him, and he *could not* break through the concept obsession to get at the intuitive awareness of her. Except with his wife – and in his wife he did at least know the appleyness. But with his housekeeper he failed somewhat. She was a bit cliché, especially the face. So really is M. Geffroy.

With men Cézanne often dodged it by insisting on the clothes, those stiff cloth jackets bent into thick folds, those hats, those blouses, those curtains. Some of the *Card-Players*, the big ones with four figures, seem just a trifle banal, so much occupied with painted stuff, painted clothing, and the humanness a bit cliché. Not good colour, nor clever composition, nor 'planes' of colour, nor anything else will save an emotional cliché from being an emotional cliché, though they may, of course, garnish it and make it more interesting.

Where Cézanne did sometimes escape the cliché altogether and really give a complete intuitive interpretation of actual objects is in some of the still-life compositions. To me these good still-life scenes are purely representative and quite true to life. Here Cézanne did what he wanted to do: he made the things quite real, he didn't deliberately leave anything out, and yet he gave us a triumphant and rich intuitive vision of a few apples and kitchen pots. For once his intuitive consciousness triumphed, and broke into utterance. And here he is inimitable. His imitators imitate his accessories of tablecloths folded like tins, etc. – the unreal parts of his pictures – but they don't imitate the pots and apples, because they can't. It's the real appleyness, and you can't imitate it. Every man must create it new and different out of himself: new and different. The moment it looks 'like' Cézanne, it is nothing.

But at the same time Cézanne was triumphing with the apple and appleyness he was still fighting with the cliché. When he makes Madame Cézanne most *still*, most appley, he starts making the universe slip uneasily about her. It was part of his desire: to make the human form, the *life* form, come to rest. Not static – on the contrary. Mobile but come to rest. And at the same time he set the unmoving material world into motion. Walls twitch and slide, chairs bend or rear up a little, cloths curl like burning paper. Cézanne did this partly to satisfy his intuitive feeling that nothing is really *statically* at rest – a feeling he seems to have had strongly – as when he watched the lemons shrivel or go mildewed, in his still-life group, which he left lying there so long so that he *could* see that gradual flux of change: and partly to fight the cliché, which says that the inanimate world *is* static, and that walls *are* still. In his fight with the cliché he denied that walls are still and chairs are static. In his intuitive self he *felt* for their changes.

And these two activities of his consciousness occupy his later landscapes. In the best landscapes we are fascinated by the mysterious *shiftiness* of the scene under our eyes; it shifts about as we watch it. And we realize, with a sort of transport, how intuitively *true* this is of landscape. It is *not* still. It has its own weird anima, and to our wide-eyed perception it changes like a living animal under our gaze. This is a quality that Cézanne got marvellously.

Then again, in other pictures he seems to be saying: Landscape is not like this and not like this and not like this and not ... etc. – and every *not* is a little blank space in the canvas, defined by the remains of an assertion. Sometimes Cézanne builds up a landscape essentially out of omissions. He puts fringes on the complicated vacuum of the cliché, so to speak, and offers us that. It is interesting in a *repudiative* fashion, but it is not the new thing. The appleyness, the intuition has gone. We have only a mental repudiation. This occupies many of the later pictures: and ecstasizes the critics.

And Cézanne was bitter. He had never, as far as his *life* went, broken through the horrible glass screen of the mental concepts, to the actual *touch* of life. In his art he had touched the apple, and that was a great deal. He had intuitively known the apple and intuitively brought it forth on the tree of his life, in paint. But when it came to anything beyond the apple, to landscape, to people, and above all to nude woman, the cliché had triumphed over him. The cliché had triumphed over him, and he was bitter, misanthropic. How not to be misanthropic when men and women are just clichés to you, and you hate the cliché? Most people, of course, love the cliché – because most people *are* the cliché. Still, for all that, there is perhaps more appleyness in man, and even in nude woman, than Cézanne was able to get at. The cliché obtruded, so he just abstracted away from it. Those last water-colour landscapes are just coloured sort of edges. The blank is vacuum, which was Cézanne's last word against the cliché. It is a vacuum and the edges are there to assert the vacuity.

And the very fact that we can reconstruct almost instantly a whole landscape from the few indications Cézanne gives, shows what a cliché the landscape is, how it exists already ready-made, in our minds, how it exists in a pigeon-hole of the consciousness, so to speak, and you need only be given its number to be able to get it out, complete. Cézanne's last water-colour landscapes, made up of a few touches on blank paper, are a satire on landscape altogether. *They leave so much to the imagination!* – that immortal cant phrase, which means they give you the clue to a cliché and the cliché comes. That's what the cliché exists for. And that sort of imagination is just a rag-bag memory stored with thousands and thousands of old and really worthless sketches, images, etc., clichés.

We can see what a fight it means, the escape from the domination of the ready-made mental concept, the mental consciousness stuffed full of clichés that intervene like a complete screen between us and life. It means a long, long fight, that will probably last for ever. But Cézanne did get as far as the apple. I can think of nobody else who has done anything.

When we put it in personal terms, it is a fight in a man between his own ego, which is his ready-made mental self which inhabits either a sky-blue, self-tinted heaven or a black, self-tinted hell, and his other free intuitive self. Cézanne never freed himself from his ego, in his life. He haunted the fringes of experience. 'I who am so feeble in life' – but at least he knew it. At least he had the greatness to feel bitter about it. Not like the complacent bourgeois who now 'appreciate' him!

So now perhaps it is the English turn. Perhaps this is where the English will come in. They have certainly stayed out very completely. It is as if they had received the death-blow to their instinctive and intuitive bodies in the Elizabethan age, and since then they have steadily died, till now they are complete corpses. As a young English painter, an intelligent and really modest young man, said to me: 'But I do think we ought to begin to paint good pictures, now that we know pretty well all there is to know about how a picture should be made. You do agree, don't you, that technically we know almost all there is to know about painting?'

I looked at him in amazement. It was obvious that a newborn babe was as fit to paint pictures as he was. He knew technically all there was to know about pictures: all about two-dimensional and three-dimensional composition, also the colour-dimension and the dimension of values in that view of the composition which exists apart from form: all about the value of planes, the value of the angle in planes, the different values of the same colour on different planes: all about edges, visible edges, tangible edges, intangible edges: all about the nodality of form-groups, the constellating of mass-centres: all about the relativity of mass, the gravitation and the centrifugal force of masses, the resultant of the complex impinging of masses, the isolation of a mass in the line of vision: all about pattern, line pattern, edge pattern, tone pattern, colour pattern, and the pattern of moving planes: all about texture, impasto, surface, and what happens at the edge of the canvas: also which is the aesthetic centre of the canvas, the dynamic centre, the effulgent centre, the kinetic centre, the mathematical centre, and the Chinese centre: also the points of departure in the foreground, and the points of disappearance in the background, together with the various routes between these points, namely, as the crow flies, as the cow walks, as the mind intoxicated with knowledge reels and gets there: all about spotting, what you spot, which spot, on the spot, how many spots, balance of spots, recedence of spots, spots on the explosive vision and spots on the co-ordinative vision: all about literary interest and how to hide it successfully from the policeman: all about photographic representation, and which heaven it belongs to, and which hell: all about the sex-appeal of a picture, and when you can be arrested for solicitation, when for indecency: all about the psychology of a picture, which section of the mind it appeals to, which mental state it is intended to represent, how to exclude the representation of all other states of mind from the one intended, or how, on the contrary, to give a hint of complementary states of mind fringing the state of mind portrayed: all about the chemistry of colours, when to use Winsor & Newton and when not, and the relative depth of contempt to display for

Lefranc on the history of colour, past and future, whether cadmium will really stand the march of ages, whether viridian will go black, blue, or merely greasy, and the effect on our great-great-grandsons of the flake white and zinc white and white lead we have so lavishly used: on the merits and demerits of leaving patches of bare, prepared canvas, and which preparation will bleach, which blacken: on the mediums to be used, the vice of linseed oil, the treachery of turps, the meanness of gums, the innocence of the unspeakable crime of varnish: on allowing your picture to be shiny, on insisting that it should be shiny, on weeping over the merest suspicion of gloss and rubbing it with a raw potato: on brushes, and the conflicting length of the stem, the best of the hog, the length of bristle most to be desired on the many varying occasions, and whether to slash in one direction only: on the atmosphere of London, on the atmosphere of Glasgow, on the atmosphere of Rome, on the atmosphere of Paris, and the peculiar action of them all upon vermilion, cinnabar, pale cadmium yellow, mid-chrome, emerald green, Veronese green, linseed oil, turps, and Lyall's perfect medium: on quality, and its relation to light, and its ability to hold its own in so radical a change of light as that from Rome to London – all these things the young man knew – and out of it, God help us, he was going to make pictures.

Now, such innocence and such naïveté, coupled with true modesty, must make us believe that we English have indeed, at least as far as paint goes, become again as little children: very little children, tiny children: babes: nay, babes unborn. And if we have really got back to the state of the unborn babe, we are perhaps almost ready to be born. The English *may* be born again, pictorially. Or, to tell the truth, they may begin for the first time to be born: since as painters of composition pictures they don't really exist. They have reached the stage where their innocent egos are entirely and totally enclosed in pale-blue glass bottles of insulated inexperience. Perhaps now they *must* hatch out!

'Do you think we may be on the brink of a Golden Age again in England?' one of our most promising young writers asked me, with that same half-timorous innocence and naïveté of the young painter. I looked at him – he was a sad young man – and my eyes nearly fell out of my head. A golden age! He looked so ungolden and though he was twenty years my junior, he felt also like my grandfather. A golden age! in England! a golden age! now, when even money is paper! when the enclosure in the ego is final, when they are hermetically sealed and insulated from all experience, from any *touch*, from anything *solid*.

'I suppose it's up to *you*,' said I.

And he quietly accepted it.

But such innocence, such naïveté must be a prelude to something. It's a *ne plus ultra*. So why shouldn't it be a prelude to a golden age? If the innocence and naïveté as regards artistic expression doesn't become merely idiotic, why shouldn't it become golden? The young might, out of sheer sort of mental blankness, strike the oil of their live intuition, and get a gusher. Why not? A golden gush of artistic expression! 'Now we know pretty well everything that can be known about the technical side of pictures.' A golden age!

Lawrence and Magnus

THE LATE MR MAURICE MAGNUS

A LETTER

New Statesman, 20 February, 1926

To the Editor of The New Statesman:

SIR, – Referring to the review published in your last issue of Mr Norman Douglas's *Experiments*, will you give me a little space in which to shake off Mr Douglas's insinuations – to put it mildly – regarding my introduction to Maurice Magnus's *Memoirs of the Foreign Legion*? When Mr Douglas's 'pamphlet' first appeared I was in New Mexico, and it seemed too far off to trouble. But now that the essay is enshrined in Mr Douglas's new book, *Experiments*, it is time that I said a word. One becomes weary of being slandered.

The whole circumstances of my acquaintance with Maurice Magnus, and the facts of his death, are told in my introduction as truthfully as a man can tell a thing. After the suicide of Magnus, I had continual letters from the two Maltese, whom I had met through Magnus, asking for redress. I knew them personally – which Douglas did not. Myself, I had not the money to repay Magnus's borrowings. All the literary remains were left to Douglas, in the terms of Magnus's will. But then, after his death, all Magnus's effects were consficated, owing to his debts. There was really nothing to confiscate, since the very furniture of the house had been lent by the young Maltese, Borg. There were the MSS. – the bulk of them worthless. Only those *Memoirs of the Foreign Legion*, which I had gone over previously with Magnus, might be sold.

I wrote to Borg that Norman Douglas would no doubt get the *Memoirs* published. The reply came from Malta, Borg would never put anything into the hands of Douglas. I then wrote to Douglas – and, remembering the care with which he files all his letters, I kept his reply. Parts of this reply I quote here:

Florence,
26th December, 1921.

Dear Lawrence,

So many thanks for yours of the 20th.

Damn the Foreign Legion ... I have done my best, and if Borg had sent it to me the book would have been published by this time, and Borg £30 or £50 the richer. Some folks are hard to please. By all means do what you like with the MS. As to M. himself, I may do some kind of memoir of him later on – independent of Foreign Legions. Put me into your introduction if you like ...

Pocket all the cash yourself. Borg seems to be such a fool that he doesn't deserve any.

I'm out of it and, *for once in my life*, with a clean conscience ...

Yours always,
NORMAN DOUGLAS.

The italics in this letter are Douglas's own. As for his accusation of my 'unkindness' to Magnus, that too is funny. Certainly Magnus was generous with his money when he had any; who knew that better than Douglas? But did I make it appear otherwise? And when Magnus wanted *actual* help – not post-mortem sentiment – where did he look for it? To the young Maltese who would have no dealings whatsoever with Norman Douglas, after the suicide.

Then I am accused of making money out of Magnus's effects. I should never have dreamed of writing a word about Magnus, save for the continual painful letters from the Maltese. Then I did it solely and simply to discharge a certain obligation. For curiously enough, both Borg and S— seemed to regard me as in some way responsible for their troubles with Magnus. I had been actually there with them and Magnus and had driven in their motor-car. To discharge an obligation I do not admit, I wrote the Introduction. And when it was written, in the year 1922, it started the round of the publishers, as introducing the *Memoirs of the Foreign Legion*, and everywhere it was refused. More than one publisher said: 'We will publish the Introduction alone, without the Magnus Memoirs.' To which I said: 'That's no good. The Introduction only exists for the Memoirs.'